Public–Private Partnerships for Sustainable Development

Public–Private Partnerships for Sustainable Development

Emergence, Influence and Legitimacy

Edited by

Philipp Pattberg, Frank Biermann, Sander Chan and Ayşem Mert

VU University Amsterdam, The Netherlands

Edward Elgar

Cheltenham, UK • Northampton, MA, USA

Published by
Edward Elgar Publishing Limited
The Lypiatts
15 Lansdown Road
Cheltenham
Glos GL50 2JA
UK

Edward Elgar Publishing, Inc.
William Pratt House
9 Dewey Court
Northampton
Massachusetts 01060
USA

A catalogue record for this book
is available from the British Library

Library of Congress Control Number: 2012930580

ISBN 978 1 84980 930 6 (cased)

Typeset by Servis Filmsetting Ltd, Stockport, Cheshire
Printed and bound by MPG Books Group, UK

Contents

Contributors

Karin Bäckstrand is associate professor (tenured) of political science, Lund University, Sweden. Her research interests are global environmental politics and the role of scientific expertise in environmental negotiations. Her dissertation explored the role of scientific advice and dominant framings of risk and scientific uncertainty in transboundary air pollution diplomacy. Her postdoctoral work examined the normative dimension of scientific expertise, encapsulated in calls for public participation in scientific decision making. Her research has been published in *Environmental Politics* and *Global Environmental Politics* as well as numerous book chapters. She teaches at the Department of Political Science as well as in the Lund University International Master's Program in Environmental Studies and Sustainability Science at the Lund University Center for Sustainability Studies (LUCSUS), where she has developed and taught a range of courses in environmental politics since 1997.

Frank Biermann is professor of political science and of environmental policy sciences at VU University Amsterdam, The Netherlands, and visiting professor of earth system governance at Lund University, Sweden. He specializes in global environmental governance with an emphasis on climate negotiations, UN reform, global adaptation governance, public–private governance mechanisms, the role of science and North–South relations. Biermann holds a number of research management positions, including head of the Department of Environmental Policy Analysis at VU University Amsterdam and director-general of the Netherlands Research School for Socioeconomic and Natural Sciences of the Environment (SENSE), a national research network of nine research institutes with 150 scientists and 400 PhD students. He is also the founding chair of the annual series of Berlin Conferences on the Human Dimensions of Global Environmental Change; founding director of the Global Governance Project, a long-term joint research programme of 12 European research institutions; and chair of the Earth System Governance Project, a 10-year core project of the International Human Dimensions Programme on Global Environmental Change.

Sander Chan is a doctoral candidate in international environmental governance with the Department of Environmental Policy Analysis, Institute for Environmental Studies, VU University Amsterdam, The Netherlands. He is also a research fellow under the EU Science and Technology Fellowship Program in China (STF China), hosted by Renmin University of China (RUC), School of Environment and Natural Resources, and a fellow of the Global Governance Project. He specializes in the application of global environmental governance instruments in China's sustainable development. Currently he is conducting research on the effectiveness and legitimacy of partnership governance in China's forestry and biodiversity. The research is part of a project on partnerships for sustainable development at VU University Amsterdam, funded by the Netherlands Organisation for Scientific Research, which included the development of the Global Sustainability Partnerships Database. He also organized a 2009 EU Roundtable on the Future of Environmental Governance in China and coordinates the China network of the Earth System Governance Project.

Daniel Compagnon is a full professor of political science and international relations at Sciences Po, University of Bordeaux, and a researcher at the CNRS centre Science Politique Relations Internationales Territoire (SPIRIT). He teaches on the environment in international relations and global environmental governance, with a special interest in developing countries. With significant fieldwork expertise on Africa, his research currently focuses on the actual and potential contribution of 'fragile' states and 'areas of limited statehood' to global environmental governance. He holds a BA in political science, a Master's degree in social sciences and a PhD in political science, all from French universities. He previously served as director of the French Institute for Africa in Harare, Zimbabwe, and as professor at the University of the French West Indies. His latest book is *A Predictable Tragedy: Robert Mugabe and the Collapse of Zimbabwe* (University of Pennsylvania Press, 2010).

Eleni Dellas is a doctoral candidate with the Department of Environmental Policy Analysis at the Institute for Environmental Studies (IVM), VU University Amsterdam, The Netherlands. Her research interests include the distributive effects of market-based environmental governance and the legitimacy and effectiveness of public–private partnerships for sustainable development. She also acts as communication officer of the Global Governance Project.

Ayşem Mert is a postdoctoral researcher at the Amsterdam Global Change Institute (AGCI), VU University Amsterdam, The Netherlands.

She holds master's degrees in international relations and environmental sciences. Her doctoral studies focused on partnerships for sustainable development and the discourses of environment and democracy in global environmental governance. Among other things, she has been manager of the 2007 Amsterdam Conference on the Human Dimensions of Global Environmental Change and managing editor of the working paper series of the Global Governance Project. Her research has appeared in *Forest Policy and Analysis* and in the edited book *Partnerships for Sustainable Development* (Edward Elgar, 2008).

Christina Müller is a PhD fellow at Bremen International Graduate School of Social Sciences (BIGSSS), specializing in the area of international relations. She holds a Master's degree in political science from the University of Bremen and is a member of the European COST Action 'The Transformation of Global Environmental Governance: Risks and Opportunities'. Her research interests include global environmental governance, the role of non-state actors in international politics and corporate social responsibility (CSR). Her doctoral dissertation focuses on social and environmental self-regulation of transnational corporations in the global garment industry.

Philipp Pattberg is an associate professor (tenured) of transnational environmental governance with the Department of Environmental Policy Analysis, Institute for Environmental Studies, VU University Amsterdam, The Netherlands. He also serves as the deputy-director and research coordinator of the Global Governance Project. Further, he is Management Committee Chair of the European COST Action 'The Transformation of Global Environmental Governance: Risks and Opportunities' and one of three speakers of the Environmental Policy and Global Change section of the German Political Science Association (DVPW). He is the author of *Private Institutions and Global Governance: The New Politics of Environmental Sustainability* (Edward Elgar, 2007); co-editor of *Global Climate Governance beyond 2012: Architecture, Agency and Adaptation* (Cambridge University Press, 2010) and co-editor of *Global Environmental Governance Reconsidered* (MIT Press, 2012).

Kacper Szulecki is a researcher at the Cluster of Excellence 'Cultural Foundations of Integration' and a doctoral candidate in political sociology at the University of Constance, Germany. Further, he is Board President and research coordinator of the Environmental Studies and Policy Research Institute (ESPRi), Wroclaw, Poland. He holds an MSc in International Relations from VU University in Amsterdam, where he also conducted a research internship at the Institute for Environmental Studies. From 2003 until 2007 he studied political science, international relations and sociology at the Universities of Warsaw and Oslo, as well as social psychology at the Warsaw School of Humanities and Social Sciences. His research interests include environmental politics, global governance, social movements and dissent (with a focus on East-Central Europe).

Preface

Public–private partnerships for sustainable development are today widely seen as the most prominent outcome of the 2002 World Summit on Sustainable Development in Johannesburg, South Africa. Governments could then not agree on major new legislative initiatives to mitigate global environmental change and to advance sustainable development. Instead, they opted to focus on the implementation of existing policies and on the support of 'type-2' outcomes of the summit, with 'type-2' denoting a new model of global governance that complements traditional, 'type-1' modes of intergovernmental cooperation. Several hundred 'partnerships for sustainable development' have been agreed before, during and in the few years after the Johannesburg summit. While the idea of public–private partnership at the global level was not new in 2002, the high number of the newly agreed partnerships, as well as the prominence and, in parts, enthusiasm that surrounded this mechanism of global governance, was surely unprecedented. And yet, the eventual role and relevance of these partnerships remains open to debate till today.

Now, exactly 10 years after the Johannesburg summit, it is time to take stock and to provide a comprehensive assessment of what the hundreds of Johannesburg partnerships could achieve, of the reasons they emerged, and of the problems and potentials associated with this new governance mode. This 10-year assessment is the main goal of this book.

The research presented here is the result of a long-term research programme developed in 2004/05 by Frank Biermann and implemented from 2006 to 2010 under the co-leadership of Biermann and Philipp Pattberg at the Institute for Environmental Studies of the VU University Amsterdam, The Netherlands. As such, the programme was part of the Global Governance Project, the long-term joint research programme of 12 leading European research institutions in the field of global environmental governance that lasted from 2001 to 2011.

Most of the research presented in this book was generously funded by the Netherlands Organization for Scientific Research (grant number 450-04-313), where it was part of the larger Netherlands-based research programme on 'Shifts in Governance'. We are grateful for this core support from the main funding body in the Netherlands, for the flexibility of its staff members and programme chairs in adjusting programme planning under changing circumstances, and for the overall intellectual stimulation from the Shifts in Governance programme community. Additional financial support for our research in China was provided by the EU-STF programme.

The core project team included the four editors of this volume, as well as a vibrant group of visiting researchers, students and research interns, many of whom gave invaluable support to the creation and coding of the Global Sustainability Partnerships Database. In particular, we are grateful for the contributions of our (former) team members Tanja Abendschein, Hilko Blok, Eleni Dellas, Okechukwu Enechi, Kenneth Bergsli Hansen, Anna Kalinowska, Stefan Koeppe, Johanna Castro Mendoza, Marta Miros, Christina Müller, Sara Pologno, Kacper Szulecki, Rui Sequeira Veras, Cheeney Zhao Qin and Ruben Zondervan.

In addition, a number of close colleagues provided important critique, valuable insights and useful comments throughout the duration of the programme. We wish to thank here in particular Karin Bäckstrand of Lund University; Jem Bendell of Griffith Business School; Daniel Compagnon of Sciences Po Bordeaux (who also joined the team as visiting professor in 2006); Jia Wenhua of the China University of Political Science and Law; Ma Zhong of Renmin University of China; Henk Overbeek of the VU University Amsterdam; Patrick Schroeder of CANGO; and Derek Vollmer of the US National Academies.

Our research is based, among others, on an expert survey and a series of interviews with leading experts on and stakeholders of public–private partnerships. We cannot thank all interviewees here by name, but wish to extend our gratitude especially to Zehra Aydin, Patricia Chavez, Neth Dano, Felix Dodds, Pamela Franklin, David Hall, Norichika Kanie, Sylvia Karlsson, Lauren Kelly, Ton Boon von Ochssée, Federica Pietracci, Jan Pronk, Diane Quarless, Jan-Gustav Strandenaes, Ann Zamit, and the entire UN-CSD partnership team. We acknowledge financial assistance by COST (European Cooperation in Science and Technology).

Special thanks go to Alex Pettifer and the entire team of Edward Elgar Publishing.

The Editors
Amsterdam, October 2011

Acronyms and abbreviations

ACCA	Association of Chartered Certified Accountants
ADEME	French Agency for Environment and Energy Management
CBFP	Congo Basin Forest Partnership
CDC	Center for Disease Control and Prevention
CEO	Chief Executive Officer
CEPF	Critical Ecosystem Partnership Fund
CGIAR	Consultative Group on International Agricultural Research
COMESA	Common Market for Eastern and Southern Africa
COMIFAC	Central Africa Forests Commissions
CPC	Communist Party of China
CSR	corporate social responsibility
DRHI	Desert Rainwater Harvesting Initiative
ECOSOC	United Nations Economic and Social Council
EPA	Environmental Protection Agency/Authority
GGSD	Good Governance in Sustainable Development
GIF	Generation IV International Forum
GITSI	Global Initiative Towards a Sustainable Iraq
GNESD	Global Network on Energy and Sustainable Development
GONGO	governmentally organized non-governmental organization
GSPD	Global Sustainability Partnerships Database
GVEP	Global Village Energy Partnership
IAEA	International Atomic Energy Agency
IR	International Relations
ITT	infrastructure and technology transfer
LDCs	Least Developed Countries
LPG	Liquid Petroleum Gas
MEDA	Maharashtra Energy Development Agency
MNC	multinational corporations
MoU	Memorandum of Understanding
NGO	non-governmental organization
NWO	Netherlands Organization for Scientific Research
ODA	official development assistance
OECD	Organisation for Economic Co-operation and Development
PAWS	Partners for Water and Sanitation

PEFC	Programme on the Endorsement of Forest Certification
PEPS	Partnership Promoting an Energy-Efficient Public Sector
PROASNE	Projeto Água Subterrânea no Nordeste do Brasil/North-eastern Brazil Groundwater Project
PVC	polyvinyl chloride
QCA	qualitative comparative research
R&D	research and development
REEEP	Renewable Energy and Energy Efficiency Partnership
REN 21	Renewable Energy Policy Network for the 21st Century
SADC	Southern African Development Community
SAPP	Southern African Power Pool
SARD	sustainable agriculture and rural development
STS	science and technology studies
SWS	safe water system
TNC	transnational corporation
UN	United Nations
UNCSD	United Nations Commission on Sustainable Development
UNDESA	United Nations Department of Economic and Social Affairs
UNDP	United Nations Development Programme
UNEP	United Nations Environment Programme
UNICEF	United Nations Children's Fund
USAID	United Nations Agency for International Development
WAWI	Western African Water Initiative
WSSD	World Summit on Sustainable Development
WHO	World Health Organization
WNU	World Nuclear University
WSUP	Water and Sanitation for the Urban Poor

1. Introduction: partnerships for sustainable development

Philipp Pattberg, Frank Biermann, Sander Chan and Ayşem Mert

Partnerships for sustainable development are often hailed as a vital new element of the emerging system of global sustainability governance. In policy and academic debates alike, partnerships are promoted as a solution to deadlocked intergovernmental negotiations, to ineffective treaties and overly bureaucratic international organizations, to power-based state policies, corrupt elites and many other real or perceived current problems of the sustainability transition. Partnerships for sustainable development are now ubiquitous. They have been promoted in particular at the 2002 Johannesburg World Summit on Sustainable Development (WSSD), where partnerships have emerged as a 'type-2 outcome' of the summit, along with the traditional outcomes of the intergovernmental diplomatic process. As of August 2011, 348 partnerships for sustainable development have been registered with the United Nations Commission on Sustainable Development (UNCSD). In addition, many similar agreements are in place across the globe but not formally registered.

And yet, the role and relevance of these partnerships remains contested. Some observers view the new emphasis on public–private partnerships – also referred to as multi-stakeholder or intersectoral partnerships (see Bitzer, Francken and Glasbergen 2008; Morsink, Hofman and Lovett 2011) – as problematic, since voluntary public–private governance arrangements might privilege more powerful actors, in particular 'the North' and 'big business', and consolidate the privatization of governance and dominant neo-liberal modes of globalization (Ottaway 2001; Corporate Europe Observatory 2002; IISD 2002; SDIN 2002). Also, some argue that partnerships lack accountability and (democratic) legitimacy (Meadowcroft 2007). Yet others see public–private partnerships as an innovative form of governance that addresses deficits of interstate politics by bringing together key actors of civil society, governments and business (e.g. Reinicke 1998; Benner, Streck and Witte 2003; Streck 2004).

In this perspective, public–private partnerships or similar governance networks for sustainable development are important new mechanisms to help resolve a variety of current governance deficits. Such governance deficits have been discussed from different conceptual perspectives (e.g. Andonova and Levy 2003; Haas 2004; Martens 2007). While some scholars regard governance deficits as a generic phenomenon in international relations (Haas 2004), others focus on a particular governance deficit, for example, the democratic deficit and problems of legitimacy (Bäckstrand 2006).

This book seeks to contribute to resolving several of the questions and debates in the current academic and policy discourse, as laid out in more detail in this introduction. The following section discusses existing definitions within and beyond the context of the WSSD and introduces our conceptualization of public–private partnerships. Then, a review of existing scholarship on partnerships for sustainable development is provided. Here we outline in what way this book goes beyond existing studies on partnerships for sustainable development. In the section that follows, we introduce the various methods employed to study partnerships for sustainable development, including a large-n database, while the final section provides an outlook on the remainder of this book.

DEFINING TRANSNATIONAL PUBLIC–PRIVATE PARTNERSHIPS

Public–private partnerships are by no means a novel phenomenon. Before taking centre stage in scholarship on global governance and international relations in the early 2000s, public–private partnerships have enjoyed sustained attention in domestic policy, in areas ranging from health to infrastructure and urban services. Public–private partnerships have been promoted as an instrument to increase governance effectiveness as part of New Public Management that gained ground in the early 1980s. Since the 1990s, public–private partnerships at the international level have been promoted as tools for good governance, increasing the legitimacy and effectiveness of multilateral policies. Partnerships in areas ranging from environmental protection and sustainable development to global health have even been analysed as instruments to promote global deliberative democracy (Börzel and Risse 2005). However, despite this rather long-standing tradition of research on public–private partnerships, the vast and growing literature on public–private partnerships suffers from conceptual confusion, rival definitions, disparate research traditions and oftentimes a normative and value-laden agenda of promoting partnerships. This state of conceptual vagueness has led some scholars even to dismiss the term 'public–private partnership' as 'conceptually empty and merely politically expedient' (Brinkerhoff and Brinkerhoff 2011: 31).

The conceptual broadness of the term, with its multitude of usages, has not prevented a prolific literature on these novel entities of global governance. Public–private partnerships, both national and transnational, have been analysed in multiple ways as hybrid governance arrangements for the provision of collective goods that lead to the transformation of political authority from government and public actors towards non-state actors, such as business and NGOs (Pattberg and Stripple 2008; Schäferhoff, Campe and Kaan 2009). In this book, we are interested in public–private, multi-stakeholder partnerships for sustainable development as a form of global governance beyond traditional forms of international cooperation.

Despite the lack of a broadly agreed definition of this phenomenon, most scholars agree on several features that constitute public–private partnerships (see also Schäferhoff, Campe and Kaan 2009: 455). Important shared characteristics of partnerships include: transnationality (involving cross-border interactions and non-state relations); public policy objectives (as opposed to public bads or exclusively private goods); and a network structure (coordination by participating actors rather than coordination by a central hierarchy). While this common understanding is quite narrow, it still covers a wide range of phenomena. For example, the functions of partnerships are varied and include agenda setting, rule making, advocacy, implementation, and service provision (Bull and McNeill 2007; Martens 2007). Furthermore, public–private partnerships appear in different sectors such as sustainable development, health, human rights, development, security and finance and vary in degree of institutionalization and permanence. Finally, partnerships have different geographical scopes from the local, national, regional to the global level (see also Appendix, this volume). It is therefore necessary to further delimit the empirical scope of this book. We are interested here predominantly in a specific sub-set of transnational public–private partnerships, namely those that (1) operate in the field of sustainable development, and (2) aim at the implementation of agreed international policy goals (such as the Agenda 21 or the Millennium Development Goals). While the overall number of these partnerships is unknown, we further limit our empirical analysis to the sub-set of partnerships that have been agreed upon in the context of the 2002 WSSD, and consequently have been registered with the UNCSD. For this specific sample, we use the term 'partnerships for sustainable development' throughout the book ('WSSD partnerships' and 'UNCSD partnerships' being used synonymously).

STATE OF THE ART AND RESEARCH QUESTIONS

While there are frequent claims that partnerships for sustainable development offer a viable solution to real or perceived deficits in sustainability governance (both in terms of effectiveness and legitimacy), there is surprisingly little systematic research in their support. Evidence for the actual role and relevance of partnerships in global sustainability governance is scarce and inconclusive. This lacuna impairs a better understanding of transnational public–private partnerships in global governance. Are partnerships a sign of a new model of world politics in which intergovernmental negotiations are complemented and sometimes even replaced by networked governance of non-state actors? Or is the contribution of partnerships rather limited? To what extent, if at all, are partnerships superior to traditional ways of international cooperation, such as the negotiation of legally binding agreements among governments and their subsequent national implementation? To what extent are partnerships for sustainable development new and additional initiatives designed to address pressing problems of global governance, or are they rather 'old wine in new bottles'? And to what extent do partnerships for sustainable development democratize current structures and processes of environmental governance beyond the state?

The current literature on transnational public–private partnerships is still not sufficiently evolved both theoretically and empirically to answer these questions, even though important pioneering work has been done (Andonova and Levy 2003; Witte, Streck and Benner 2003; Hale and Mauzerall 2004; Bäckstrand 2006). Yet the literature continues to be hampered by fragmented research agendas, inconsistent conceptualizations across different studies, and the absence of large-*n* studies.

A quick glance at the existing case study literature on partnerships (in and beyond sustainable development) illustrates this point. Most empirical studies on partnerships differ, for example, regarding the policy level they analyse. Some studies examine partnerships that work at the local level (Bassett 1996; De Rynck and Voets 2006), others those at the national level (Jimenez et al. 1991; Selin 1999), others again transnational partnerships, while only few papers discuss interaction between levels (Börzel 1997). At local and national levels, the focus is on patterns of shifts in governance, namely towards non-regulatory policy instruments and voluntary measures that have emerged with the debate on government-overload in the 1970s. At the level of governance 'beyond the nation state', many studies look at the European Union (Marks 1993; Bache, George and Rhodes 1996). In these studies, the necessity to research pieces of a complex framework led to a strong emphasis on very specific aspects, such as on notions of centre and periphery (Bomberg 1994); on structural funds (Heinelt and Smith 1996); or on the role of European agencies (Dehousse 1997).

Empirical studies also differ in terms of the functions of partnerships that are studied. Some partnerships serve as mechanisms of rule and standard setting. An example is the Forest Stewardship Council, in which stakeholders from industry, environmental organizations and local communities set standards for sustainable forest management (see Pattberg 2005). Other partnerships serve as mechanisms of rule implementation and service provision (Börzel and Risse 2005). Again, other partnerships function as mechanisms for information provision and dissemination. Tully (2004), for example, suggests that partnerships typically emerge out of operational requirements for information through informal contacts and mature into a formal memorandum of understanding on the conditions of engagement including the use of information. Also Glasbergen and Groenenberg (2001) suggest, in their definition of product-oriented partnerships, that partners mostly focus on exchanging knowledge and information. In any case, it is open to debate whether findings on partnerships in one functional arena can be generalized to other arenas as well.

Empirical studies further differ regarding the policy area in which partnerships operate, ranging from studies in the various fields of sustainable development and environment, to a variety of other issues including security (Considine 2002; Krahmann 2003), economy (Kenis and Schneider 1987; Considine and Lewis 2003), tourism (Selin 1999), or health (Jimenez et al. 1991; Altenstetter 1994). The predominant case-study approach often results in a bias towards the most visible and most successful public–private partnerships, which tends to paint a universe that is more partnership-dominated than reality may warrant.

This book remedies a number of shortcomings in the existing literature on partnerships for sustainable development. First, the research reported in this book is based on a clearly defined sample of partnerships (the overall universe of UNCSD-registered partnerships), thereby avoiding conceptual and empirical confusion. Second, by employing a large-*n* database in combination with qualitative approaches such as expert interviews and comparative case studies, we are not only able to observe and explain variation in partnership effectiveness, but also analyse the precise functional pathways of how partnership success is realized. Third, the research presented here provides a holistic overview of the partnership phenomenon by analysing the total universe of partnerships for sustainable development along with sectoral and geographic samples. Finally, our aspirations with this book do not stop at explaining observations, but focus on a critical assessment of the fundamentally normative questions underlying partnerships for sustainable development.

In particular, our research is motivated by the existing knowledge gaps in relation to three distinct areas (see also Schäferhoff, Campe and Kaan 2009 for a recent literature review): first, our research scrutinizes the *emergence* of partnerships for sustainable development, including questions such as: What was the political context surrounding the emergence of partnerships for sustainable development? Who benefitted from the emerging partnerships regime? How can the observed variation in sectoral, functional and geographic spread of partnerships be explained?

Second, we are interested in measuring and explaining the *impacts and effects* of partnerships for sustainable development (both as an aggregate phenomenon of more than 340 partnerships and as individual partnerships), including questions about their concrete problem-solving effectiveness (i.e. partnerships' contribution to the Millennium Development Goals, Agenda 21 or the Johannesburg Plan of Action) and their broader influence in global environmental governance (including unintended effects).

Third, we analyse the *legitimacy* of partnerships for sustainable development, including questions such as: how do partnerships perform in terms of their input and output legitimacy? Are partnerships for sustainable development effectively closing the participation gap in global environmental politics? Are partnerships democratizing environmental governance? How legitimate are specific technologies and practices promoted through partnerships for sustainable development? Taken together, this book offers a comprehensive assessment of partnerships for sustainable development, inquiring into their historic and political context, their effectiveness and broader influence as well as into the question of legitimacy of governing beyond the state.

METHODS AND APPROACHES

In this book, we employ four methods to understand the partnership phenomenon in global sustainability governance: a database approach, an expert survey, semi-structured interviews and narrative analysis. Each approach will be outlined in more detail below.

Database Approach

Most research on transnational public–private partnerships has so far been conducted in the form of single- or small-*n* case studies. We believe that this is insufficient to generate convincing knowledge on the role and relevance of partnerships in local and global politics. The existing clusters of case studies suffer from the lack of a consensus definition and are thus difficult to compare in their results. All single and small-*n* case studies cover only a part of the entire kaleidoscope of partnerships with regard to the level, policy area, and function of partnerships. It is thus unclear whether findings from one level, policy area or function can be extrapolated to a more general understanding of the partnership phenomenon. A database has here a number of advantages: it allows for a better understanding of the entire phenomenon of transnational governance beyond the restricted look at single cases. In addition, a database can help to put into perspective individual, intensively studied cases, thus making sense of the relevance of particular partnerships within the overall universe of partnerships. Likewise, database research can help to understand correlation between variables, and thus allow for the generation or rough testing of hypotheses that would later be complemented by qualitative work.

A first and important step towards such a quantitative study programme has been made by Liliana Andonova and Marc Levy (2003) with their early analysis of WSSD partnerships as a potentially innovative governance mechanism. However, at that time, their work remained limited to only a relatively small set of variables at the level of the partnerships themselves, and it has been largely discontinued after publication of first results, which were at that time based on only roughly half of all partnerships that are now officially registered with the UNCSD. Given the speed of developments in this area, most data in their database is now increasingly outdated. In addition, Andonova and Levy's work concentrated on the partnerships themselves and hence did not include systematic information on the output and outcome of partnership policies.

To overcome these limitations, we have embarked upon a large-*n* research programme that evolved around the Global Sustainability Partnerships Database (GSPD) that was developed between 2006 and 2009 at the Institute for Environmental Studies, VU University Amsterdam. Based on data provided by the UNCSD, extensive desk studies, and numerous expert interviews, the GSPD provides information on descriptive categories such as partnership name, existence of website, number of countries in which partnerships implement their activities, number of and type of partners, type of lead partners, area of policy implementation and functions performed, geographical scope, duration, date of establishment, and resources reported to be required for each of the 330 partnerships registered with the UNCSD at the time the coding was completed in 2009. In addition, the GSPD also contains information about individual partnership output, that is, the concrete activities and programmes of partnerships for sustainable development. All data was coded by a team of researchers for whom an inter-rater reliability check has been performed.

Partnerships registered with the UNCSD are rather comparable on issue areas and geographical scope, actor constellation and so forth, although they are diverse in terms of the concrete policies and organizational models employed. More importantly, their main goals are comparable, in the sense that these are defined by the Millennium Development Goals and the other documents resulting from international summits and negotiations.

At a practical level, the UNCSD website and database provide information regarding the basic characteristics of partnerships. However, the data on partnerships provided through the UNCSD is not necessarily accurate, up-to-date, or complete. More importantly, many details are interpreted differently by each partnership when reporting to the UNCSD. While including some of this information into the GSPD, it was crucial that a limited group of researchers have coded partnerships. In many cases, the categorization that was used by the UNCSD has been changed. For instance, while the UNCSD statistics often show abundant major group participation, a closer analysis reveals that most of these major groups belong to only a few of the categories and that the most vulnerable groups are often excluded. On the other hand, most of the data on the dependent variables, such as functions and output originated from the partnership websites, professional publications, contact with partnerships, as well as the expert surveys conveyed throughout 2007–08 (see below). The experts' insights into partnerships have been included in order to critically refine our data.

The measurement of our main dependent variable, the function-output fit, is derived almost exclusively from sources independent of the UNCSD database. By comparing what the partnerships claim as their goal and function with their actual activities and products (output), the function–output fit reveals the accuracy and consistency of these declarations without bringing in another set of biases resulting from our own ideas of effectiveness. To do this, a group of researchers studied the UNCSD information pages and websites of partnerships and subsequently categorized their declared goals, aims, and functions (Table 1.1). Up to three declared functions were coded in the GSPD. Then, different types of output (ranging from publications, training, fund raising, to technology transfer) were conceptualized, and the outputs of each partnership were coded according to this list, adding new types of output when necessary (Table 1.2). Finally, these two lists of 15 types of outputs and 11 functions were linked, on the basis that the presence of a specific output would indicate at least partial fulfilment of the related functions (Table 1.3).

The database approach of the GSPD is complemented by a range of

Table 1.1 List of functions of partnerships in GSPD

Function	Explanation
Knowledge production (innovation)	Production of knowledge, information, innovation (scientific or applied)
Knowledge dissemination	Dissemination of knowledge, including dissemination of 'good practices'
Technical implementation	Implementation of previously existing technologies, plans, and policies, including pilot projects
Institutional capacity building	Building new social institutions (with or without legal status) or expanding existing support organizations
Norm setting	Setting up new norms or standards or spreading the use of such new norms, including the certification of products
Campaigning	Campaigns, including raising public awareness on a given topic, and education of the public at large
Lobbying	Lobbying, restricted to pressure applied on governmental actors from non-governmental ones
Technology transfer	Transfer of technology and methodology (including the transfer of science-based evaluation or monitoring methods)
Participatory management	Participatory management and involvement of local communities in policy programmes
Training	Training of employees, other social actors, or students (including school training if new curriculum is introduced with a specific sustainable development content)
Planning	Planning at national or regional levels (including the production of large policy plans, development or planning of policy instruments)

additional research methods such as expert surveys, in-depth and semi-structured interviews, text analysis and narrative analysis.

Expert Survey

Throughout 2007 and 2008, the research team conducted expert surveys to collect detailed information on partnerships and their perceived effectiveness by experts. Respondents to these surveys were representatives of partnerships, major groups or sectors, as well as UN officials and diplomats or academics that work on partnerships or the UNCSD process. To this end, all partnerships were categorized into 14 clusters based on their thematic focus. Each expert was shown a list of partnerships in their respective area of expertise.

Table 1.2 List of output codes and their explanations in GSPD

Output code	Explanation
OUT_PUB	Publications (research, advocacy, standards, training, policy and reports); Documents found on the Internet and at partnership meetings pertaining to:
_RES	*Research: Any publication by the partnership (not by individual partners) documenting academic research, data-gathering for implementation and policy, and action research.*
_ADV	*Advocacy and public awareness-raising: Any publication by the partnership (not by individual partners) arguing in favour of the partnership cause with a wider audience than policy makers (public); campaign material, newsletters, petitions, and promotion material (posters, leaflets, brochures).*
_STA	*Standards: Any publication by the partnership (not by individual partners) setting out policy and/or procedural standards (except internal operating procedures) for application to a sustainable development issue.*
_TRA	*Training: Any publication by the partnership (not by individual partners) aimed at training, including best practice manuals; and instruction materials.*
_POL	*Policy: Any publication by the partnership (not by individual partners) arguing for specific policies (whether regional, national, or trans-national) with policy makers (public) to regulate and manage sustainable development issues.*
_REP	*Self-Reports: Any publication by the partnership (not by individual partners) pertaining transparency and accountability towards the partners, stakeholders and wider audiences (such as annual reports, and evaluations of the partnership).*
_OTH	*Other publications.*
OUT_DTB	Database and systematically organized retrievable information (except databases of self-reports).
OUT_WSC	Workshops/seminars/conferences including training seminars, exhibitions, stakeholder consulting events and courses organized by the partnership (excluding events organized during the 2002 WSSD).
OUT_ITT	Infrastructure and technology transfer: Construction or improvement of new and existing physical facilities as well as the application and transfer of new technologies (including the exchange of grassroot innovations).
OUT_WBS	Website: An active and operational website.
OUT_CNS	Consultancy service (excludes implementation).
OUT_PRT	Conference and workshop participation (excluding conferences and workshops organized by the partnership or the UN CSD, WSSD processes).
OUT_NEW	New institutions, organizations and new partnerships.
OUT_OTHER	Other activities and fundraising.

Table 1.3 Functions and fitting outcomes

Function	Fitting outputs			
Knowledge production (innovation)	Output_PUB_RES	Output_DTB		
Knowledge dissemination	Output_PUB_TRA	Output_DTB	Output_WSC	Output_PRT
Technical implementation	Output_ITT		Output_NEW	
Institutional capacity building	Output_PUB_TRA	Output_WSC		
Norm setting	Output_PUB_STA			
Campaigning	Output_PUB_ADV	Output_WSC		
Lobbying	Output_PUB_POL	Output_PRT		
Technology transfer	Output_PUB_TRA	Output_WSC	Output_ITT	Output_CNS
Participatory management	Output_PUB_REP	Output_WSC		
Training	Output_WSC			
Planning	Output_PUB_POL	Output_WSC	Output_CNS	Output_PRT

In line with a predetermined Expert Survey Protocol, respondents were asked about their affiliations, areas of specialization, and roles and functions in the partnerships they work with. Subsequently, experts were asked to rate (on a scale from 1, low, to 5, high) the performance of each partnership within their area of expertise in terms of

- their contribution towards the achievement of one of the Millennium Development Goals;
- their achievement in addressing a problem that is insufficiently covered by intergovernmental agreements;
- their achievement in mobilizing additional financial resources for sustainable development;
- their performance in generating innovative solutions for sustainable development;
- their contribution towards addressing an urgent issue within this area;
- and finally, their achievements in including all relevant stakeholder groups.

The survey continued until all thematic clusters were evaluated by at least one expert. A total of 34 surveys have been completed in 2007 and a total of 30 surveys in 2008. In total, 64 experts have evaluated the thematic partnership clusters, providing assessments on 149 partnerships in 2007 and 158 partnerships in 2008, respectively. Of the total data points, 71 were self-assessments. As they were in line with the assessment of other experts, they are included in our assessment. In sum, 210 partnerships were assessed through our expert survey.

Semi-structured Interviews

In addition to the GSPD and the expert survey, the research team conducted more than 50 semi-structured in-depth interviews with partnerships experts and policy-makers in order to supplement the quantitative data with background information and to shed light on the formation process out of which UNCSD partnerships emerged. The respondents were representative of various viewpoints, but were mostly involved in the WSSD process, the UNCSD, or both. Interviewees included government delegates, non-governmental organization (NGO) representatives, representatives of major groups during the PrepComs to WSSD and the WSSD summit, employees of UNCSD and United Nations Department of Economic and Social Affairs (UNDESA), representatives of individual partner organizations of UNCSD partnerships, representatives of environmental NGOs, representatives of business groups and representatives of partnerships not registered with the UNCSD. Most interviews were held during the UNCSD 16 and 17 meetings at the United Nations Headquarters, New York.

Text and Narration Analyses

In addition to the quantitative and qualitative approaches described above, we have also employed text and narrative analyses on a wide range of documents, including scientific reports, texts resulting from major UN Conferences on the environment (Stockholm, Rio and Johannesburg Summits), texts from the PrepCom meetings, as well as relevant documents on partnerships such as brochures, websites of partnerships and websites of donor agencies. This data has been used to reconstruct the emergence of the partnerships regime, contextualizing the diverse accounts revealed by the in-depth interviews.

STRUCTURE OF THE BOOK

This book is organized in four parts, following this introduction.

Part I analyses the emergence of partnerships for sustainable development and the political bargains behind the WSSD summit. Part II then focuses on the overall influence and problem-solving effectiveness of partnerships. Part III addresses partnerships for sustainable development beyond the OECD world, with a particular focus on Asia and Africa. Finally, Part IV engages with the question of the legitimacy of partnerships for sustainable development.

Chapter 2 provides an overview of the political negotiations in and around the Johannesburg Summit and the resulting type-2 agreement on partnerships for sustainable development. In more detail, while partnerships have been portrayed by the United Nations as mere implementation instruments in global sustainability governance, they also have a strong political dimension. The negotiation process that resulted in partnerships as the type-2 outcome of the WSSD was marked by contestations over partnerships between different country, business and civil society delegations. In addition, partnerships exert considerable influence on sustainable development at different levels of governance and in different issue areas.

Chapter 3 takes a closer look at the existing geographical and functional patterns of partnerships for sustainable development. Based on hypotheses derived from major theoretical perspectives in political science, such as functionalism, institutionalism and policy network theories, this chapter explains the observable patterns of partnerships with regards to their geographical scope, the policy area in which they operate and the participation of various actors. We find that, in contrast to many functionalist accounts, partnerships are not necessarily filling functional gaps; in particular, they do not necessarily emerge in the geographic spaces where they are most needed. Policy network accounts go a long way in explaining the geographic dimension of emergence, with partnerships emerging in countries that are member to many international organizations and most activities being implemented in urban, densely populated areas. However, especially the transnational advocacy network account does not seem to be applicable to the participatory dimension of partnerships.

Chapter 4 analyses the overall partnerships for sustainable development regime, i.e. the more than 340 partnerships that emerged from the Johannesburg summit and have been registered with the Commission on Sustainable Development. The assessment of the overall effectiveness and influence of the partnership regime is based on three hypothetical global governance deficits that partnerships are supposed to close: the regulatory deficit, the implementation deficit and participatory deficit.

Chapter 5 takes a sectoral approach and subsequently scrutinizes the problem-solving effectiveness of partnerships in the renewable energy sector. The key puzzle addressed is the following: why do some partnerships within the issue area of renewable energy perform remarkably well while others have hardly any traceable output? In more detail, this chapter argues that the variation in the problem-solving effectiveness of public–private partnerships in the energy sector is predominantly explained by organizational variables such as decision-making procedures, staff and organizational resources, while power and material capabilities of individual actors have less influence on the effectiveness of partnerships.

Chapter 6 compares two leading Asian countries – India and China – with regards to their role and relevance in the overall partnerships for sustainable development regime. In particular, this chapter investigates whether partnerships can be successfully implemented in a political/ administrative context that is different from the one in which partnerships have originally developed. In more detail, we provide a comparative analysis that allows for an assessment of political and institutional contexts as factors in the transposition and organization of partnerships beyond the OECD context. We find that the potential for partnership governance in sustainable development varies by country, depending on the political, societal and economic contexts. In China, where formal political participation exists but there is a lack of political pluralism, the potential for partnerships on the basis of equality between governmental and nongovernmental partners is rather limited. In contrast, the relative freedom and autonomy of civil society allows for more partnership initiatives that include NGOs and social organizations in India. Within the same partnership, organization can be differentiated depending on whether activities take place in China or India.

Chapter 7 provides a second perspective on partnerships for sustainable development beyond the OECD world, with a geographical focus on Sub-Saharan Africa. This chapter concludes that, while partnerships attracted a growing academic attention since 2002 and enjoyed widespread popularity among policy-makers, they are by no means the magic wand for overcoming Africa's development and governance conundrums, contrary to what several observers have expected. Partnerships for sustainable development in Africa are largely as effective as states and national elites allow them to be, and their development as a policy instrument should not distract our attention from the persistent challenge of state reform on the continent.

Chapter 8 addresses the question of the legitimacy of partnerships for sustainable development and contends that partnerships can be considered democratically legitimate if they fulfil core democratic values such as participation, accountability, transparency and deliberation. A conclusion from almost a decade of research on the Johannesburg partnerships is that their democratic credentials are weak in terms of incorporation of core democratic values. The Johannesburg partnerships consolidate rather than transform asymmetrical patterns of participation between North and South, between established and 'marginalized groups', and between state and non-state actors. Furthermore, the accountability mechanisms are weak and the deliberative potential of partnerships is limited.

Chapter 9 addresses the broader implications of private sector involvement in UNCSD water partnerships for input and output legitimacy. The chapter concludes that partnerships with private sector participation have particularly good prerequisites for high performance and thus output legitimacy: they tend to have more resources available than other water partnerships, they produce more output, and also implement more effectively, as it is indicated by their higher function–output fit. However, this does not necessarily translate into a focus on project activities that actually benefit the groups and regions with the lowest level of water access.

Chapter 10 takes issue with the widely held assumption that the legitimacy of partnerships can be assessed independently from the technologies and governance practices that are embedded within individual partnerships. In more detail, technology transfer through water partnerships is often presented as a tool not only to combat water scarcity, but also to alleviate poverty, ensure gender equality and improve health and environment indicators. However, the implications of technological improvements are not straightforward, as different technologies have varying implications for the autonomy, flexibility and self-reliance of communities.

Chapter 11 summarizes the overall findings of this volume along the three main research questions presented in the introduction and presents a number of policy recommendations.

REFERENCES

Altenstetter, C. (1994), 'European Union responses to AIDS/HIV and policy network in the pre-Maastricht era', *Journal of European Public Policy*, **1**(2), 413–40.

Andonova, L.B. and M.A. Levy (2003), 'Franchising global governance: making sense of the Johannesburg Type II Partnerships', in O.S. Stokke and O.B. Thommessen (eds), *Yearbook of International Co-operation on Environment and Development*, Oxford, UK: Earthscan, pp. 19–31.

Bache, I., D. George and R.A.W. Rhodes (1996), 'Policy networks and policy making in the European Union: a critical appraisal', in L. Hooghe (ed.), *Cohesion Policy and European Integration: Building Multi-Level Governance*, Oxford: Oxford University Press, pp. 367–87.

Bäckstrand, K. (2006), 'Multi-stakeholder partnerships for sustainable development: rethinking legitimacy, accountability and effectiveness', *European Environment*, **16**(5), 290–306.

Bassett, K. (1996), 'Partnerships, business elites and urban politics: new forms of governance in an English city?', *Urban Studies*, **33**(3), 539–56.

Benner, T., C. Streck, and J.M. Witte (eds) (2003), *Progress or Peril? Networks and Partnerships in Global Environmental Governance. The Post-Johannesburg Agenda*, Berlin: Global Public Policy Institute.

Bitzer, V., M. Francken and P. Glasbergen (2008), 'Intersectoral partnerships for a sustainable coffee chain: really addressing sustainability or just picking (coffee) cherries?', *Global Environmental Change*, **18**, 271–84.

Bomberg, E. (1994), 'Policy networks on the periphery: EU environmental policy and Scotland', in S. Baker, K. Milton and S. Yearley (eds), *Protecting the Periphery: Environmental Policy in Peripheral Regions of the EU*, London: Frank Cass, pp. 45–61.

Börzel, T.A. (1997), *Policy Networks. A New Paradigm for European Governance?* Florence, Italy: European University Institute.

Börzel, T.A. and T. Risse (2005), 'Public–private partnerships: Effective and legitimate tools of international governance?', in E. Grande and L.W. Pauly (eds), *Complex Sovereignty: Reconstituting Political Authority in the Twenty-first Century*, Toronto, Canada: Toronto University Press, pp. 195–216.

Brinkerhoff, D.W. and J.M. Brinkerhoff (2011), 'Public–private partnerships: perspectives on purposes, publicness, and good governance', *Public Administration and Development*, **31**, 2–14.

Bull, B. and D. McNeill (2007), *Development Issues in Global Governance. Public–Private Partnerships and Market Multilateralism*, New York: Routledge.

Considine, M. (2002), *Joined at the Lip? What Does Network Research Tell us*

About Governance? Knowledge Networks and Joined-Up Government, Melbourne, Australia: University of Melbourne, Centre for Public Policy.

Considine, M. and J.M. Lewis (2003), 'Bureaucracy, network, or enterprise? Comparing models of governance in Australia, Britain, the Netherlands, and New Zealand', *Public Administration Review*, **63**(2), 131–40.

Corporate Europe Observatory (2002), *From Rio to Johannesburg: Girona Declaration*. London: Corporate Europe Observatory.

De Rynck, F. and J. Voets (2006), 'Democracy in area-based policy networks: the case of Ghent', *The American Review of Public Administration*, **36**, 58–78.

Dehousse, R. (1997), 'Regulation by networks in the European Community: the role of European agencies', *Journal of European Public Policy*, **4**(2), 245–61.

Glasbergen, P. and R. Groenenberg (2001), 'Environmental partnerships in sustainable energy', *European Environment*, **11**(1), 1–13.

Haas, P.M. (2004), 'Addressing the global governance deficit', *Global Environmental Politics*, **4**(4), 1–15.

Hale, T.N. and D.L. Mauzerall (2004), 'Thinking globally and acting locally: can the Johannesburg Partnerships coordinate action on sustainable development?', *The Journal of Environment and Development*, **13**(3), 220–39.

Heinelt, H. and R. Smith (1996), *Policy Network and European Structural Funds*, Survey, UK: Avebury.

IISD (International Institute for Sustainable Development) (2002), *A Snap-shot of the Summit: General News*. WSSD Info. Linkages Series, Winnipeg, Canada: International Institute for Sustainable Development.

Jimenez, R., M.I. Scarlett, et al. (1991), 'Improving community support for HIV and AIDS prevention through national partnerships', *Public Health Reports*, **106**.

Kenis, P. and V. Schneider (1987), 'The EC as an international corporate actor: two case studies in economic diplomacy', *European Journal of Political Research*, **15**(4), 437–57.

Krahmann, E. (2003), 'Conceptualizing security governance, cooperation and conflict', *Journal of the Nordic International Studies Association*, **38**(1), 5–26.

Marks, G. (1993), 'Structural policy and multilevel governance in the European Community', in A. Cafruny and G. Rosenthal (eds), *The State of the European Community II: The Maastricht Debates and Beyond*, Boulder, CO: Lynne Rienner, pp. 391–410.

Martens, J. (2007), *Multistakeholder Partnerships: Future Models of Multilateralism?* Occasional Paper Series, Berlin.

Meadowcroft, J. (2007), 'Democracy and accountability: the challenge for cross-sectoral partnerships', in P. Glasbergen, F. Biermann and A.P.J. Mol (eds), *Partnerships, Governance and Sustainable Development: Reflections on Theory and Practice*, Cheltenham, UK: Edward Elgar, pp. 194–213.

Morsink, K., P.S. Hofman and J.C. Lovett (2011), 'Multi-stakeholder partnerships for transfer of environmentally sound technologies', *Energy Policy*, **39**(1), 1–5.

Ottaway, M. (2001), 'Corporatism goes global: international organizations, non-governmental organization networks, and transnational business', *Global Governance*, **7**(3), 265–92.

Pattberg, P. (2005), 'The institutionalization of private governance: how business and nonprofit organizations agree on transnational rules', *Governance*, **18**(4), 589–610.

Pattberg, P. and J. Stripple (2008), 'Beyond the Public and Private Divide: Remapping Transnational Climate Governance in the 21st Century', *International Environmental Agreements: Politics, Law and Economics,* **8**(4), 367–88.

Reinicke, W.H. (1998), *Global Public Policy. Governing without Government?* Washington DC: Brookings Institution Press.

Schäferhoff, M., S. Campe and C. Kaan (2009), 'Transnational public–private partnerships in international relations: Making sense of concepts research frameworks, and results', *International Studies Review,* **11**(3), 451–74.

SDIN (Sustainable Development Issues Network) (2002), *Taking Issue: Questioning Partnerships*. SDIN Paper No.1, Sustainable Development Issues Network.

Selin, S. (1999), 'Developing a typology of sustainable tourism partnerships', *Journal of Sustainable Tourism,* **7**(3–4), 260–73.

Streck, C. (2004), 'New partnerships in global environmental policy: the clean development mechanism', *The Journal of Environment and Development,* **13**(3), 295–322.

Tully, S.R. (2004), 'Corporate–NGO partnerships and the regulatory impact of the Energy and Biodiversity Initiative', *Non-State Actors and International Law,* **4**(2), 111–33.

Witte, J.M., C. Streck and T. Brenner (2003), 'The road from Johannesburg: what future for partnerships in global environmental governance?' in T. Benner, C. Streck, J. Martin Witte (eds), *Progress or Peril? Networks and Partnerships in Global Environmental Governance. The Post-Johannesburg Agenda,* Berlin: Global Public Policy Institute, pp. 59–84.

PART I

Emergence of partnerships for sustainable development

2. The politics of partnerships for sustainable development

Ayşem Mert and Sander Chan

Partnerships for sustainable development have been negotiated, endorsed and implemented in a contested political arena, serving a multitude of political goals. While partnerships for sustainable development explicitly refer to sustainable development objectives, they generate effects beyond their explicit goals. Only a part of these effects are intended. New political challenges may result from these implicit, unintended consequences. Partnerships, therefore, are not neutral implementation tools: they are employed in a political context, serve political goals and generate political challenges.

Interviews with partnership experts from different sectors reveal that partnerships are predominantly understood as short-term projects aimed at implementing the Millennium Development Goals, in which different sets of actors share risks and contribute their expertise. This common view of partnerships is difficult to support with factual evidence: 30 per cent of partnerships for sustainable development have an undetermined duration or take the form of open-ended projects. Many do not focus on specific implementation goals. Most importantly, there is little evidence to suggest that risks are shared among partners. The lack of written protocols, contracts and memoranda of understanding among partners make accountability and risk-sharing particularly difficult. As instruments that bring partners together with different interests, goals, abilities and priorities, partnerships do not only represent collaborative arrangements, they also become a ground for competition over meanings, resources and ultimately hegemony. However, even if the process of building partnerships is flawed, or if partnerships themselves are ineffective, it does not mean that they do not exert influence.

This chapter examines the political dimension of partnerships for sustainable development. The first section focuses on the process that resulted in partnerships as the official outcome of the WSSD. The second section looks into the political influence of partnerships at several levels of governance in the field of sustainable development. Finally, the third section examines the influence of specific partnerships on their respective issue areas.

NEGOTIATION OF PARTNERSHIPS

Partnerships for sustainable development were defined as 'voluntary multi-stakeholder initiatives which contribute to the implementation of inter-governmental commitments' in Agenda 21, as well as in the Programme for the Further Implementation of Agenda 21 and in the Johannesburg Plan of Implementation.[1] A set of guidelines, the so-called Bali Guiding Principles, were added, detailing what is meant by partnerships within the UN governance system. The definition of partnerships as voluntary implementation instruments and the Bali Guiding Principles were both settled in the preparatory process to the WSSD, during PrepComs II, III and IV; they are the result of long consultation, negotiation and lobbying processes. These processes did not only involve delegates and UN representatives, but also non-state actors. The resulting conceptualization was a compromise; the guidelines were non-binding criteria that neither defined screening, monitoring or reporting procedures, nor was a central body designated to oversee the evolving partnerships regime. Nonetheless, partnerships became an official part of the UN environmental governance system as they were accepted as an official outcome of the WSSD, despite opposition from several major groups and country delegations.

Although the term 'partnership' has belonged to the UN jargon since 1992, partnerships were only considered as official (type-2) outcomes of an intergovernmental process in the preparatory phase of the WSSD, because pressure to produce a concrete deliverable at the WSSD in Johannesburg was mounting.[2] Shortly after the WSSD organization bureau at the UNDESA proposed partnerships as a possible outcome, 'the US expressed appreciation for the non-binding type-2 outcomes and called for "space" at the WSSD to allow for related dialogues.'[3] The concept had earlier been developed by UNDESA to increase NGO involvement and reflect on a past decade of environmental governance. But most importantly, partnerships were meant to break through existing donor fatigue: 'Every responsibility was being put at the feet of the governments. There was a strong push that this [responsibility to implement] should be shared.'[4]

UNDESA's intended format of a UN partnerships regime was very different from the end result. First and foremost, expectations about type-1 and type-2 outcomes as complementary processes changed:

> This was our [UNDESA's] concept of what would be the outcome of Johannesburg: a commitment among the governments to go forward within that intergovernmental framework, and the type-2 outcome was to be the expressed, demonstrable commitment of donors and the wider community to help developing countries through a range of partnership initiatives, which would express the broader participatory approach to development support.[5]

According to this original intention, the commitment of donors and the international community to realize the Millennium Development Goals in developing countries would be assured, while intergovernmental agreements would continue to address new and more challenging issues. However, partnerships were not matched by a binding outcome, as governments failed to agree on most issues at the WSSD. In fact, partnerships were the only tangible outcome of the Johannesburg Summit.

Secondly, the function of type-2 outcomes was reduced to mere implementation, despite initial aims to conceptualize them as instruments to enhance participation in global sustainable development:

> [In the run up to the WSSD] we were talking about outcomes. An outcome needs not to be implementation, but it has been narrowly defined as implementation. Partnership was intended to be more of a coordinated and collective approach to provide development support. The question is how you define that development support. Unfortunately, because we were dealing with very specific concerns, we ended up attaching the guideline to an entity which became a project or programme.[6]

In sum, the initial conceptualization of partnerships for sustainable development differed from the end result, owing to decisions made at the PrepComs about the concept of partnerships, the specific terms of the Bali Guidelines and the negotiation results at the WSSD.

During PrepCom III, the US and major group representatives of business and industry explicitly supported a vaguely defined partnerships process, which raised suspicions with both NGOs and developing countries. The first lines of contestation were drawn as a response to US support for partnerships:

> We had a meeting with the US delegation at PrepCom 2, [in which] we lectured them on what it is and all kinds of activity would come out and we would be able to do things that would go beyond intergovernmentally made decisions. We must have done such a good job that they became champions of partnerships, which can backfire in this house because there are well set perceptions about the governments and their decisions. When the US overly supports something, everybody starts wondering why. [. . .] The minute the US government started talking close to the partnerships, the other parties suspicions expanded all of a sudden. In fact we had to go and tell them quietly not to do it anymore.[7]

According to another respondent, US support for the partnerships process had opened a space for other countries to avoid binding decisions:

> [Partnerships are] another thing that kills any initiative [and are to be] seen as an opportunity to opt out of responsibility [. . .] [The United States was] the most visible advocate of these partnerships. The concern of the developing countries was that the States would not agree to [any binding agreements]. And it was seen as opting out of responsibilities on both sides.[8]

In other words, US support for partnerships at PrepCom III had signalled to developing countries that the United States would either not agree to new multilateral environmental agreements or fail to ratify them, as it had been the case with other conventions. Hence, developing countries re-focused their strategies to avoid potential loss that could result from the adoption of partnerships as type-2 outcomes, both in terms of loss in Official Development Assistance (ODA) and in terms of loss in autonomy in environmental decision-making. According to a Southern country delegate,

> [When] the secretariat released a paper introduc[ing] the concept of Type I and Type II [outcomes], the developing countries had the biggest concern, because they felt that this is going to bypass binding obligations of states and that this was a way to channel money outside of governments. [. . .] Instead of money flowing bilaterally or multilaterally it would be easier for [the donors] to pick a project and bypass the government. Because in some cases the players in the partnerships were other NGOs. If you look at the US partnership in the Congo Basin, the Forest Partnership, it basically bypasses all the governments; [the money] goes straight to WWF. This is against what has been done for years in funding conservation. There never was [this way of funding of] US-based NGOs, US-based consultancies. So there was a big concern that this was going to happen through partnerships.[9]

Additional suspicion was raised when the broad business support for partnerships became evident. According to Diane Quarless, the chair person of the partnership negotiations at PrepCom IV,

> business was absolutely supportive. [. . .] Here was an opportunity for particularly large business actors. There is a tremendous cache attached to the UN's acknowledgement. At the time [. . .] there was a developing country knocking heads with a big oil multinational. G77's concern was that [this could] whitewash them: You give these companies the UN stamp, a green stamp of approval of CSR. The MNCs have done [much environmental damage], and now they will be absolved of these crimes by virtue of partnerships. There were those among the developing countries that were feeling very strongly about this.[10]

All respondents from within the organizing committee, United Nations Economic and Social Council (ECOSOC) and UNDESA agree that the concerns of the South were being forcefully expressed, draining the enthusiasm (particularly from business actors). In addition to the bypassing of governments by substituting ODA, resistance was building on two issues:

> That the secretariat was taking the responsibility over from those who are responsible, which usually means the industrialized countries, and [. . .] loading it on to major groups. [The other was that] we were making it easier for CSD not to make more heart breaking decisions because [delegations] could easily have said 'we have a partnership on this, we don't need to decide'.[11]

In a similar vein, EU delegations and environmental NGOs were worried that partnerships could become an instrument to repudiate international environmental agreements. Another concern of the NGO community was the increasing business involvement in the UN, and the green-/blue-washing of invasive corporate activities. Finally, a further and largely unforeseen concern also surfaced during the PrepComs III and IV, once again frustrating the organizing committee's initial formulation of partnerships: delegations from the South had started to perceive partnerships as a threat to their sovereignty. Developing country delegations (China, Indonesia and Malaysia were specifically mentioned), had become increasingly worried about the possibility that developmental projects within their national borders would pick and choose which international or national NGOs to work with. As a result, some delegations raised questions about non-state actor participation, and China went even as far as to delineate which NGOs were acceptable and which were not.

The framework that was negotiated at PrepCom IV was meant to address various governmental concerns in order to make partnerships an agreeable outcome to all parties involved. However, the negotiation process was long and cumbersome. According to Diane Quarless, co-chair of that meeting, one of the reasons for this frustration had been the alienation of business from the process:

> All of these big corporations [had] an interest in CSR, therefore the process had to be selective. So the idea was first to make the corporations sign the CSR code of conduct through the process of registration. That, I think, was the principle reason for the draining of the enthusiasm from the private sector. These [concerns] leading up to the Bali guidelines killed the initiative. Bali was critical, the enthusiasm that has been built evaporated.[12]

Another reason was that the concerns of developing countries slowed down the process resulting in a loss of momentum. Jan Pronk argued that the idea of an inclusive process within the UN was frustrating because the guidelines were particularly discouraging new and big initiatives to be effectively created in the short-term.[13] Diane Quarless agreed that the negotiations took too long: 'It all changed at Bali. That's where [the initiative] was killed . . . we have taken so long to reach an agreement on [. . .] the Bali Guidelines, [which] were supposed to be the basis on which you form a partnership.'[14]

The resulting document, the Bali Guiding Principles[15] (or the Bali Guidelines) forms the framework that guides the arrangement and registration of partnerships with the UNCSD. While respondents from partnerships often thought they were ambiguous, UN representatives and experts focusing on governance regarded them as a failure, for several reasons. Part of the critique concerned the way in which the issues above were addressed. Another part concerned the content of the guidelines: what they invoked and what they left out.

Although the Bali Guidelines reflected the concerns of several parties, the final document did not effectively address them. For instance, one guideline defines partnership objectives, clarifying that partnerships were only to contribute to the implementation of intergovernmental decisions, implying that newly emerging issues on the environmental agenda would not be tackled through partnerships. In a later study, Gunningham (2007) noted that partnerships are most effective and influential in newly emerging issue areas. But without an institutional body to initiate or invite partnerships on these new issues, and under the condition that partnerships can only address issues with intergovernmental consensus, this was not possible in practice.

Negotiations also concentrated on the inclusion of business actors into the decision-making process. Two criteria were proposed: a code of conduct to be signed by all corporate actors involved and a strict commitment to CSR. Both of these proposals were ultimately turned down. Regarding the involvement of NGOs, some delegations agreed to type-2 outcomes only if they had the chance to approve the list of all NGOs from their country that could be partners. According to a respondent from the organizing committee,[16] although partnerships were 'not sufficiently significant to raise havoc', if any Southern government wished to nullify the registration of a partnership, they could. This was because the only partnerships that were actually negotiated and agreed upon would be those registered during the WSSD, in other words, what was agreed upon was not a process but a list of partnerships at a certain point in time. Moreover, conceptualizing partnerships as implementation mechanisms as opposed to decision-making mechanisms or means to ensure participation of non-state actors remedied some concerns. The outcome was that partnerships were no longer envisaged as an instrument to increase inter-sectoral and multi-stakeholder participation, but rather a straightforward implementation tool.

The Bali Guidelines were, however, successful in framing an ideal-type of partnership, even when they did not provide the mandate to reach this ideal. For example, it was highlighted that partnerships should address economic, social and environmental dimensions of sustainable develop-ment both in their design and in their implementation activities. This very broad scope of issues accounts for a rather ambitious framing if one con-siders that partnerships are mere implementation mechanisms that could not go beyond intergovernmental decisions. The broad scope of issues to be addressed has been one of the reasons why in the partnerships registry partnerships are asked to list multiple aims and functions in the social, economic and ecological spheres. While most partnerships reported func-tions across such a wide issue area, they did not have the means to fulfil all of those promises, resulting in partnerships that only elusively relate to the environmental aspect of poverty reduction or vice versa.

While addressing the three pillars of sustainable development, part-nerships should also fit into the sustainable development strategies and poverty reduction strategies of the countries, regions and communities where implementation takes place. This statement assumes that appropri-ate strategies are in place and operational in countries of implementation. On this account, partnerships are not supposed to lead to significant political changes and reform, or to move beyond the existing frames of reference.

While it was stated in the Bali Guidelines that partnerships should be multi-stakeholder initiatives with equal say among partners in the design and management of projects, they should 'preferably involve a range of significant actors in a given area of work' (UN 2002). In other words, partnerships potentially reassert existing power imbalances by only involving actors that are already seen as significant in a given issue area. This is particularly relevant for local communities on the recipient side. Introducing new technologies, governance schemes, or ways of living into communities is often accompanied by hegemonic relations that can be further exacerbated. Another guideline that contradicts the intended empowerment of the recipient communities suggests that 'while the active involvement of local communities in the design and implementation of partnerships is strongly encouraged (bottom-up approach), partnerships should be international in their impact' (UN 2002), which allows for the empowerment of transnational and international instead of local actors. While the guidelines suggest that all partners should be involved in the design of the partnerships, they also advised that 'as partnerships evolve, there should be an opportunity for additional partners to join on an equal basis' (UN 2002).

Another set of problems regarding the content of the Bali Guidelines arises from what was not explicitly outlined. While partnerships should be voluntary, self-organizing, transparent and accountable, the Guidelines did not stipulate any screening or monitoring mechanisms to ensure these qualities. Instead, partnerships should prove to be transparent and accountable by self-reporting. Moreover, the Bali Guidelines refer to the need to identify funding resources, formulate tangible goals and specify clear timeframes. However, the Guidelines do not explicate on how to fulfil these needs.

According to Quarless,

> There were lengthy discussions within the bureau as to how we were going to monitor these partnerships. [In the two-year UNCSD cycle] there was sup-posed to be one year where we would do nothing more than reviewing these partnerships. [. . .] That has not happened. [In the end], we got the lowest common denominator, which has broken my heart, really. Because what they said is that 'we do not want DESA to take a leadership role in conceptualizing partnerships'.[17]

Neither UNDESA nor the UNCSD were given authority to effectively review and monitor partnerships. The UNCSD's authority was limited to screening and selection at a very minimal level. Despite all the contradictions above, the Bali Guidelines could have had significant effects, had there been a central partnerships body in place overseeing the reviewing and the monitoring of partnerships. With a stronger UNCSD mandate, a more balanced focus on different issue areas, an even geographical distribution and balanced multi-stakeholder participation in partnerships could have emerged. Furthermore, if there had been binding rules, the UNCSD could have better maintained the qualities of partnerships as an instrument for sustainable development. The ideal-type partnership sketched in the guidelines may have been practically impossible for every partnership to achieve, yet ideals would still be better reflected in the partnerships regime. Unfortunately, as non-binding principles, the Guidelines mostly reflected disagreement among parties than anything else.

In sum, the Bali Guidelines consisted of conflicting suggestions regarding the role, function and nature of partnerships; while warning about potential negative effects, they failed to address and avoid them. While framing partnerships in an ideal form, they simultaneously restricted partnerships to evolve towards such a limited ideal. Most importantly, the partnerships process remained non-binding and it was not accompanied by a monitoring mechanism, resulting in a weak screening process for registration.

GOVERNANCE THROUGH PARTNERSHIPS

In the previous section we noted that there is a discrepancy between the ideal of partnerships and the partnerships regime as an outcome of the WSSD. This gap widened as some established stakeholders in international negotiations sought to tune down the potential of a future partnerships regime. At the same time, ambitions for binding rules on partnerships registration were watered down in the process, leaving a rather weakly defined process. However, many scholars (e.g. Witte, Streck and Benner 2003) and interviewees in our survey agreed on the great potential of partnerships in sustainable development governance. That is, had they been well defined, accompanied by strict requirements with regards to e.g. corporate social responsibility, and if there were a monitoring process in place, partnerships potentially could have been a more effective instrument to achieve sustainable development. This assumption is difficult to put to test, since it concerns a hypothetical situation. Yet, the question of how partnerships impact on the institutional and political environment of sustainable development remains relevant: an individual partnership or a group of partnerships can still significantly impact a policy field at different levels of governance. In the following sections, we discuss the extent to which partnerships change established political configurations at different levels of governance, in particular at the UN level, the domestic level and the level of the partnerships regime.

Partnerships and the UN System

Despite the weak partnerships regime defined at the UN level, partnerships have had a significant effect on the workings of the UN. The emergence of partnerships as official governance mechanisms within the UN is a manifestation of a discursive shift in governance, but it is also instrumental to a closer association between the UN and business (Zammit 2003). Since the WSSD, the annual meetings of the Commission on Sustainable Development have (often) been accompanied by 'Partnership Fairs'. According to the UN, these fairs provide 'a venue for partnerships for sustainable development to network, identify partners, create synergies between partnerships and learn from each other's experiences'.[18] The fairs aim to support partnerships and build capacities, but also to broker more partnerships. However, no new partnerships have actually been announced at or during these meetings. Moreover, registration seems to be slowing down: in 2009, only two new partnerships were registered, and none were registered in 2010. Therefore, in terms of building partnerships, the process appears rather unsuccessful. Yet, partnership fairs also provide the opportunity for NGOs and business to enter the UN venue during the UNCSD meetings, as country delegations meet and discuss selected themes of sustainability politics. Therefore, rather than building new partnerships, representatives of partnerships aim to reach officials and delegates to the UNCSD. The partnerships regime has the effect of opening political space for a closer association between the UN, NGOs and business. This does not lead to new partnerships or increased governance without government (Rosenau and Czempiel 1992; Peters and Pierre 1998). Rather, it confirms the position of the UNCSD as an intergovernmental body that is relatively open to third parties to influence, but not to directly partake in decision-making. This has also been observed by Witte and colleagues (2003); the UN and other international organizations do not have a coherent policy to embed or mainstream partnerships in their operations, even when partnerships have been discussed in the broader context of Global Public Policy Networks (Reinicke 1998), and international organizations have widely adopted a discourse that prefers partnerships.

Partnerships and the Domestic Level

One impact that partnerships have at the domestic level of governance is that they can be instrumental in the strengthening of non-governmental actors in public service and goods provision vis-à-vis the state. It has been argued that, especially in developing countries, business has taken over many government tasks, sometimes in the form of business–government or business–NGO partnerships. Idemudia (2008), for instance, discusses the role of multinational oil companies engaging in development in the Niger Delta through various types of partnerships. He observes that community investments driven by business logic results in an uneven distribution of social infrastructure, for example in the field of tap water provision. The strengthening of business interests through partnerships has led to a broader claim that partnerships are a vehicle in the further expansion of neo-liberalism. Miraftab (2004) argues that partnerships often end up reinstating or even reinvigorating for-profit interests, since the introduction of partnerships is often accompanied by a programme of privatization (cf. Savas 2000). While partnerships are set up to service the poor, they also are used to break down state responsibility for equitable development. After a partnership ends its activities, the state has faded away and instead of promised power sharing, the poor end up with even graver dispossession. Therefore, Miraftab compares partnerships to a Trojan horse: presented as a gift, they actually break down state responsibility and capability for equitable development and, as a result, reinstate private and corporate interests.

On the other hand, some scholars associate partnerships with reforms in political institutions and policies, seeing them as a tool for democratization. Bäckstrand (2006) finds that 'deliberative stakeholder practices with general democratic potential' are exemplified in global sustainability governance, in particular in the process surrounding the WSSD. Similar reform is observed at the local and domestic level (e.g. Johnson and Wilson 2000; Barret and Usui 2002). However, in the sample of partnerships registered with the UNCSD, only few are explicitly concerned with promoting democratic practices and practices of good governance. An exception is the Good Governance in Sustainable Development (GGSD) partnership, which explicitly aims at assisting societies 'to develop effective government within a democratic system, and to implement sustainable development principles through global partnership'[19] through local city networks. At the same time, GGSD sets its own limits to influence democratization processes, as it departs from a minimal basic assumption that 'the country [where the partnership implements its activities] must politically practice a democratic system'.[20] Another exception is the partnership for the Promotion of Sustainable Development in the Lake Victoria Basin, which also refers to democratic governance as a goal, although it does not explicitly refer to government reform. Whether the work of these partnerships has actually led to more (deliberative) democracy remains to be investigated, since both have not reported back to the UNCSD. The only partnership that has claimed to have achieved more democratic governance is Partners for Water and Sanitation (PAWS), which declares it facilitated 'the development of more inclusive, democratic and adaptive governance processes for water management involving historically disadvantaged communities'[21] in South Africa. Of course, a partnership does not need to influence policy processes at a level and a scale where it can claim democratic change. Some partnerships will seek to strengthen civil society or business vis-à-vis 'old government'. For instance, the Critical Ecosystem Partnership (CEPF) seeks to strengthen civil society in local biodiversity governance, by implementing grant programmes to support local NGOs' biodiversity conservation activities.

In some cases, partnerships even question the sovereignty of existing government entities. The CEPF, again, represents an interesting case because it defines 'biodiversity hotspots' as implementation areas, rather than countries or areas within countries. For instance, the 'Western Ghats' biodiversity hotspot encompasses both areas in India and Sri Lanka, and the 'Indo-Burma' hotspot even encompasses five countries: Cambodia, Lao P.D.R., Thailand and Vietnam, as well as Hainan Island and parts of southern China. Such a transregional focus has far reaching implications with regards to political organization. The CEPF promotes transnational areas as entities of global governance, instead of sovereign states and sub-ordinated regions and localities.

The Organizational Field of Partnerships

While the number of partnerships for sustainable development registered with the UNCSD hardly increases, outside of the UNCSD, partnerships are continuously brokered. As the number of partnerships grows, they increasingly interact, collaborate, and sometimes even create new partnerships. Among partnerships, a certain politics is therefore also evolving. Partnerships can exist in isolation from each other, but more likely – when they are active in the same geographical and issue area – they adopt political strategies. For instance, partnerships may compete for dominance, or partnerships adopt collaborative strategies. Among the UNCSD-registered energy partnerships, there are intensive collaborations. For example, the Renewable Energy Policy Network for the 21st Century (REN 21) and the Renewable Energy and Energy Efficiency Partnership (REEEP) are both partners and founders of a search engine for renewable energy and energy efficiency. Another example of a collaborative strategy among partnerships is memorandums of understanding for instance between the Global Village Energy Partnership (GVEP), The Global Network on Energy for Sustainable Development (GNESD) and REEEP.

On the other hand, it is reasonable to expect that competitive strategies among partnerships will also become more common; following the example in private rule making, where standard setting and labelling have at times been negatively affected by competition. One of the most significant examples of this development is visible in the field of sustainable forestry. The Forest Stewardship Council, successful at gaining considerable recognition by various actors across various sectors, soon found itself competing against alternative forest certification schemes (such as, the Programme for the Endorsement of Forest Certification Schemes [PEFC]) leading to considerable fragmentation in the field of private rule making in sustainable forestry (Chan and Pattberg 2008).

INTRODUCTION OF CONTROVERSIAL TECHNOLOGIES AND INSTITUTIONS

In this section we look at the political use of partnerships in several issue areas. Due to the lack of a strict screening and follow-up process, partnerships create a platform for highly controversial technologies to gain recognition at the UN level (e.g. nuclear energy, biotechnologies, biofuels and PVC and vinyl partnerships). In this section we present cases where partnerships are employed as a tool to relate politically controversial sectors and contexts.

Global Initiative Towards a Sustainable Iraq (GITSI)

The flexible nature of partnerships and the lack of criteria for formation and registration of UNCSD partnerships make them particularly prone to reflect the preferences of powerful actors in the politics of sustainable development. An example is the Global Initiative towards a Sustainable Iraq (GITSI). GITSI is an initiative launched at the UN Headquarters in May 2008 by Sustainable Development International and the United Nations Development Programme (UNDP); its partners are local governments in Iraq, a number of stakeholders from the Gulf region, and the United States government. GITSI's information page on the UNCSD website[22] indicates that its aim is to

> improve knowledge and awareness of the Iraqi society about sustainable development for the sake of achieving a sustainable Iraq so as to have a sustainable, stable and prosperous Iraq where all present and future generations can live in peace and harmony with other nations and where all resources are utilized in a sustainable manner catering to the well-being of Iraq's current and future generations and ecosystems.

GITSI's goals appear rather lofty, even though the causality established here can be challenged: improving knowledge of sustainability does not necessarily result in or even contribute to a country's stability, prosperity, peace and harmony. It could be argued that US occupation (supported by the very regional governments that gained considerable power vis-à-vis the central government) has not contributed to stability, nor to the peace and harmony or the sustainability of Iraq. Moreover, GITSI aims to achieve this goal mainly by capacity building, technology transfer, raising awareness and subcontracting, some of the main strategies of US development aid in the past two decades. This raises the question how development aid relates to US hegemony, and, in this case, what the consequences and the intentions are of a partnership like GITSI. A United States Agency for International Development (USAID) text on its website is a telling example of the linking of development with a wider political reform agenda:

> The United States has a long history of extending a helping hand to those people overseas struggling to make a better life, recover from a disaster or striving to live in a free and democratic country. It is this caring that stands as a

hallmark of the United States around the world [. . .] and shows the world our true character as a nation. US foreign assistance has always had the twofold purpose of furthering America's foreign policy interests in expanding democracy and free markets while improving the lives of the citizens of the developing world (USAID).

In sum, GITSI's aim cannot be seen apart from a wider political agenda. GITSI is aiming at the necessary institutions, human and economic resources, technological means and public opinion for Iraq's modernization towards a political system that is fully integrated into existing global power constellations.

Nuclear Energy

At the UNCSD-15 meeting held in New York in May 2007, some of the UNCSD partnerships had their stands at the Partnerships Fair, an exhibition to showcase success in partnership projects. The last two partnerships registered to the UNCSD before the meeting also participated in this fair: Generation IV International Forum (GIF) and World Nuclear University (WNU), both promoting different aspects of nuclear energy. Until 2007, the UNCSD did not have any nuclear energy partnerships in its portfolio. However, UNCSD-15 was particularly about energy in the context of sustainable development, and the Partnerships Team's call for new registries has caught the attention of these initiatives. Generation IV refers to the latest generation of nuclear power plants and advocates their safety advantages compared to earlier technologies. The WNU focuses on educating nuclear engineers while simultaneously 'correcting the misunderstandings [of the public] regarding nuclear energy.'[23] To this end, the WNU organized a high profile side event at the UNCSD, titled 'The Contribution of Nuclear Energy to Sustainable Development', advocating the use of nuclear energy for the cause of sustainable development. While two speakers focused their presentations on the ways in which nuclear energy could be publicized, the opening speech of Susan Eisenhower was distinctly politically motivated. She claimed that under the pressures of climate change nuclear energy was under review again, since 'it has been and will continue to be the largest source of emission-free energy. [. . .] Nuclear energy is the only source of energy that can provide consistent and substantial levels of energy while reducing. . . [correction:] while producing emission-free.'[24]

Eisenhower's correction was important, as nuclear power plants were not reducing carbon emissions – in fact, they did not even result in the reduction of overall carbon emissions of the United States, which according to her, were 'responsible for half of the total voluntary reductions in greenhouse gas emissions reported by US companies in 2001'.[25] The voluntary reductions and the voluntary reporting scheme aside, in 2001 (and during all the years since then) there has been no reduction in carbon emissions of the United States. Second, she was employing the term emission-free, which can be questioned from a technical point of view, as electricity production through nuclear power plants results in water vapour emissions, if not carbon. But most importantly, Eisenhower was introducing nuclear technologies as a sustainable and environmentally friendly source of energy at the UN Headquarters, when there is no agreement on the status of nuclear energy and sustainable development.

Eisenhower's argument was based on three points. First, that nuclear energy production is safe, especially compared to other security and environment concerns: 'You have to live near a nuclear power plant for over 2000 years to get the same amount of radiation that you get at a standard medical X-ray. So I challenge everyone here to look into the facts about this, because there are too many other issues on the table that threaten our long-term security that could be addressed by nuclear energy.' Second, solving climate change, nuclear energy production would also be the solution to proliferation problems:

> I know we're talking about sustainable development but everybody has to be deeply concerned about those developing nations and the potential of their access to nuclear technologies that may, as we discuss in Washington and elsewhere, lead to proliferation concerns. Rather ironically, I may be one of these security experts who feel very strongly that we will not be able to address proliferation problems without nuclear energy. Few people realise here today that 20 per cent of the nuclear energy that is generated in this country comes from Soviet era war heads that have been blended for reactor use. [. . .] I myself have been in and out of these nuclear weapons facilities and I can tell you I know something about the disposition of nuclear materials. We have a perfect storm, a perfect opportunity to be able to use excess nuclear materials and to make them appropriate for reactor use thus solving some of the deep concerns we have about the misuse of nuclear materials.

Thus in the heart of her vision about nuclear energy was her grandfather President Dwight Eisenhower's Atoms for Peace Program, which not only suggested peaceful use of nuclear technologies through the establishment of the International Atomic Energy Agency (IAEA) but also sharing nuclear technologies (but not necessarily weapons) with the developing countries, some of which later on refused to sign the Nuclear Non-Proliferation Treaty.

In the context of the WNU, this vision of 'peaceful and sustainable use of nuclear technologies' was supported by other important figures such as John Ritch (Director General of World Nuclear Association),

James Lovelock (author of the Gaia Theory), Hans Blix (IAEA Director General-Emeritus), Mohamed El-Baradei (Director General of IAEA and Nobel Peace Prize Laureate), Sir David King (Chief Science Advisor to the Government of the United Kingdom), and representatives of the nuclear energy industry. At the inaugural ceremony of the WNU, Blix[26] pointed out the security threats of climate change, proposing a transition from Atoms for Peace to Atoms for Sustainable Development, while El-Baradei[27] suggested the necessity of nuclear power for development. Lovelock[28] too emphasized that climate change made nuclear energy indispensible, and that 'it is a foolish fantasy to think that we could [produce sufficient renewable energy] soon enough to avoid risking a greenhouse catastrophe'. Finally, Geoffrey Ballard, the CEO of General Hydrogen linked all concerns into one, in a way framing the reasoning behind the 'nuclear renaissance': As economic progress increased per capita energy consumption, and since all other forms of social progress are dependent on this,

> for society to continue its progress in medicine, social responsibility, science, education and quality of life, we must assure that there is an ever increasing supply of energy per capita. With human populations still on the rise, progress will not be sustained if we attempt to further reduce, or even stabilize, our energy production by reducing the emissions of the current energy source mix. We must increase our supply of energy, not reduce it.[29]

It is important to note how the discourse around clean energy production is increasingly subdued to concerns over climate change. Both GIF and WNU regard climate change and sustainable energy production as their primary goals and argue that nuclear energy production is sustainable on the basis that it is free of carbon emissions (cf. UN 2004). While the GIF maintains that the partnership contributes to the implementation of Agenda 21 by protecting the atmosphere (cf. UN 2004), the WNU states its mission as 'increasing use of nuclear power as the one proven technology able to produce clean energy on a large, global scale'; it also refers to contributing to Agenda 21 by protecting the atmosphere, the quality and supply of freshwater resources, and the transfer of environmentally sound technology, while contributing to science for sustainable development (UN 2004).

While the UNFCCC and the Kyoto Protocol do not recognise nuclear energy as a suitable and sustainable way of mitigating climate change, lack of screening and monitoring of UNCSD partnerships allows for a controversial technology to gain recognition in UN circles, by reducing sustainable development to climate change, and climate change to carbon emissions. Political moves of the WNU not only include the linking of security and environmental issues, but also the reduction of sustainability to low emission energy production. Another result is that other issues on the UNCSD agenda, such as changing unsustainable patterns of consumption and production, end up being subjugated to doubtful techno-fixes suggested to remedy climate change. The more general implications of this discursive shift have been noted in a BBC opinion article by O'Hara (2007), who argued that focusing merely on reducing carbon emissions was setting aside the common cause of many other problems, simply put, unsustainable lifestyles.

Biotechnology

In his study of biotechnology partnerships, Shuji Hisano (2005) lists some of the major problems with biotechnology partnerships. For instance, although the official goal of many biotech partnerships is poverty alleviation, they focus on economically interesting products, which are mostly grown by larger- and medium-scale farmers. Similarly, genetic engineering technologies donated by corporations were not developed to cope with the viruses that caused the most pressing problems for farmers. Moreover, the stated aim of the same partnership could vary from one media channel or platform to the other, raising questions about the beneficiaries of the projects: while on some platforms the partnership would be profiled as a development aid project, on another one its aim would be stated as negotiating sales rights.

The Consultative Group on International Agricultural Research (CGIAR) Centres that Hisano studied are among the UNCSD partnerships. Their partners are also involved in other partnerships and projects under the UNCSD. One of the specified aims of CGIAR is to improve dialogue among stakeholders from the private sector and civil society on the issues regarding biotechnology and genetically modified agricultural production. According to various NGO representatives, the process resulted in the sidelining of alternative viewpoints prevalent in civil society and in a deeper engagement of the centres with the private sector. On the other hand, in partnerships between CGIAR and the private sector, the technologies and proprietary genes were mostly provided free of charge by corporations.

This closely resembles the spread of nuclear technologies when they were made freely available to recipient countries by the US government through the Atoms for Peace Programme. With or without developmental or humanitarian aims, the projects subscribe to the spread of genetic modification technologies to the recipient countries. The partnerships neither give voice to any of the opposition or critique from the users of these products (farmers and consumers alike), nor do they acknowledge the importance of traditional ways of agriculture as opposed to the cultivation of crops that require chemicals, insecticides and other kinds of inputs. Similarly, Deibel (2009) suggests that public–private partnerships between corporations and research networks of biotechnology working under humanitarian licenses limit the possibilities for alternative ways of economic and scientific organization. Most visibly, they reproduce existing hierarchies that exclude small-scale and/or poor farmers. More subtly, by giving away a technology it is also acknowledged that the technology is privately owned by the donor, even when ownership is sometimes highly contested, especially in some of the beneficiary countries. Such a combination of ownership and technology transfer with humanitarian aims could undermine the potential of alternatives, for example alternatives that explicitly support individuals that chose to live and work with genetic materials (Deibel 2009).

PVC

According to the Greenpeace International website, 'the production of PVC creates and releases one of the most toxic chemicals – dioxin'.[30] Greenpeace International has been campaigning with considerable success against PVCs, contributing to their restriction (and complete ban in children's toys) in northern Europe as well as in the products of corporations such as Nike, IKEA and The Body Shop. It could be argued that the success of their campaign is a result of their focus on the production, as opposed to consumption or waste management aspects. Dioxin is emitted in the production and incineration process of PVC products. Its dissemination through the atmosphere results in their large-scale consumption, while accumulation in the food chain causes eco-systemic concentration. This has even been the case in mammals and birds with no exposure to plastics (such as polar bears and penguins), as well as the marine aquatic environment (De Rooij et al. 2004). The harmful health and eco-systemic effects of PVC production and consumption have been well-documented, particularly in the last decade (cf. Lithner et al. 2009), although these effects have been downplayed owing to the 'substantial input from the chemical industry' in consultative and stakeholder processes (cf. Sass, Castleman and Wallinga 2005).

Vinyl 2010 is a Belgium-based partnership registered with the UNCSD that aims to 'provide the organizational and financial infrastructure to manage and monitor the actions undertaken as part of the Voluntary Commitment [by PVC manufacturers]'.[31] It is an initiative of four European lobby groups.[32] Although their representative to the UNCSD-15 session suggested in a speech that 'transparency and working with stakeholders is key for industry initiatives,'[33] the partnership neither has consumer groups nor NGOs on board. The UNCSD website suggests that the partnership aims to 'improve production processes and products, invest in technology, minimise emissions and waste and boost collection and recycling, according to the guidelines of the EU institutions, and progressing towards sustainability'.[34] Nonetheless its target of cutting raw material and energy consumption would be applied 'where economically and ecologically warranted'.[35] When asked how they specified the criteria for 'economically and ecologically viable', a respondent from the partnership answered that there were indeed no criteria, and that reduction of production was not one of their main goals.[36]

Water Purification Chemicals

While the issue area of water will be studied in more detail in Chapters 9 and 10 (this volume), Procter and Gamble's water purification product 'PUR' is another example of politics of technology transfer through partnerships. While being regarded as a research and development and/or marketing failure until 2003,

> 'PUR' was relaunched as a CSR product in 2004 within the Safe Drinking Water Alliance, a partnership comprising Procter and Gamble and the Johns Hopkins University Bloomberg School of Public Health's Center for Communication Programs (CCP), Population Services International (PSI) and UK charity Care. The Safe Drinking Water Alliance was the first in a series of partnerships between Procter and Gamble and non-profit organizations featuring 'PUR' and was designed as a pilot programme to test three marketing strategies: social marketing, commercial marketing and disaster and humanitarian relief networks (Hanson 2007).

Indeed, the Alliance was designed as a pilot project to test marketing strategies, which Procter and Gamble continued to use in its later partnerships such as the UNCSD registered Safe Water System (SWS) and Community Water Initiative partnerships. Similar to the humanitarian licenses in biotechnology (cf. Deibel 2009), utilizing a humanitarian relief strategy, Procter and Gamble partnered first with CARE in Ethiopia in 2004, and later with the United Nations Children's Fund (UNICEF) in the aftermath of the Indian Ocean tsunami, where Procter and Gamble would provide 'PUR' at low cost, while the funds would be provided by NGOs as well as Procter and Gamble employees. As Greg Allgood from the corporation's consumer health products unit stated,

Before this date, we'd sold only 3 million sachets in three years. After the tsunami hit, we sold 15 million sachets in 48 hours. AmeriCares used two of its cargo planes: one went to Sri Lanka and the other to Indonesia. We increased production: we went to 24-hour shifts and we installed an additional packing machine (Hanson 2007).

By 2006, 'PUR' had 10 social markets and its distribution totalled 54 million sachets, turning an R&D failure into a marketing victory.

In our interviews with respondents from different sectors, 'PUR' has been repeatedly mentioned, both as a success story and a scam. The reason for such controversial comments was not only the questionable ethics of these business strategies. They were also concerning the nature of the product: although Procter and Gamble and the US CDC advertise 'PUR' as a product that supplies 'safe drinking water' in developing countries, one respondent suggested that it only cleansed the water from certain contaminants and not others. Therefore, it was regarded as misinformation. In fact, the language used in the advertisements of 'PUR' is cautious about the removal process (e.g. 'proven to remove the vast majority of bacteria, viruses, and protozoa' without suggesting complete removal, or avoiding the term 'proven' regarding heavy metals and chemical contaminants which are also presumably removed).[37] 'Safe drinking water' is a term that is more often used to describe the resulting mixture, which indeed suggests misinformation.[38]

CONCLUSIONS

This chapter examined the political dimension of partnerships. We focused on three related aspects. First, the process that resulted in partnerships emerging as the official outcome of the WSSD was scrutinized. During their negotiation, partnerships became the object of political contestations. Second, while the WSSD resulted in a weak overall partnerships regime, individual partnerships still have considerable impact and political influence at several levels of governance. Finally, we presented cases in which partnerships, due to the lack of a strict screening and follow-up process, create a platform for highly controversial technologies to gain recognition at the UN level. These technologies and practices introduced by partnerships for sustainable development include nuclear energy, biotechnologies, biofuels, PVC and vinyl, to name a few. On this account, partnerships are not just neutral instruments for implementing internationally accepted sustainability norms, such as the Millennium Development Goals and Agenda 21, but rather sites of contestation over distinct technologies and practices. We contend that this broader critical view on partnerships beyond problem-solving is helpful in estimating the overall contribution of the partnership regime to the much required sustainability transition (see also Chapter 4, this volume).

NOTES

1. UN DESA website: http://www.un.org/esa/dsd/dsd/dsd_faqs_partnerships.shtml (retrieval: 15.08.2011).
2. The final decision of PrepCom IV mentions partnerships as 'events' to take place before the summit.
3. IISD website: http://www.iisd.ca/vol22/enb2219e.html (retrieval: 21.09.2008).
4. Interview with a DESA representative at the time of the WSSD, May 2007, New York.
5. Interview with a DESA representative at the time of the WSSD, May 2007, New York.
6. Interview with a DESA representative at the time of the WSSD, May 2007, New York.
7. Interview with UN representative, May 2008, New York.
8. Interview with DESA representative, May 2007, New York.
9. Interview with Southern country delegate to the CSD and the WSSD, December 2006, Denpasar.
10. Interview with Diane Quarless, May 2007, New York.
11. Interview with Southern country delegate to the CSD and the WSSD, December 2006, Denpasar.
12. Interview with Diane Quarless, May 2007, New York.
13. Interview with Jan Pronk, 21 April 2008, The Hague.
14. Interview with Diane Quarless, May 2007, New York.
15. UN DESA website: http://www.un.org/esa/dsd/dsd_aofw_par/par_mand_baliguidprin.shtml (retrieval: 15.07.2009).
16. Interview with UN representative, May 2008, New York.
17. Interview with Diane Quarless, May 2007, New York.
18. cf. http://www.un.org/esa/dsd/dsd_aofw_par/par_csdfair.shtml (retrieval: 15.03.2011).
19. UNCSD Partnerships for Sustainable Development database available at: http://webapps01.un.org/dsd/partnerships/public/partnerships/228.html (retrieval: 16.03.2011).
20. UNCSD Partnerships for Sustainable Development database, http://webapps01.un.org/dsd/partnerships/public/partnerships/228.html (retrieval: 16.03.2011).
21. UNCSD Partnerships for Sustainable Development database, http://webapps01.un.org/dsd/partnerships/public/partnerships/92.html (retrieval: 16.03.2011).
22. UNCSD website: http://webapps01.un.org/dsd/partnerships/public/partnerships/2407.html (retrieval: 5.03.2009).
23. Transcribed from the presentations made in the side event to the CSD-15, 1 May 2007.
24. Transcribed from the presentations made in the side event to the CSD-15, 1 May 2007.
25. Transcribed from the presentations made in the side event to the CSD-15, 1 May 2007.
26. WNU website: http://www.world-nuclear-university.org/about.aspx?id=15904 (retrieval: 16.11.2009).
27. WNU website: http://www.world-nuclear-university.org/about.aspx?id=15906 (retrieval: 16.11.2009).
28. WNU website: http://www.world-nuclear-university.org/about.aspx?id=15902 (retrieval: 16.11.2009).
29. WNU website: http://www.world-nuclear-university.org/about.aspx?id=15928 (retrieval: 16.11.2009).
30. Greenpeace International website: http://www.greenpeace.org/international/campaigns/toxics/polyvinyl-chloride (retrieval: 03.12.2009).
31. UNCSD website: http://webapps01.un.org/dsd/partnerships/public/partnerships/1132.html (retrieval: 05.03.2009).

32. The European Council of Vinyl Manufacturers (ECVM), the European Plastics Converters (EuPC), the European Council for Plasticisers and Intermediates (ECPI) and the European Stabiliser Producers Associations (ESPA).
33. *Partnerships Wire*, 4 May 2007, available at: UN DESA website: http://www.un.org/esa/sustdev/csd/csd15/PF/wire_May_4.pdf (retrieval: 14.06.2008).
34. UNCSD website: http://webapps01.un.org/dsd/partnerships/public/partnerships/1132.html (retrieval: 05.03.2009).
35. UNCSD website: http://webapps01.un.org/dsd/partnerships/public/partnerships/1132.html (retrieval: 05.03.2009).
36. Interview with business respondent, May 2007, New York.
37. US CDC website: http://www.cdc.gov/safewater/publications_pages/options-pur.pdf (retrieval: 01.02.2010).
38. US CDC website: http://www.cdc.gov/safewater/publications_pages/options-pur.pdf (retrieval: 01.02.2010).

REFERENCES

Bäckstrand, K. (2006), 'Democratizing global environmental governance? Stakeholder democracy after the World Summit on Sustainable Development', *European Journal of International Relations*, **12**(4), 467–98.
Barret, B. and M. Usui (2002), 'Local Agenda 21 in Japan: transforming local environmental governance', *Local Environment*, **7**(1), 49–67.
Chan, S. and P. Pattberg (2008), 'Private rule-making and the politics of accountability: analyzing global forest governance', *Global Environmental Politics*, **8**(3), 103–121.
Deibel, E. (2009), *Common Genomes: On Open Source in Biology and Critical Theory beyond the Patent*, Amsterdam: VU/Ridderprint.
De Rooij, C., C. Defourny, R.S. Thompson, V. Garny, A. Lecloux and D. Van Wijk (2004), 'Vinyl chloride marine risk assessment with special reference to the Osparcom region: North Sea', *Environmental Monitoring and Assessment*, **97**, 57–67.
Gunningham, N. (2007), 'Environmental partnerships in agriculture: reflections on the Australian experience, in F. Biermann, P. Glasbergen and A.P.J. Mol, *Partnerships, Governance and Sustainable Development: Reflections on Theory and Practice*, Cheltenham, UK: Edward Elgar, pp. 115–37.
Hanson, M. (2007), 'Pure Water', *Management Today*, 01 April 2007, available at: http://www.managementtoday.co.uk/news/647187 (retrieval: 01.02.2010).
Hisano, S. (2005), 'A critical observation on the mainstream discourse of "biotechnology for the poor"', *Tailoring Biotechnologies*, **1**(2), 81–106.
Idemudia, U. (2008), 'Oil extraction and poverty reduction in the Niger Delta: a critical examination of partnership initiatives', *Journal of Business Ethics*, **90**(1), 91–116.
Johnson, H. and G. Wilson (2000), 'Biting the bullet: civil society, social learning and the transformation of local governance', *World Development*, **28**(11), 1891–906.
Lithner, D., J. Damberg, G. Dave and A. Larsson (2009), 'Leachates from plastic consumer products: screening for toxicity with *Daphnia magna*', *Chemosphere*, **74**, 1195–200.
Miraftab, F. (2004), 'Public–private partnerships. The Trojan horse of

neoliberal development', *Journal of Planning Education and Research*, **24**(1), 89–101.

O'Hara, E. (2007), 'Focus on carbon "missing the point"', BBC News Online, 30 July 2007, available at: http://news.bbc.co.uk/2/hi/science/nature/6922065.stm (retrieval: 13.08.2007).

Peters, B.G. and J. Pierre (1998), 'Governance without government? Rethinking public administration', *Journal of Public Administration Research and Theory*, **8**(2), 223–43.

Reinicke, W.H. (1998), *Global Public Policy. Governing without Government?* Washington, DC: Brookings Institution Press.

Rosenau, J.N. and E.O. Czempiel (eds) (1992), *Governance without Government: Order and Change in World Politics*, Cambridge, UK: Cambridge University Press.

Sass, J.B., B. Castleman and D. Wallinga (2005), 'Vinyl chloride: a case study of data suppression and misrepresentation', *Environmental Health Perspectives*, **113**(7), July 2005, 809–812.

Savas E.S. (2000), *Privatization and Public–Private Partnerships*, New York: Chatham House.

United Nations (2002), Guiding principles for Partnerships for Sustainable Development ('type 2 outcomes') to be elaborated by interested parties in the context of the World Summit on Sustainable Development (WSSD), Fourth Summit Preparatory Committee (PREPCOM 4), 27 May–07 June 2002, Bali, Indonesia, available at: htttp://www.johannesburgsummit.org/html/documents/prepcom4docs/bali_documents/annex_partnership.pdf (retrieval: 03.05.2011).

United Nations (2004), UN CSD Partnerships Database, available at: http://webapps01.un.org/dsd/partnerships/public/welcome.do (retrieval: 03.05.2011).

Witte, J.M., C. Streck and T. Brenner (2003), 'The road from Johannesburg: what future for partnerships in global environmental governance?' in T. Benner, C. Streck and J. Martin Witte (eds), *Progress or Peril? Networks and Partnerships in Global Environmental Governance. The Post-Johannesburg Agenda*, Berlin: Global Public Policy Institute, pp. 59–84.

Zammit, A. (2003), *Development at Risk: Rethinking UN–Business Partnerships*, Geneva: The South Centre and UNRISD.

3. Explaining the geographic, thematic and organizational differentiation of partnerships for sustainable development

Sander Chan and Christina Müller

Transnational public–private partnerships have become a preferred instrument of global governance for sustainable development. At the 2002 WSSD, the failure to achieve sustainable development goals was blamed on an implementation gap that could be countered by intensifying and increasing partnership arrangements. Following Chapter 2 that analyses in more detail the political bargaining process involved, this chapter focuses on the emergence of partnerships for sustainable development. While the rise of public–private partnership as a distinct form of governance has been widely acknowledged in the governance and public policy literature, the question of how such partnerships emerge at the global stage has yet to be answered.

In the first part of this chapter we review various suggestions concerning the emergence of partnerships for sustainable development from a number of theoretical perspectives, including rationalism, functionalism, policy network theory and institutionalism.

The second part of this chapter examines the patterns of emergence of partnerships for sustainable development. The theories discussed here are expected to have specific implications for the geographic scope of partnerships, the policy area in which they emerge as well as for the participation of different actors in partnerships. Hence, discrepancies between the theoretical expectations about the emergence of partnerships and the empirically observed patterns of emergence raise the question of whether current theories provide a sufficient analytical framework for the appraisal of partnerships. The empirical assessment is based on the GSPD (see Chapter 1, this volume).

WHY DO PARTNERSHIPS EMERGE? THEORETICAL PERSPECTIVES

There seems to be a discrepancy between the rationale of the emergence of individual partnerships and the emergence of partnerships as an aggregate phenomenon in global environmental governance. The emergence of individual partnerships is often explained from a rationalist standpoint that depicts partners as rational self-interested agents, seizing every opportunity to create and profit from win–win constellations. Existing theoretical perspectives on the emergence of partnerships, however, go beyond this atomized rationalist reasoning. This chapter does not offer a solution to this disagreement; however, by formulating hypotheses on patterns of emergence of partnerships for sustainable development, it will put some theoretical assumptions to the empirical test.

Functionalism

According to the functionalist perspective, partnerships emerge as a reaction to perceived needs, manifested in an institutional void: an empty institutional space (Arts 2003: 34) made up by multiple functional governance gaps. Haas (2004) specifies the governance gap by listing nine governance functions (agenda setting; framing; monitoring; verification; rule making; norm development; enforcement; capacity building and financing) that are unevenly addressed in current global environmental governance. Some scholars stress the changing role of traditional *foci* of governance, for instance, Biermann and Dingwerth (2004) observe that states, in spite of considerable efforts, often fail to effectively address global environmental change, leaving a functional demand for non-state actors to assume a more prominent role. As traditional institutions fail to deliver effective governance, new institutional arrangements come forward. As a result, non-state institutions increasingly supplement old *loci* of global governance, namely nation-states and international organizations.

The functionalist argument, therefore, seems to hinge both on the empirical observation that there are gaps in global governance, and on the consequentialist reasoning that new actors and institutions will fill those gaps. As a result, normative and empirical questions of emergence become interlinked. Some scholars observe a de facto system of global environmental governance consisting of state and non-state actors, while at the same time appraising the emergence of new and alternative governance arrangements as something advantageous. This confusion often occurs subtly, for instance, Najam and colleagues (2004) suggest that global environmental governance 'remains incomplete', implying that there is something as 'complete' environmental governance. Similarly, Haas (2004: 8) stresses the need for new decentralized, densely networked institutions and a division of labour between 'governments, NGOs, the private sector, scientific networks and international institutions'. Other scholars even see proof of a replacement: a shift in governance from a confrontational model to a collaborative model on a win–win basis, from sovereign governance to post-sovereign governance (Karkkainen 2004: 75). These functionalist arguments may be reasonable, however, in terms of emergence they lack a solid empirical basis. The shift in governance from older institutional forms to newer ones may prove not to be as clear-cut as has been suggested.

Policy Network Theory

The emergence of public–private partnerships has also been viewed as the constitution of new policy networks. However, network explanations suffer from considerable conceptual confusion. For instance, Börzel (1998) noted the Babylonian confusion about the term 'policy network'. Börzel observed that the term 'network' was used to refer to widely varying notions such as analytical models, theories and methods. Moreover, a policy network could refer to a meso-economic structure applying to all kinds of relations between private and public actors, or it could refer to a specific set of relations among actors.

In this chapter specific policy networks of governance are highlighted, as these coincide with the empirical focus with concrete UNCSD registered partnerships. From a network perspective, these network/partnerships are enabled by societal change and technological advancement (functional disaggregation, differentiation, communication revolution). In sociology and in international relations literature, the advent of networks has also been attributed to the somewhat opaque process of globalization (Kenis and Schneider 1991; Kooiman 1993; Reinicke 1998; Knill and Lehmkuhl 2002).

In connection with the UN partnerships, Wolfgang Reinicke's Global Public Policy Institute has been especially influential, not only by conducting research focusing on the connection between the emergence of global public policy partnerships and globalization, but also by providing consultancy and advice to government and UN agencies. Reinicke (1997) understands globalization as a progressing micro-economic linking of markets, corporations, and units within firms. This form of globalization reflects in an organizational structure resembling a network including various non-state and state actors. From this perspective, government is still necessary, but instead of being the lead actor in traditional international relations, it is only one of many nodes in a much wider policy network. The 'rational choice' for a network-type of organization is informed by their ability to better coordinate dispersed resources under conditions of societal change. Consequently, public policy networks emerge where other forms of steering (through government hierarchy or market) are unable to deliver optimal resource mobilization and coordination.

With regard to policy networks as a meso-economic structure, the emergence of transnational public policy partnerships has often been explained by market mechanisms. According to this explanation, coordination and distribution in the environment of free markets is best served by network-types of organization (Cutler, Haufler and Porter 1999). While this account shares a rationalist perspective with functionalism, its vantage point is not functional gaps; rather it understands the emergence of new institutions deriving from economic coordination and distribution problems.

Confusion between the empirical and the normative remains. For instance, Reinicke (1998: 228) refers to empirical occurrences of global public policy networks in the fields of financial markets, organized crime and global corporations, while also arguing for 'the next step toward global public policy network [. . .] to fill the most important gaps and establish the missing links identified in each policy domain'. The public policy network method turns up in various reform strategies by international organizations such as the OECD, the UN and the EU, for instance the European Commission's White Paper on governance (Commission of the European Communities 2001). This repetitive progression, generated by blueprinting of public policy networks, seems to be somewhat at odds with the network assumption that this form of governance is preferred for its ability to better coordinate and mobilize resources in a globalized world.

Institutionalism

Rationalist theories are goal-oriented, and take the actor's self-interest as a vantage point. These theories assume explanatory power with actors themselves. Even though an actor focus may seem 'reasonable', rationalism has encountered much criticism. The ability for actors to foresee costs and benefits and their ability to act upon what they deem reasonable is restricted. Nobel Prize laureate Herbert Simon (1955) argues that there are limits to the rationality of people, who are also emotional and at times irrational beings. This multifacetedness of people is inevitably reflected in their actions.

The limits to rationality apply also to organizations and institutions. In the field of international relations, actor-rationality has been widely assumed in the so-called realist theories, which presume that power-maximizing states are the ultimate actors in world politics. However, in the same vein, one could argue that state actors are also restricted in maximizing their interests by traditions, by institutions, by non-state actors. Such a bounded environment gives leeway to a whole set of institutionalist explanations.

Notwithstanding the relative late-coming of partnerships in international governance, the partnership model of governance seems remarkably well established. This may relate to the fact that partnerships are often heralded as a highly flexible type of institutional arrangement. However, partnerships are not necessarily optimally adapted to meet every demand for governance. In fact, partnerships in global environmental governance are not necessarily better than the 'old school' international regimes at filling functional gaps, nor do they necessarily emerge where the need for governance is greatest. One explanation that better accounts for these 'irrational' patterns of emergence is institutionalism.

According to the institutionalist account, partnerships do not always emerge as a result of intentional efforts; rather, the emergence takes place in an organizational context. The institutional model of partnerships is copied after initial success in other policy fields. Policy-makers often lack time and resources to look for optimal solutions; instead they turn to a steady flow of best practices, and choose for the beaten track.

A public-administrative variant of institutionalism also refers to partnerships as carriers of certain societal norms. On this account, policy-makers decide not on the basis of rational or comprehensive analysis, but based 'on a partial review . . . of a number of preconceived normative judgments and assumptions' (Flinders 2005: 236). These normative judgements and assumptions take shape in a (policy) network context, where ideas of social fitness and standard models emerge, which in turn result in certain preferred types of institutional arrangements (Dingwerth and Pattberg 2009). Moreover, from a public administrative perspective, the emergence of institutional collaboration can also be seen as a confluence of problem, policy, organizational and socio-economic streams (Kingdon 1984). This theory has mainly been applied within national political systems; however collaborative windows of opportunity could also be discerned in global governance (Lober 1997).

The institutionalist perspective provides a wide array of explanations for the emergence of partnerships and similar institutional arrangements. However, these explanations are often typically void of (political) power as an important factor; rather they focus upon the structure as the context where reorganization of global governance occurs.

PATTERNS OF EMERGENCE: GEOGRAPHIC SCOPE

For each of the theories discussed above, we have formulated hypotheses concerning the expected topical, geographic, policy area and participatory patterns of emergence. Observed discrepancies between theoretically expected patterns and the actual patterns of emergence render insight into the plausibility of different theoretical arguments on the emergence of transnational partnerships.

The emergence of partnerships is often explained in the context of a globalization, which is understood as a distinctly de-territorialized process. Indeed, in terms of communications, physical space does not seem to matter anymore. In terms of governance, however, most new governance arrangements that emerge are not less territorial than before. In fact, according to Saskia Sassen (2002), globalization is a distinctly territorialized process, taking place, for instance, in financial centres, and in the so-called global cities. Similarly, Kobrin (2002) also advances territorialization as an attribute of globalization. Moreover, domestically we still observe territorial concentrations of partnerships, to give an example, the ones on the densely populated Chinese east coast (Chan 2009).

Given the territoriality of globalization and the shifts in governance, it is reasonable to expect that partnerships do not emerge evenly across the globe. Instead, some political spaces make a better environment for the emergence of partnerships than others. Table 3.1 summarizes various hypotheses regarding the geographic patterns of emergence.

Table 3.1   Geographic patterns of emergence

Theoretical perspective	Hypotheses	Indicators
Functionalism	Partnerships emerge in places where government capability is decreasing.	More partnerships emerge in Sub-Saharan Africa than in the BRICs.
Policy network theories	Partnerships emerge in places where organizational density is higher.	More partnerships emerge in South Africa and India, playing hosts to the WSSD process.
Institutionalism	Partnerships are active in countries that are most embedded in international institutions.	More partnerships in countries with high degrees of IO membership.

Functionalism

From functionalism we derived the hypothesis that partnership govern-ance would emerge in places where government capacity is decreasing. We arrived at this hypothesis because functionalism assumes a rational emergence process: partnerships emerge to fill a certain gap in the govern-ance process. While acknowledging that government capacity is very hard to measure, we chose to compare two sets of partnerships, from the Sub-Saharan African region and from the BRICs (Brazil, Russia, India and China). Since the BRICs have undergone high economic growth over the last decades we assume that governments have increased capacity through higher tax and trade revenues, but also through administrative reforms. The relatively stagnant development of Sub-Saharan Africa, excluding South Africa, results in relatively low revenues and few increased means for government reform. Therefore, we would expect the governance gap to be greater in Sub-Saharan Africa than in the BRICs; resulting in a major incentive and demand for partnerships.

Table 3.2 shows frequencies on the number of partnerships registered with the UNCSD by region and by geographic scope. Countries in the Sub-Saharan African region host 152 partnerships as countries of imple-mentation, while the BRICs are countries of implementation for 117 partnerships. Considering the small number of countries that the BRICs represent, the fact that they attract more than one third of all 344 partner-ship activities is remarkable. Therefore, we do not unequivocally observe that more partnerships emerge in regions where the governance gap is greatest, for instance, Sub-Saharan Africa. However, interpreting these figures is difficult: do we look at the number of countries or at the popula-tion that the countries represent? Yet, generated frequencies clearly indi-cate that partnerships are not overwhelmingly emerging where governance gaps are greatest.

Policy Network Theories

Policy network theories assume that emergence of partnerships is more likely to occur in places where organizational density is high. Since the set of partnerships we are looking at are part of one political process, we iden-tified geographical nodes, where policy-makers met to broker partnerships and to decide on partnerships as an official outcome, namely South Africa and Indonesia, hosts to the WSSD and its related preparatory process. Consequently, we expect more partnerships in these countries compared to other countries in their respective regions.

South Africa is a country of implementation for 84 UNCSD-partnerships

Table 3.2   *Geographic scope and partnerships per region*

		Number of PFSDs registered with the UN CSD				
		Global scope	Regional scope	Sub-Regional scope	National scope	Local scope	Total
Countries of Implementation (CoI)*	Northern Africa	41	7	10	–	1	59
	Sub-Saharan Africa	109	24	13	6	–	152
	(excl. South Africa)	(87)	(22)	(13)	(5)		(127)
	Latin America & Caribbean	99	9	19	3	2	132
	(excluded Brazil)	(89)	(9)	(19)	(2)	(2)	(121)
	East Asia (excl. China)	45	13	4	1	–	63
		(18)	(8)	(3)	(–)		(29)
	South Asia (excl. India)	67	14	2	1	1	85
		(41)	(7)	(2)	(1)	(–)	(51)
	South-East Asia	67	27	12	2	–	108
	West Asia	30	3	7	1	–	41
	Oceania	15	6	18	1	–	40
	CIS (excl. Russia)	32	4	4	1	–	41
		(19)	(2)	(4)	(1)		(26)
	Developed regions	121	32	37	2	1	193
	(excl. lower-middle income countries)	(118)	(32)	(37)	(2)	(1)	(190)
	BRICs	87	18	8	3	1	117

Note: *Partnerships that have more Countries of Implementation are counted as separate partnerships in every region. (Regional groupings according to the official United Nations site for the MDG Indicators: http://mdgs.un.org/unsd/mdg/Host.aspx?Content=Data/RegionalGroupings.htm)

(see Table 3.2). This corresponds to more than half (55 per cent) of all partnerships active in Sub-Saharan Africa. Without South Africa, the countries of this region would represent 25 fewer UNCSD-partnerships (which equals to a drop of 16.4 per cent). South Africa is therefore clearly overrepresented as a country of implementation, even though other countries may have more urgent sustainable development needs.

Indonesia is a country of implementation for 58 UNCSD-partnerships, which means that more than a half (54 per cent) of all partnerships in the South-East Asian region are implementing projects in this country. In South-East Asia, 108 partnerships are implemented, without Indonesia there would be 12 less (−11.1 per cent). Although the difference is less pronounced than in the case of South Africa, Indonesia is also clearly overrepresented in its region as country of implementation.

This finding may relate to a higher organizational density during the WSSD and its preparatory process. Indeed, we also point out that these countries were playing hosts to the WSSD, and that their respective governments had higher reputational stakes in the (apparent) success of it. Therefore, emergence of this particular set of public–private partnerships may not only be a manifestation of the rise of international or transnational policy networks, but a result of the stronger incentives for host countries to have visible outcomes.

Institutionalism

Institutionalism assumes an organizational context that is more or less enabling for partnerships. In the case of partnerships for sustainable development, the institutional arrangement is often reproduced through international organizations, who are actively promoting the model through programmes and the provision of steady flows of 'best practices'. Accordingly, we expect more partnerships in countries with a high number of memberships in international organizations. Analysis is however complicated by an intervening variable, namely that the most connected countries tend to be industrialized countries that often assume a specific role as funding partners within partnerships. Therefore we apply the comparisons within the group of the most connected countries and within the group of countries with the lowest membership in international organizations (Figures 3.1 and 3.2, Source: Own data and CIA 2009).

Among the countries most connected to international organizations, which also are the donor countries (see Figure 3.1), we observe no remarkable relation between membership in international organizations and the number of partnerships they are partner in as a country of implementation.

Among the least connected countries, however, we observe a marked

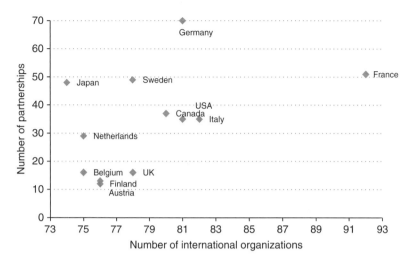

Figure 3.1   Membership in international organizations and number of partnerships in most-connected countries

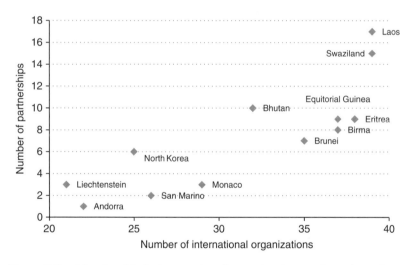

Figure 3.2   Membership in international organizations and number of partnerships in least-connected countries

tendency (see Figure 3.2). Higher membership in international organizations seems to be a good indicator for higher involvement in partnerships as a country of implementation. It should be noted that most of the least connected countries also happen to be some of the smallest countries in the world. We should therefore be cautious when drawing our conclusions, since there are more factors that might determine a country's partnership activities. Nevertheless, it seems that the number of memberships in international organizations matters for the prevalence of partnerships in countries that have not yet reached the high degree of membership in international organizations that is common for industrialized countries.

PATTERNS OF EMERGENCE: POLICY AREAS

The structure and features of a particular policy area can affect the emergence of partnerships. Cutler and colleagues (1999) have argued that a market structure encourages private governance. However, do markets provide a sufficient coordination mechanism to provide public goods? It has been argued that oligarchic market structures are more suitable for private and hybrid governance than markets with an indefinite number of players. The fewer players in a certain sector, the more visible they are for e.g. consumer organizations and NGOs to scrutinize and to pressure for self-regulation. Ronit and Schneider (1999: 262), for instance, suggest that 'in general, an effective sanctioning system seems more manageable in small or federated organizations, where the visibility of each member is high'.

Therefore, partnerships emerge in and across existing policy areas, but some policy areas are probably more supportive to governance by transnational public policy partnerships than others.

When formulating hypotheses around policy area patterns of emergence of partnerships, we are confronted with the fact that policy areas are rarely fixed, often overlap and partnerships often cut across various areas. Nor have we found a systematic formulation of hypotheses on policy areas in current partnership literature. In the Table 3.3 we attempted to formulate some hypotheses regarding the policy area patterns of emergence, along with some possible indicators, by theoretical category. The theories discussed and hypotheses derived are not exhaustive, but we deem it useful to emphasize theoretical implications of the policy area patterns of emergence of transnational public policy partnerships.

Functionalism

From a functionalist perspective we could assume that the emergence of partnerships occurs in policy areas that are deemed most urgent. To test this functionalist hypothesis, we focus on the overarching theme of water (see also Chapters 9 and 10, this volume). This theme contains a variety

Table 3.3   Policy area patterns of emergence

Theoretical perspectives	Hypotheses	Indicators
Functionalism	Partnerships emerge in policy areas that are (deemed) most urgent.	More partnerships emerge in areas related with MDG priorities.
Policy network theories	Partnerships emerge in policy areas where organizational density is high.	More partnerships emerge within policy areas that are the focus of the UNCSD.
Institutionalism	Partnerships emerge in policy areas that are most regulated.	More partnerships emerge in areas that are governed by international law.

of issues with varying levels of perceived urgency. We expect that more partnerships emerge in sub-themes that are considered more urgent. To determine the level of urgency, we use the Millennium Development Goals indicators, since they reflect the international policy priority setting. The Millennium Development Goals explicitly stress the need for access to drinking water and sanitation. Figure 3.3 shows 48 partnerships within the water theme. Moreover, water partnerships often relate to other Millennium Development Goal themes, such as poverty and health.

The pattern of emergence within the water theme seems to coincide with the hypothesis that there are more water-partnerships in issues that are considered most urgent in international politics (see Figure 3.3). We observe a consistent tendency towards Millennium Development Goal-related topics such as drinking water-, poverty- and sanitation-related issues.

Policy Network Theories

According to policy network theories, the partnerships emerge where organizational density is highest. For an empirical test of this assumption we focus on partnerships in policy areas which were featured in recent policy cycles of the UNCSD. The UNCSD works with a biannual focus on one or a few policy areas. In the preparation of these UNCSD meetings, many policy-makers, politicians and stakeholders gather. The density of potential partners may result in partnership agreements.

We concretely focus on partnerships with climate change as a theme, looking at whether the number of these climate-related partnerships increased after climate change was featured as the main theme of the UNCSD-policy cycle, during which many potential partners in climate change gathered at the UNCSD meetings.

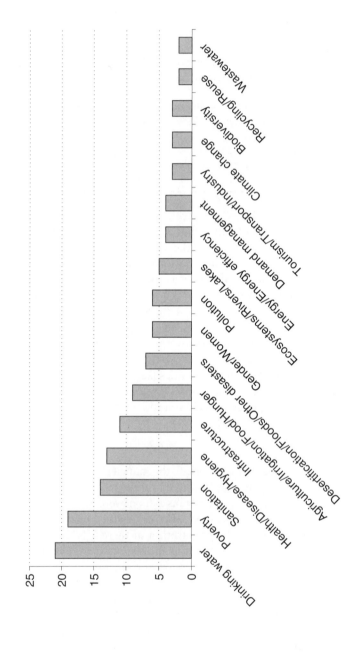

Figure 3.3 Water partnerships by function area

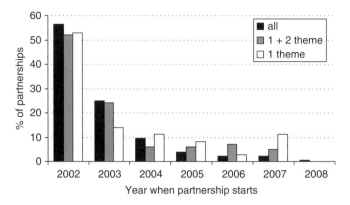

Figure 3.4   Percentage of partnerships registered in all themes and with climate (as a primary or secondary) theme

Figure 3.4 shows that generally fewer partnerships have been registered over the years. The spike we observe in 2002 reflects the moment when partnerships were first registered with the UNCSD. In the UNCSD-cycle (2006–07), climate change was featuring as the main thematic focus. In view of the first year of the cycle (2006), one can see a little increase of partnerships, with climate change as a primary or secondary theme. But more interesting is the second year of the cycle (2008), when 11 per cent of the partnerships addressing climate change as primary theme were registered. In fact, half of the partnerships that registered in 2007 had climate change as primary theme. Therefore, the increase of climate partnerships is considerable compared to other partnerships.

We observe that when the UNCSD deals with a thematic area like climate change, partnerships in the same field are registered. This can be partly explained by the density of the climate policy-makers and practitioners at a certain point in time. However, an additional explanation is that the Partnerships Team, the coordination and partnerships registration unit at the UNCSD, is actively looking for partnerships, inviting them to register when it fits the theme of the upcoming cycle.[1] Moreover, in other policy areas, the density of the network seems to matter less, for instance, the 2008–09 cycle (UNCSD 16/17) dealt with agriculture, however, only two additional partnerships with agricultural themes were registered.

Institutionalism

Institutionalism would suggest that partnerships are most likely to emerge in policy areas that are most regulated. This assumption is further

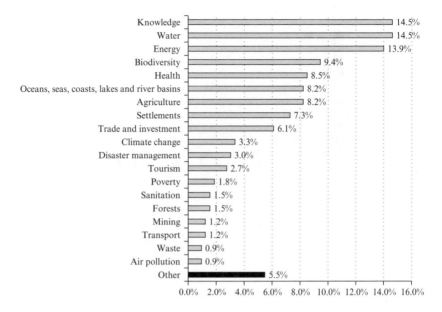

Figure 3.5   Distribution of partnerships across policy areas

supported by the notion of partnerships as implementation instruments, pertaining to better implementation of internationally agreed outcomes. Therefore, more partnerships are to be expected when there are more internationally agreed outcomes, for instance treaties, to implement. Figure 3.5 shows the distribution of partnerships across policy areas.

Indeed, we find fewer partnerships in fields that are regulated domestically such as poverty reduction, sanitation, forests, mining, and waste and air pollution. However, areas that are subject to international law, such as oceans and seas as well as trade and investment do not necessarily feature the highest number of partnerships, although still more than average.

PATTERNS OF EMERGENCE: PARTICIPATION

A distinctive element of partnership governance is the participation of multiple (non-state) actors. In contrast to the discussion about geographic scope and policy areas, the literature on participatory patterns of emergence of partnerships is abundant. Corporate social responsibility (CSR) new public management, and transnational advocacy network literature each provide distinct perspectives on why certain actors get involved in partnerships.

In the CSR literature, the evidence for partnerships lies with changed attitudes and behaviour of business actors (Hartman and Stafford 1997; Hartman, Hofman and Stafford 1999). Partnerships have increasingly become a corporative strategy (Juniper and Moore 2002). An early example of business-initiated partnerships is from 1996, when the WBCSD initiated the International Business Action on Climate Change campaign, calling for public–private partnerships (see the 2001 International Business Action on Climate Change executive summary). Interestingly, most business actors involved in global governance partnerships concern big multi-national companies. Indeed, the membership of the WBCSD consists solely of MNCs. This could give rise to the idea that highly visible business actors are more inclined to initiate partnerships, since they are under closer scrutiny by consumers' associations and NGOs.

New public management and similar perspectives (e.g. Hood 1991) explain the emergence of partnerships from the presumed inefficiency of traditional government and the alleged efficiency of the private sector. The conjuncture of economic liberalization, increasing complexity of public management and budget constraints, has pressured governments (at different levels) to acquire resources to conduct and implement policies. Public–private arrangements answer to the demands for more resources and higher implementation capacity. On a more critical note, public–private arrangements could also defer politically sensitive issues to mere management and resources issues. The new public management perspective has especially taken off in the context of national government, especially the UK and the United States. However, the perspective is also applied at the level of international relations and intergovernmental organizations (such as the UN) and supranational organizations (such as the EU). For instance, in the 1990s the UN suffered a severe lack of funding, partly attributable to payment arrears by some of its most prominent members. In an effort to revive and reinvigorate the organization, Secretary-General Kofi Annan sought alternative resources through partnerships. Annan's strategy has been much credited for this political-administrative move.

The emergence of partnerships in global governance has also been attributed to the rise of transnational advocacy networks (Keck and Sikkink 1998; Hudson 2001). NGOs and other interested organizations become more and more accustomed to the language of business and international organizations. Moreover, some NGO representatives find business actors more responsive to their causes than traditional governments.

In the context of the WSSD, one could ask how much support the partnerships process really enjoyed from civil society actors. Applauded by some, partnerships for sustainable development were also heavily

Table 3.4   Participatory patterns of emergence

Theoretical perspectives	Hypotheses	Indicators
Functionalism	Partnerships are emerging to fill participatory gaps.	Most partnerships involve increased business and NGO participation.
Policy network theories	Partnerships emerge in a context of transnational linking, they are initiated bottom-up by non-state actors.	Partnerships are mostly led by civil society actors.
Institutionalism	Partnerships mimic each other and are therefore similar in their organization.	Many partnerships feature similar types and number of actors and divisions of tasks.

criticized by others. For instance, Friends of the Earth International (FOE 2003) refused to take part in them. The rift between advocacy organizations on partnerships may be pointing towards a division of labour in the non-profit sector. Moreover, the emergence of partnerships in countries with a restricted civil society, like China (see Chapter 6, this volume), would suggest that the role of NGOs and other interest organizations is actually more limited than often suggested in transnational advocacy literature.

Observations in CSR, new public management and transnational advocacy networks literature are not necessarily tied to one of the theories discussed earlier. However, many commonalities are found between the respective literature and some of the theories discussed. For instance, new public management and corporate social responsibility literature seem to have more in common with rationalist theoretical arguments, while transnational advocacy arguments seem to share more with institutional–rationalist explanations, as it can be understood as the institutionalization of a global civil society. However, a rationalist reading of transnational advocacy arguments is also possible, as transnational advocacy coalitions could also be seen as a form of network coordination. Table 3.4 suggests some hypotheses and indicators regarding the participatory patterns of emergence, without being exhaustive.

Functionalism

According to functionalists, partnerships are initiated to answer to participatory shortcomings contingent on intergovernmental processes. It is argued that non-state actors are underrepresented in the governance of

Table 3.5   Performance of partnerships rated by experts

	Frequency	Percent
Good performance	60	47.2%
Neutral performance	44	34.6%
Bad performance	23	18.1%
Total	127	100%

sustainable development, and therefore partnerships should fill this short-coming and include business and civil society.

Evidence from the GSPD shows considerable participation of non-state actors. The average partnership registered with the UNCSD consists of about six corporations or other for-profit organizations and about seven scientific institutions or non-profit NGOs. These findings are consistent with our 2007–08 expert survey that shows that most expert-rated partnerships are performing well at involving all relevant stakeholders (Table 3.5; see Chapter 1, this volume).

While the involvement of non-state actors is substantial, it is still much lower than the involvement of state actors. It seems like partnerships are successful at increasing participation, but one could also argue quite the opposite; there may be no functional need for participation by more non-state actors, because even a little more participation by non-state actors is considered to be sufficient.

Policy Network Theories

Since partnerships, in participatory terms, are networks themselves, the question is not whether network theory is applicable, but which variant of network theory explains best. For instance, traditional policy network theory attributes a greater role to government actors than theories on transnational advocacy networks. In this analysis, we looked at whether partnerships were a manifestation of a denser civil society. In other words, are partnerships mostly initiated by non-state actors?

Findings point toward a different answer: less than one third of all UNCSD-partnerships are led by civil society actors (NGOs, business partners, researchers/scientists and stakeholders) (see Figure 3.6). More are led by 'traditional' actors in international relations: states (23.8 per cent), UN organizations (16.7 per cent) and intergovernmental organizations (IGOs) (12.5 per cent).

While non-state actors play an important role, they do not seem to be the main initiators of partnerships. Observed participatory patterns

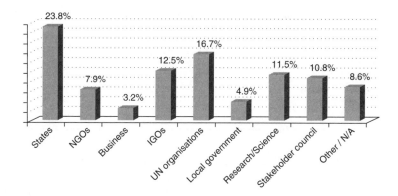

Figure 3.6   Type of lead actor

of emergence seem to suggest that international organizations and state actors play a greater role in emergence of partnerships than theories on transnational networks would suggest.

Institutionalism

Institutionalism assumes that partnerships in the same policy process (like the WSSD) show similar characteristics, since a certain partnership model is copied and referred to as 'best practice'. The institutional replication of partnerships is attractive, since it does not incur the cost of 'reinventing the wheel'. However, partnership models could be replicated according to models that may not work in diverging contexts. Partnerships share commonalities, even when these features may not be 'rational' at the level of the individual partnership. An indication of such institutionalist prom-ulgation of partnerships would be the predomination of commonalities as opposed to institutional differences within the set of WSSD partnerships analysed in this book.

While Table 3.6 is not a comprehensive list of all possible institutional features of partnerships, there are observable differences with regard to their internal organization, size, type and number of partners and leading actors, type of membership, duration and the number of countries of implementation. Subsequently, the institutionalist hypothesis does not seem to be supported within our set of partnerships. In other words, there is not a clear best practice model in the set that is replicated. However, it may be that more models are featured within the WSSD process. In some policy areas, like renewable energy, we observe that partnerships have become institutionally linked to one another. GVEP and REEEP, for

Table 3.6   Institutional commonalities and differences within the set of partnerships for sustainable development

Commonalities	Differences
The majority is global (but 48% are not).	The internal organization varies.
Mostly OECD-countries are donors, while developing countries are receiving.	The size of partnerships varies considerably: the number of partners ranges from 1 to 514.
Pertaining implementation of international sustainable development priorities	The types of partners and lead actors varies: states, UN organizations, IGOs, researchers, stakeholders, NGOs, business etc.
	The type of membership varies: 37% are closed, 3% are open and 55.8% are semi-open.
	The duration varies: some are pre-WSSD, some are open-ended, others have not been indicated.
	The regional coverage of partnership activities ranges from 1 to 200.
	The themes vary: there are more than 19 themes (+ 5 WEHAB-areas) that partnerships deal with.

instance, share projects and collaborate closely. This might be an indication of a development towards meta-partnerships or at least a more institutionalized organizational field of partnerships.

CONCLUSIONS

Discussing the geographic, policy area and participatory patterns of emergence, allowed for systematic formulation and testing of hypotheses. We highlighted some possible implications of theoretical assumptions on patterns of emergence. We examined actual patterns of emergence of partnerships. Finally, we observe discrepancies between the theoretical discussions and actual patterns of emergence, which raises the question whether current theories sufficiently provide an explanation for the emergence of partnerships.

In contrast to many functionalist accounts, partnerships are not necessarily filling functional gaps; in particular, they do not necessarily emerge in the geographic spaces where the demand for partnerships is greatest. Policy network accounts go a long way in explaining the geographic dimension of emergence, with partnerships emerging in countries that are member to many international organizations and most activities being implemented in urban, densely populated areas. However, in particular the transnational advocacy network account does not seem to be applicable to the participatory dimension of partnerships. While non-state actor representation is considerable, most partnerships are still led by traditional players in international relations. Some evidence for institutionalism may be found in the observation that partnerships are often dealing with issues that are already subject to international law and agreements. However, no prevailing organizational model is repeated throughout the WSSD process. To some extent, many partnerships may have reinvented the wheel repeatedly.

The diversity of theories reflects the current state of knowledge on the emergence of transnational public–private partnerships. There is a lively theoretical discussion, but there is scarce empirical evidence pointing towards a specific theory, while some of the theories could be compatible.

The sample of partnerships that have emerged around and after the 2002 WSSD summit provides a unique opportunity to understand patterns of emergence, as it represents a comparable and delimited set of partnerships belonging to the same political and institutional process. In the specific case of the emergence of WSSD partnerships, we found that none of the theories could fully account for the observed patterns of emergence. One shortcoming of the theories discussed may be a too narrow focus on partnerships as a separate institutional entity. In fact, partnerships are emerging in a politically heavily contested context.

That partnerships are overrepresented in South Africa and Indonesia cannot be seen apart from the political process that the countries were hosting. The strong support from UN and other international organizations is apparent. Also partnerships seem to follow the international political agenda, with more partnerships being registered in areas that are higher on the international political agenda (see Chapter 2, this volume).

While the political motivation in the emergence question is obvious, this does not necessarily mean that partnerships are a mere political instrument. The emergence of partnerships is often politically motivated. However, in their operations, partnerships are increasingly collaborating, resulting in an increasingly densely institutionalized organizational field of partnerships for sustainable development.

NOTE

1. Interview with Patricia Chavez, officer at the UNCSD Partnerships Team, May 2008, UNHQ, New York.

REFERENCES

Arts, B. (2003), *Non-state Actors in Global Governance. Three Faces of Power*, Köln: Max Planck Institute for Research on Collective Goods.

Biermann, F. and K. Dingwerth (2004), 'Global environmental change and the nation state', *Global Environmental Politics*, **4**(1), 1–22.

Börzel, T.A. (1998), 'Organizing Babylon: on the different conceptions of policy networks', *Public Administration*, **76**(2), 253–273.

Chan, S. (2009), 'Partnerships for sustainable development in China: adaptation of a global governance instrument', *European Journal of East Asian Studies*, **8**(1), 121–134.

Central Intelligence Agency (CIA) (2009), *The World Factbook*, available at: https://www.cia.gov/library/publications/the-world-factbook, (retrieval: 03.05.2011).

Cutler, A.C., V. Haufler and T. Porter (1999), *Private Authority and International Affairs*, Albany, NY: State University of New York.

Commission of the European Communities (CEC) (2001), 'European governance: a white paper', Brussels, 25.7.2001 COM(2001) 428 final, available at: http://eur-lex.europa.eu/LexUriServ/site/en/com/2001/com2001_0428en01.pdf, (retrieval: 03.05.2011).

Dingwerth, K. and P. Pattberg (2009), 'World politics and organizational fields: the case of sustainability governance', *European Journal of International Relations*, **15**(4), 707–743.

Flinders, M. (2005), 'The politics of public–private partnerships', *The British Journal of Politics and International Relations*, **7**(2), 215–239.

Friends of the Earth (eds) (2003), *That's all Very Well But. . .Friends of the Earth's Guide to Partnerships*, Washington DC: Friends of the Earth.

Haas, P.M. (2004), 'Addressing the global governance deficit', *Global Environmental Politics*, **4**(4), 1–15.

Hartman, C.L. and E.R. Stafford (1997), 'Green alliances: building new business with environmental groups', *Long Range Planning*, **30**(2), 184–196.

Hartman, C.L., P.S. Hofman and E.R. Stafford (1999), 'Partnerships: a path to sustainability', *Business Strategy and the Environment*, **8**(5), 255–266.

Hood, C. (1991), 'A public management for all seasons?', *Public Administration*, **69**(1), 3–19.

Hudson, A. (2001), 'NGOs' transnational advocacy networks: from "legitimacy" to "political responsibility"?', *Global Networks*, **1**(4), 331–352.

Juniper, C. and M. Moore (2002), 'Synergies and best practices of corporate partnership for sustainability', *Corporate Environmental Strategy*, **9**(3), 267–276.

Karkkainen, B.C. (2004), 'Post-sovereign environmental governance', *Global Environmental Politics*, **4**(1), 72–96.

Keck, M.E. and K. Sikkink (1998), *Activists Beyond Borders. Advocacy Networks in International Politics*, Ithaca, NY: Cornell University Press.

Kenis, P. and V. Schneider (1991), 'Policy networks and policy analysis: scrutinizing a new analytical toolbox' in B. Marin and R. Mayntz (eds), *Policy Networks: Empirical Evidence and Theoretical Considerations*, Boulder, CO: Westview Press, pp. 25–59.

Kingdon, J.W. (1984), *Agendas, Alternatives and Public Policies*, Boston, MA: Brown and Company.

Knill, C. and D. Lehmkuhl (2002), 'Private actors and the state: internationalization and the changing patterns of governance', *Governance: An International Journal of Policy, Administration, and Institutions*, **15**(1), 41–63.
Kobrin, S.J. (2002), 'Economic governance in an electronically networked global economy', in R.B. Hall and T.J. Biersteker (eds), *The Emergence of Private Authority in Global Governance*, Cambridge, UK: Cambridge University Press, pp. 43–75.
Kooiman, J. (eds) (1993), *Modern Governance: New Government-Society Interactions*, London: Sage.
Lober, D.J. (1997), 'Explaining the formation of business–environmentalist collaborations: collaborative windows and the Paper Task Force', *Policy Sciences*, **30**(1), 1–24.
Najam, A., I. Christopoulou and W.R. Moomaw (2004), 'The emergent system of global environmental governance', *Global Environmental Politics*, **4**(4), 23–35.
Nölke, A. (2005), 'Introduction to the special issue: the globalization of accounting standards', *Business and Politics*, **7**(3), 1–7.
Reinicke, W.H. (1997), 'Global public policy', *Foreign Affairs*, **76**(6), 127–138.
Reinicke, W.H. (1998), *Global Public Policy. Governing Without Government*, Washington DC: Brookings Institution Press.
Ronit, K. and V. Schneider (1999), 'Global governance through private organizations', *Governance: An International Journal of Policy and Administration*, **12**(3), 243–266.
Sassen, S. (2002), 'The state of globalization', in R.B. Hall and T.J. Biersteker (eds), *The Emergence of Private Authority in Global Governance*, Cambridge, UK: Cambridge University Press, pp. 91–114.
SDIN (2002), 'Taking issue: questioning partnerships', SDIN Paper No.1, Sustainable Development Issues Network (SDIN).
Simon, H.A. (1955), 'A behavioral model of rational choice', *The Quarterly Journal of Economics*, **69**(1), 99–118.
United Nations (2003), *Partnerships for Sustainable Development*, New York: Department of Public Information and the UN Department of Economic and Social Affairs.
World Business Council for Sustainable Development (WBCSD) (2001), 'International business action on climate change. Executive summary', available at: http://www.wbcsd.org/DocRoot/sZAS90awk0RJWJ239GaU/bizoncc.pdf (retrieval: 03.05.2011).

PART II

Influence of partnerships for sustainable development

4. The overall effects of partnerships for sustainable development: more smoke than fire?

Frank Biermann, Sander Chan, Ayşem Mert and Philipp Pattberg

As the previous chapters have shown, transnational public–private partnerships have become a highly visible and highly discussed element of global sustainability governance. Especially since the 2002 Johannesburg WSSD, transnational public–private partnerships have multiplied, now counting well above 300 partnerships in the register maintained by the United Nations. In policy and academic debates alike, partnerships are promoted as solution to deadlocked intergovernmental negotiations, to ineffective treaties and overly bureaucratic international organizations, to power-based state policies, corrupt elites and many other real or perceived current problems of global governance.

The previous chapter explained in detail the emergence of partnerships as a key element of the 'post-Johannesburg process'. Yet despite the creation of hundreds of partnerships since 2002, the role and relevance of this new type of global governance remains contested. The systematic assessment of the influence of partnerships in global sustainability governance is hence one of the core tasks that we undertake in this book. We do this at different levels and by different methods. Chapters 5 and 9 look in detail at the effects that partnerships have in specific sectors, notably energy governance and water governance. Chapters 6 and 7 analyse the effects of partnerships in specific regions, that is, Asia and Africa. Chapters 8, 9 and 10 study specific elements of partnerships that might help explain, among other things, their effectiveness in resolving pressing problems of global governance, looking in particular at the legitimacy of partnerships.

This chapter provides the background to these later chapters by presenting a large-n assessment of the entire 'universe' of public–private partnerships (the chapter draws on Biermann et al. 2007). We focus our analysis here on three potential functions that partnerships could address.

First, partnerships are often expected to further the development of new norms and regulations in sustainability governance in areas where intergovernmental regulation is largely non-existent. Second, partnerships are believed to advance sustainability governance by helping to implement intergovernmental regulations that do exist, but that are only poorly implemented. Third, partnerships are often expected to assist in increasing the inclusiveness of global sustainability governance. In this view, intergovernmental negotiations are seen as dominated by powerful governments and international organizations, while partnerships might ensure higher participation of less privileged actors, including voices from the youth, the poor, women, indigenous people and civil society at large. Increased participation from such groups is seen as needed to improve the implementation of international agreements and to strengthen the overall legitimacy, accountability and democratic quality of governance.

While these claims of transnational partnerships as agents of norm creation, norm implementation and norm inclusiveness in sustainability governance are frequently made, there is surprisingly little systematic research in their support. Evidence for the actual role and relevance of partnerships is scarce and inconclusive. This lacuna impairs a better understanding of partnerships in global governance. Are partnerships a sign of a new model of world politics in which intergovernmental negotiations are complemented and sometimes even replaced by networked governance of non-state actors? Or is the contribution of partnerships rather limited? To what extent, if at all, are partnerships superior to traditional ways of international cooperation, such as the negotiation of legally binding agreements among governments and their subsequent national implementation?

In order to improve understanding of the role and relevance of partnerships, this chapter offers a large-*n* empirical assessment of the entire system of partnerships for sustainable development 10 years after they were institutionalized at the WSSD. We draw on three data sources: first, a meta-analysis of empirical studies of the performance of partnerships for sustainable development; second, UNCSD database on partnerships (a basic inventory of registered partnerships based on self-reporting); and finally, data from the Global Sustainability Partnership Database that we have developed (see Chapter 1, this volume).

The remainder of our chapter is organized around the three functions that we have outlined above and that partnerships are believed to resolve: norm development, norm implementation and norm inclusiveness.

NORM DEVELOPMENT

One core claim in support of transnational partnerships for sustainable development is that they function where governments fail. When governments cannot agree on effective international agreements, or when these agreements are too general to elicit any meaningful action, non-state actors step in with the creation of multi-stakeholder partnerships. One can reformulate this claim in two hypotheses. First, if partnerships advance norm development, they should be more prominent in areas where public regulation is largely non-existent. That is, there would be a negative correlation between the frequency of partnerships in a given issue area and public regulation of that area. Alternatively, if this was not the case, then partnerships would at least be spread rather equally over a wide range of problems.

The evidence is inconclusive, but hardly supportive of either hypothesis. Partnerships are indeed unequally spread over issue areas, with some areas, such as water (75 partnerships), energy (55) and natural resource management (52), receiving most attention (based on data on their self-declared primary theme when registering with the UN, excluding 'cross-cutting issues'). From these areas with highest partnership density, at least energy and natural resource management are densely regulated at the national level, and by a large measure also internationally, for example through the climate regime and the biodiversity protection regime. Other areas of equal importance for global environmental change – mining (6), desertification (11), drought (12) or toxic chemicals (4) – are relatively neglected by partnership initiatives (see UN 2006).

A systematic comparison of the distribution of partnerships with that of multilateral environmental agreements per issue area, through an online treaty locator (CIESIN 2007), suggests that issues that are less regulated or unregulated (like mining) also attract very few partnerships. Relatively more partnerships exist in areas that are heavily regulated, such as marine resources, oceans and seas. This hypothesis has also been analysed by Liliana Andonova (2006: 48) based on older data sets from 2003. Both Andonova's and our investigations seem to contradict the hypothesis that partnerships are core agents in norm development. It seems that a fair degree of institutionalization and a relatively high density of intergovernmental agreements facilitate partnership entrepreneurship, whereas areas with obvious governance gaps have been less popular for partnerships.

A similar trend emerges from our country studies, for example in Chile (Tondreau 2005). Issues addressed by partnerships in Chile were heavily concentrated on more managerial problems, such as sustainable management of forests, improving mapping and citizen information, whereas

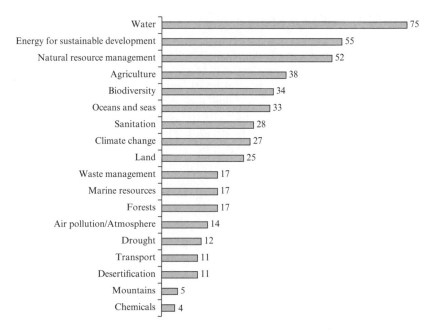

Figure 4.1   Issue areas of WSSD partnerships

almost no partnerships existed on issues of major importance but with little national and international regulation, such as mining or aquaculture. Thus, while some areas with major international conventions – such as energy and climate change – are heavily populated with partnerships, areas with no strong international agreements, such as forestry, are less well covered by partnerships.

Hale and Mauzerall (2004) explain this by the private and voluntary nature of partnerships that prevents them from sharing the macro-perspective of the UN and international partnership advocates, so that 'some key issues have not received the attention they deserve'. This could result in partnerships picking the 'low hanging fruit' in highly regulated areas, since they do not necessarily view problems in terms of urgency, but in terms of manageability.

Another important factor that might facilitate partnership agreements, and that also contradicts the claim of partnerships as norm creators, is funding. Partnerships tend to emerge in areas that receive abundant funding from governments, especially from the European Union and the United States; areas such as climate change, air pollution, energy and water (see Figure 4.1). In the Johannesburg process the United States have pledged to invest 970 million US dollars over 3 years in water and sanitation projects, and the European Union has offered to launch a 700 million US dollar partnership on energy development. Both issue areas are now also most densely populated by partnerships. The pattern of partnerships emerging in areas with such financial priorities points to a conclusion that the emergence of partnerships is rather supply-driven than responsive to a perceived lack in the institutionalization of global governance.

In sum, transnational partnerships for sustainable development do not live up to expectations that they play a major role in the development of new norms of global governance. While our current analysis and previous studies do not focus on the performance of individual partnerships in a given issue area, we can conclude that partnerships have been created rather unevenly across issues. This uneven spread across areas, however, does not negatively correlate with the regulatory density in an area. In fact, there is some evidence to suggest that partnerships emerge in areas where there is already a fair degree of regulatory institutionalization.

This is not necessarily a problem: if partnerships serve to contribute to the implementation of existing rules and regulations, it might be more effective for them to flourish in areas with substantial public regulation. However, the underlying question then is whether partnerships in fact contribute to implementation, as we analyse in the following section. In any case, at least the claim that partnerships fill regulatory gaps where governments fail to agree on taking action is hardly supported by the evidence.

NORM IMPLEMENTATION

The second claim in support of partnerships for sustainable development is that they help improve the implementation of intergovernmental treaties, agreements and programmes. In the official texts from the WSSD, strengthened implementation is generally seen as the most important rationale for partnerships. In Johannesburg, multi-stakeholder partnerships were explicitly defined as 'specific commitments by various partners intended to contribute to and reinforce the *implementation* of the outcomes of intergovernmental negotiations of the WSSD and to help the further *implementation* of Agenda 21 and the MDGs [Millennium Development Goals]' (Kara and Quarless 2002, emphasis added). The argument for partnerships asserts that international agreements are poorly implemented and that the international community should focus on this implementation deficit through public–private cooperation and voluntary action of environmental leaders (Bruch and Pendergrass 2003).

To what extent do partnerships contribute to the implementation of intergovernmental agreements and of global sustainability governance in general? Although some studies have addressed implementation (Witte, Streck and Brenner 2003; Speth 2004; Streck 2004), measuring the effectiveness of the contribution of partnerships towards the implementation of international programmes remains difficult. We have analysed four hypotheses: If partnerships were effective in helping to implement global governance norms, they should be expected: (1) to have the required capacity and in particular the human and material resources; (2) to create additional sources of funding, on top of what governments and UN agencies were already going to provide; (3) to concentrate on direct environmental improvement rather than creating new bureaucratic procedures; and (4) to implement projects in the least developed countries to prioritize the realization of the Millennium Development Goals.

Sufficient Capacity?

Regarding the first hypothesis, there are reasons to doubt that partnerships have the capacity and necessary financial and personnel means to reach their sustainable development goals. For example, 65 per cent of all partnerships registered with the UN have declared to be still looking for funds, along with 4–8 per cent of partnerships that search also for additional non-financial resources such as computers or office space. As of 2006, all partnerships together sought additional funding of 710 million US dollars, which equals 55.6 per cent of what they had in funds at that time. The community of more than 300 partnerships registered with the UN is very diverse, and there are thus several reasons that might explain why the majority of partnerships is still looking for more money: they could plan to expand because they see themselves as rather successful; they could be new and in the formation stage; or unexpected problems could require additional funds. And yet, another – and in our view more convincing – reading is that there is a more general problem and that the vast majority of all partnerships simply lacks the financial means to reach the goals they set for themselves.

New and Additional Resources?

Second, we have analysed whether partnerships create new sources of funding in addition to what governments and UN agencies were already going to provide. If partnerships generated a substantial amount of new resources, this would be a positive indicator of their effectiveness in implementing the sustainable development goals. At the end of the WSSD, all partnerships initiated around the summit had less than 250 million US dollars in resources (Hale and Mauzerall 2004: 235). In the larger context, this sum is a trifle and merely slightly more than the official development assistance of a small country such as Luxemburg. Admittedly, until 2004 – in less than 2 years – funding increased four-fold to 1.02 billion US dollars. However, the main reason for this substantial increase was the reclassification of large intergovernmental programmes as multi-stakeholder partnerships, while the programmes continue to rely on governmental funding and on existing programmes within the UN and World Bank programmes (Hale and Mauzerall 2004: 235).

In any case, this sum is still small compared to 78 billion US dollars in overall official development assistance of the OECD countries (OECD 2004). Even in the multi-sectoral partnerships funding remains largely public: business actors account for only 1 per cent of the new funding, almost the same ratio as non-governmental organizations, which has led Hale and Mauzerall (2004: 235–6) to the conclusion that 'partnerships have failed to bring a substantial amount of new, multi-sectoral resources to sustainable development activities'. Our more recent analysis indicates that not much has changed.

It is also difficult to estimate the percentage of funds that is genuinely new and that has not been allocated for sustainable development before the WSSD (Bäckstrand 2006). Partnerships were often presented to developing country representatives as a more reliable source of funding, as they were not dependent on the uncertain process of negotiations (personal communication with members of government delegations to the WSSD and to the fourth Preparatory Committee meeting, January 2007). This partially explains why developing countries agreed to the partnerships regime at the WSSD, but also supports suspicions that substantial parts of the partnership funds are in fact reclassified public development assistance.

Focus on Direct Impact?

Third, if transnational partnerships contribute to the implementation of global sustainability governance, one could expect that they concentrate on direct environmental impacts. However, in an OECD survey (2006), which looks mainly at partnerships registered with the UN that have an environmental focus, only 28 per cent of the responding partnerships considered themselves as providing direct environmental benefits. The OECD researchers interpreted this as an overestimate and suggested that at a closer look, it was more likely that 'of the 32 partnerships only three or four had direct environmental impact, with the rest facilitating impact further down the line' (OECD 2006: 24). Another critical finding of the survey is that most partnerships identify as main beneficiaries of multi-stakeholder cooperation 'the partners themselves' (79 per cent) or 'the partners as well as others' (OECD 2006: 24–25). A similar pattern is found among the 321 partnerships registered with the United Nations. For example, 165 partnerships report rather vague objectives as their primary goals, such as 'strengthening the means of implementation', 'building institutional frameworks', and 'supplying information for decision-making'. A survey by the International Food Policy Research Institute on 124 public–private partnerships in agricultural innovation in nine South American countries concludes that most of the partnerships reviewed 'are not based on genuine demand; do not produce the expected synergistic effects from complementary use of resources, co-innovation, and joint learning; and do not respond to common interests' (Hartwich, Gonzalez and Viera 2005: 30).

Likewise, our study of partnerships implemented in Chile found that only half of the partnerships list as objective the 'actual increase in coverage of services and life quality' and 'reduction of environmental impacts'. Instead, most objectives seem to have only a rather indirect impact on actual problems, for example through 'improving mapping that helps to take better public decisions', 'access to credits that allow people to improve their quality of life' or 'giving consultancy services for better and more sustainable results from agriculture' (Tondreau 2005).

Another proxy for the question of whether partnerships further the implementation of global governance is the number of partnerships that in fact monitor their progress in implementing the Millennium Development Goals. In the 250 partnerships that Hale and Mauzerall (2004) studied, merely 69 per cent had a reporting system and less than 50 per cent had a monitoring mechanism in place. Because this study was conducted shortly after the initiation of partnerships, monitoring mechanisms might have been created later. However, there is indicative evidence that the lack of monitoring persists. For example, an OECD survey (2006) states that many partnerships that focused on environmental protection had no monitoring mechanism in place. While 81 per cent of the sampled cases planned an evaluation of the effectiveness of the partnership, only 56 per cent declared that they would evaluate 'their contribution to the Millennium Development Goals'.

This seems comparable to other multi-stakeholder processes. For example, a McKinsey report on 'intermediate impacts' of the United Nations Global Compact does not find any substantial improvements towards the Compact's principles 5 years after its initiation. The results of the survey indicate that the foremost reason to sign the Global Compact for non-governmental organizations was 'to network with other organizations' (64 per cent). Companies most often claimed that they aimed at addressing humanitarian concerns (55 per cent globally) or at becoming familiar with corporate social responsibility (62 per cent in non-OECD countries). However, only 58 per cent of the companies took 'any (at least one) action' in support of global compact goals. While 67 per cent of companies indicated that their companies 'made changes' to implement the Compact's principles, only 9 per cent claimed that the Global Compact had a crucial impact on any of these policy changes (McKinsey 2004).

Of course, improving means of implementation or building institutional frameworks are important elements of the larger quest for the transition towards a more sustainable development. Yet, given these data, the suspicion arises that a sizable part of current partnership activity is not implementation per se, but rather the construction of a bureaucratic procedural universe in parallel to the existing intergovernmental processes. These activities may lay the foundation for effective implementation in the future, but this is far from certain.

Focus on Least Developed Regions?

Fourth, if partnerships were contributing to the implementation of global sustainability governance, one would expect them to focus in particular on these countries and regions where implementation is most urgently needed. One can analyse this through looking at the designated countries of implementation of partnerships registered with the United Nations. Most previous partnership studies have focused on countries as (lead) partners and neglected the category of country of implementation. This category indicates exclusively the broadness of implementation regardless of which countries the partners come from. Interestingly, we found that it is not the least developed countries but the OECD countries that are the most frequent countries of implementation, followed by Asian countries and Africa (see Figure 4.2). If partnerships exist to further the implementation of the Millennium Development Goals, such as bringing food and education to the poorest, it is striking that there is no bias in the partnership universe in favour of least developed countries as countries of implementation.

In sum, the general perception that partnerships advance the implementation of global sustainability governance seems overly optimistic. A number of indicators – the balance of issue areas and geographical areas, the lack of focus on direct environmental impact, the potential to reach goals and to attract additional funding – all point to the conclusion that the current practice of partnerships does not show strong evidence that they contribute significantly towards the implementation of global sustainability governance.

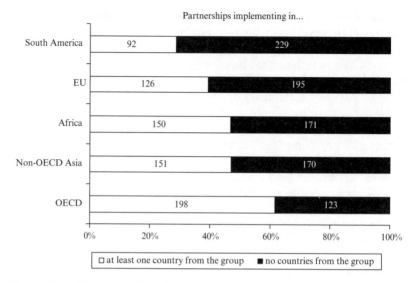

Figure 4.2   Countries of implementation

NORM INCLUSIVENESS

Transnational partnerships for sustainable development are often seen as a means to ensure larger participation of all stakeholders. Already Principle 10 of the 1992 Rio Declaration on Environment and Development stipulated that 'environmental issues are best handled with participation of all concerned citizens, at the relevant level', and at the Rio Summit the notion of major groups was introduced to acknowledge the necessity of broad-based participation in decision-making to achieve sustainable development. Thus, the Agenda 21 of 1992 urged governments to retreat 'from narrow sectoral approaches' and move towards 'full cross-sectoral coordination and cooperation' (UN 1992: paragraph 8.12).

There are various arguments that support broader participation. Some argue that ensuring participatory processes is a public good in itself (Stiglitz 2002: 168–171), while others add that participation also increases the effectiveness of projects and of decisions in general, ensures political sustainability, assists in a more acceptable development transformation and creates more transparent corporate governance (Isham, Narayan and Pritchett 1995; Isham, Kaufmann and Pritchett 1997).

Proponents of partnerships as means to increase participation offer three core arguments: First, because national governments and public agencies have limited resources, information and skills, they need to collaborate with other sectors to ensure effective governance (Reinicke and Deng 2000; Ruggie 2002; Streck 2004). Second, partnerships that bring together a variety of sectors in environmental decision-making will decrease the gap between societies and global institutions that emerges from the impossibility of a global democracy. Finally, partnerships are believed to reduce the costs of compliance to international agreements through creating consensus among the major actors. Increased participation through partnerships is often related to their assumed bridge-functions between state and non-state actors (Martens 2007: 33). Yet the assumed positive effect of partnerships also relates to their role in bridging the differences of understanding between the global 'North' and 'South' on environment and development issues.

Does this promise hold, and is the theory met by reality? We have analysed three hypotheses. We assumed that if partnerships are effective in strengthening participation, they will have: (1) an at least balanced distribution of lead partners from the global North and South and of actors from developing countries in general; (2) an at least balanced distribution of lead partners from state and non-state actors; and (3) a sufficient participation of traditionally marginalized partners.

Balance Between North and South?

First, regarding overall representation and distribution of leadership roles between North and South, this is hardly balanced among state actors in partnerships for sustainable development. In more than a quarter of all partnerships registered with the UN, industrialized countries are the only state partners involved. In 60 per cent of the registered partnerships, at least one OECD state is a partner. Developing countries are underrepresented; 56 per cent of all partnerships have no state partner from the developing world.

The leadership of partnerships lies predominantly with industrialized countries. By the end of 2006, governments that were leading partnerships registered with the UN were almost exclusively from the North. The only developing countries among the group of the ten most-often leading governments were the host countries of the last preparatory conference to the World Summit on Sustainable Development (Indonesia) and of the Summit itself (South Africa), see Figure 4.3.

The general trend that Northern actors play a major role in initiating, funding and operating private–public governance is supported also by sectoral studies. For example, Buse (2004) concludes for global health partnerships that the most active governmental partners are the United States, the United Kingdom, the Netherlands and Canada, with the

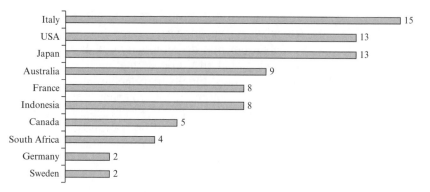

Figure 4.3   Lead partner governments

consequence that Southern governments and non-governmental organizations are systematically underrepresented in the governing bodies. Even when Southern actors are represented, leadership and initiation might mean that decision-making power remains with more powerful actors. Bartsch (2006) cites global health partnerships as cases in which no real decision-making power is granted to governments and civil society actors from the South even despite their representation.

Empirical studies of environmental partnerships have reached similar conclusions. Andonova (2006: 44–45) suggests that, 'the more countries are involved in foreign aid transactions, the more their governments and development agencies are likely to have interest and political skill to participate in public–private institutions'. On the other hand, according to Andonova, environmental stress, level of involvement in international institutions and domestic political environment have no bearing on the state partners involved (with the exception of countries with the largest populations that are more likely to build partnerships, and of the two host countries of the WSSD and the Bali preparatory meeting, South Africa and Indonesia).

Increased Participation of Non-governmental Actors?

Second, it has been argued that partnerships would create new opportunities for non-state actors and thus advance the inclusiveness of global sustainability governance. Again, this is hardly supported by data on partnership practice. Across all issue areas, state actors and intergovernmental organizations dominate the partner population of partnerships for sustainable development. Only 16 per cent of partnerships have no government as a partner. Public actors are also more likely to take the

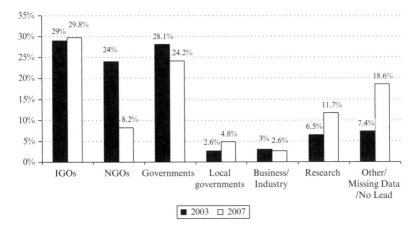

Sources: Andonova and Levy 2003; GSPD

Figure 4.4   Sectoral distribution of lead partners in 2003 and 2007

lead: national and local governments lead 29 per cent of all partner-ships, and the United Nations and other intergovernmental organiza-tions another 30 per cent. Taken together, public actors run almost 60 per cent of all partnerships that have emerged from the Johannesburg process. Business actors are in charge of only 3 per cent of all partnerships registered with the UN, which is noteworthy given that business actors were highly supportive of the partnership idea during the Johannesburg Summit. Non-governmental organizations lead an additional 8.2 per cent of all registered partnerships, with research and science organizations and networks (12 per cent) and collective actors such as partnership fora or stakeholder councils, as well as cases of missing data accounting for the rest (18.6 per cent).

Back in 2003, Andonova and Levy (2003: 23) had concluded that partnerships are mainly 'supply-driven (by what powerful actors have to offer)'. The current sets of data analysed for this study show that not much has changed since then (Figure 4.4). The only major change over the last years is a sharp decrease in the percentage of NGO-led partnerships and a moderate increase in research and science networks as lead partners. The decrease in the number of NGO-led partnerships is largely attributable to partnerships registering themselves or their previous names as the lead partner with the UN. The research and science networks that take over leading roles, on the other hand, are evenly distributed over issue areas and other basic characteristics of partnerships.

Source: UN 2006

Figure 4.5   Number of partners from different sectors and major groups

Increased Participation of Marginalized Groups?

Third, in addition to increasing participation of non-state actors in general, it has been argued that partnerships would increase participation of the often-marginalized stakeholders in global politics. These positive expectations are not supported by the data. Of all partnerships registered with the UN as of December 2006, less than 1 per cent had partners from groups such as farmers, workers and trade unions, indigenous people, women, youth or children (Figure 4.5). More institutionalized groups are better represented in partnerships, with 9 per cent of all partners in those registered with the UN coming from the scientific and technological community, 11 per cent from business and industry, 19 per cent from non-governmental organizations, and 30 per cent from governments and 18 per cent from intergovernmental organizations. This picture of partnerships contradicts the optimistic idea that they can serve as a means to ensure the inclusiveness of groups that are otherwise marginalized in global politics. Rather, partnerships seem to have created mechanisms to select state and non-state actors that are already 'part of the game', and to exclude others.

As Buse (2004: 232) quotes one informant of his research on health partnerships, '[i]f you don't have some money on the table, some time, and expertise, you are not a partner'.

Comparable imbalances are also found in the Global Compact that the UN concluded with a number of actors to improve the environmental, social or human rights performance of companies by bringing them together with UN agencies, civil society and labour unions. The impressive portfolio of the initiative, which attracted some 1430 small- and medium-sized enterprises and 1615 larger corporations, including 108 of the businesses ranked in FT Global 500, is in stark contrast to low involvement of non-governmental organizations – merely 7 per cent of all participants are NGOs – and lack of consistency in the commitments of business partners: 40 per cent of the companies listed on the Compact's database are either inactive or non-communicating participants (most of them being small- and medium-sized enterprises). Similar to partnerships for sustainable development, small businesses and civil society have a limited participation in the Global Compact.

In sum, there is empirical support for the claim that partnerships reproduce or even intensify existing relationships in the international system (Martens 2007). This is not restricted to partnerships for sustainable development. Similar patterns are visible in other governance arrangements (e.g. partnerships established through the Global Compact) and other issue areas (e.g. health partnerships). So far, partnerships for sustainable development remain dominated by states and international organizations, and are predominantly led and populated by Northern actors. Participation of 'major groups' is limited to stakeholders that have certain competitive advantages or useful resources. Traditional patterns of political exclusion of weaker groups tend to be reproduced at the transnational level of partnerships as well.

CONCLUSIONS

In sum, the balance of evidence in our large-*n* analysis of all UN-registered partnerships for sustainable development suggests that these new mechanisms of global governance fall short of the high expectations that they were to fulfil. Surely, some partnerships are highly effective and make important contributions to global sustainability governance. Chapters 6 and 7 provide ample examples of such effective partnerships, and offer some explanations why these partnerships excel. Yet overall, looking at all of the more than 300 partnerships that have been agreed around and after the 2002 Johannesburg summit, our assessment is more critical.

Many partnerships are not active. In addition, partnerships do not seem to address core functions where their particular role and comparative advantage was believed to lie: to initiate new global governance norms in areas where governments fail to take action; to help implement existing intergovernmental regulations; and to increase the inclusiveness and participation in global governance by bringing in actors that have so far been rather marginalized. While a few partnerships can be found to make useful contributions in these areas, the overall system of partnerships for sustainable development falls short of the high expectations.

How can we explain this? The following chapters will provide a host of detailed reasons that can explain the variation in effectiveness of individual partnerships in specific sectors and regions. With a view to the overall assessment of all partnerships taken together as a new type of governance mechanisms, there is contradiction, for example, between advancing the implementation and inclusiveness of global governance at the same time and to the same degree. Although partnerships are expected to effectively implement sustainable development policies and at the same time to ensure a certain level of participation, this appears difficult within the context of the WSSD and its follow-up process. If partnerships are created to advance the implementation of global governance, this will require like-minded state and non-state actors to form a partnership and implement some or all Millennium Development Goals. Yet if they aim at ensuring broadest possible participation, the chances of effective implementation could be hampered by partners with opposing interests. This contradiction from within the partnership system is reflected in the debate on the 'partnership brokers', wherein some argued that 'if the partners cannot work out a way to work together and develop mutual trust on their own, then perhaps the partnership should not be formed in the first place' (Warner 2003). It might be, in this case, more realistic and useful for partnerships to focus on implementation, and limit the ambitions with regard to participation.

Surely, the question is not whether one single partnership advances at the same time the development, implementation and inclusiveness of global standards and regulations. The question is about the overall role and relevance of the entire system of the almost 400 partnerships that have emerged in the last decade to advance sustainable development in the areas of water, energy, health, agriculture and biodiversity and to contribute to the implementation of the Millennium Development Goals. Does this entire partnership universe help to advance global sustainability governance? Given the large number and variety of partnerships, an answer to this question is difficult. Our large-*n* analysis – drawing on existing studies, on UN data and on our own GSPD – comes to a rather sombre conclusion. While some partnerships might have some positive effects, this does not seem to be the case for the entire system of partnerships, at least not in comparison with the highly optimistic claims by proponents of partnerships as a new, highly innovative type of global governance. Partnerships are most frequent in those areas that are already heavily institutionalized and regulated. They are predominantly not concerned with implementation, but rather with further institution-building. For many of them it is doubtful whether they have sufficient resources to make any meaningful contribution towards implementation in the first place. Finally, the majority of partnerships strengthens the participation of those actors that already participate: governments, major international organizations and those civil society actors that have had a say in global governance already before the partnership phenomenon emerged. The balance of evidence suggests that those that have been marginalized before have also been marginalized in the partnership process.

If the entire system of partnerships does not help much in supporting global sustainability governance, what is then their main rationale? Other reasons for partnerships to emerge have been mentioned. Dedeurwaerdere (2005: 4) for instance had suggested that 'self-regulatory institutions remain subject to takeover by opportunistic individuals and to potentially perverse dynamics'. Some of these subsidiary purposes in partnership building may be self-interest, as both public and private actors can be expected to form a partnership 'not necessarily to foster their [partnership's] main rationale, but for a subsidiary purpose' (Broadwater and Kaul 2005: 3). Considering the amount of time and funding invested in each partnership, it seems not surprising that partners themselves tend to be the primary beneficiaries of their partnerships.

REFERENCES

Andonova, L.B. (2006), 'Globalization, agency, and institutional innovation. The rise of public–private partnerships in global governance', *Goldfarb Center Working Paper No. 2006-004*, March 2006.

Andonova, L.B. and M.A. Levy (2003), 'Franchising global governance: making sense of the Johannesburg type II partnerships', in O.S. Stokke and O.B. Thommessen (eds), *Yearbook of International Co-operation on Environment and Development*, London: Earthscan, 19–31.

Bäckstrand, K. (2006), 'Multi-stakeholder partnerships for sustainable development: rethinking legitimacy, accountability and effectiveness', *European Environment*, **16**(5), 290–306.

Bartsch, S. (2006), The South in global health governance: perspectives on global public–private partnerships, International Studies Association Annual Meeting, 21–25 March 2006, San Diego, USA.

Benner, T., C. Streck and J.M. Witte (eds) (2003), *Progress or Peril? Networks and Partnerships in Global Environmental Governance. The Post-Johannesburg Agenda*, Berlin: Global Public Policy Institute.

Biermann, F., S. Chan, A. Mert, and P. Pattberg (2007), 'Multi-stakeholder partnerships for sustainable development. Does the promise hold?', in P. Glasbergen, F. Biermann, and A.P.J. Mol (eds) (2007), *Partnerships, Governance and Sustainable Development. Reflections on Theory and Practice*, Cheltenham, UK: Edward Elgar, 239–60.

Broadwater, I. and I. Kaul (2005), 'Global public–private partnerships: the current landscape (study outline)', UNDP/ODS Background Papers, Office of Development Studies, United Nations Development Programme.

Bruch, C. and J. Pendergrass (2003), 'Type II partnerships, international law, and the commons', *Georgetown International Environmental Law Review*, **15**(4), 855–86.

Buse, K. (2004), 'Governing public–private infectious disease partnerships', *Brown Journal of World Affairs*, **10**(2), 225–42.

CIESIN, UNEP, et al. (2007), Socioeconomic Data and Applications Center (SEDAC) collection of treaty texts, Columbia University, available at: http://sedac.ciesin.columbia.edu/contact.html (retrieval: 11.05.2011).

Dedeurwaerdere, T. (2005), 'The contribution of network governance to sustainable development', *Les séminaires de l'Iddri*, **13**, 1–15.

Hale, T.N. and D.L. Mauzerall (2004), 'Thinking globally and acting locally: can the Johannesburg Partnerships coordinate action on sustainable development?', *The Journal of Environment and Development*, **13**(3), 220–39.

Hartwich, F., C. Gonzalez and L.F. Vieira (2005), 'Public–private partnerships for innovation-led growth in agrichains: a useful tool for development in Latin America?', *ISNAR Discussion Paper*, **1**, 1–39.

Isham, J., D. Narayan and L.H. Pritchett (1995), 'Does participation improve performance? Establishing causality with subjective data', *World Bank Economic Review*, **9**, 175–200.

Isham, J., D. Kaufmann and L.H. Pritchett (1997), 'Civil liberties, democracy, and the performance of government projects', *World Bank Economic Review*, **11**, 219–42.

Kara, J. and D. Quarless (2002), 'Guiding principles for partnerships for sustainable development ('type 2 outcomes') to be elaborated by interested parties in the context of the World Summit on Sustainable Development (WSSD)', Fourth Summit Preparatory Committee (PREPCOM 4), Bali, Indonesia.

Martens, J. (2007), 'Multistakeholder partnerships: future models of multilateralism?', *Dialogue on Globalization Occasional Papers*, **29** (January), Bonn, Germany: Friedrich-Ebert-Stiftung.

McKinsey (2004), *Assessing the Global Compact's impact*, UN Global Compact Office, available at: http://europeandcis.undp.org/guides/poverty/spd/ras/mck insey_report_gc.pdf (retrieval: 11.05.2011).

OECD (2004), *Net Official Development Assistance in 2004*, Paris: Organization for Economic Cooperation and Development (OECD), available at: http://www.un.org/special-rep/ohrlls/News_flash2005/OECD%20ODA%20 2004%20general.pdf (retrieval: 11.05.2011).

OECD (2006), *Evaluating the Effectiveness and Efficiency of Partnerships*, Paris: Organization for Economic Cooperation and Development (OECD).

Reinicke, W.H. and F.M. Deng (2000), *Critical Choices: The United Nations*

Networks and the Future of Global Governance, Ottawa, Canada: International Development Research Centre.

Ruggie, J.G. (2002), 'The theory and practice of learning networks: corporate social responsibility and the Global Compact', *Journal of Corporate Citizenship*, **5** (Spring), 27–36.

Speth, J.G. (2004), 'Perspective on the Johannesburg Summit' in K. Conca and G. D. Dabelko (eds), *Green Planet Blues: Environmental Politics from Stockholm to Kyoto*, New York: Westview Press, pp. 156–63.

Stiglitz, J.E. (2002), 'Participation and development: perspectives from the comprehensive development paradigm', *Review of Development Economics*, **6**(2), 163–82.

Streck, C. (2004), 'New partnerships in global environmental policy: the clean development mechanism', *The Journal of Environment and Development*, **13**(3), 295–322.

Tondreau, F. (2005), 'Measuring the effectiveness of partnerships for sustainable development: what can we learn from the Chilean experience?', Report, Institute for Environmental Studies (IVM), VU University Amsterdam.

UN (1992), *Agenda 21*, United Nations Conference on Environment and Development, Rio de Janeiro, 1992.

UN (2006), CSD Partnerships Database, United Nations Commission on Sustainable Development, available at: http://webapps01.un.org/dsd/partnerships/public/welcome.do (retrieval: 11.05.2011).

Warner, M. (2003), 'Partnerships for sustainable development: do we need partnership brokers?', programme on Optimising the Development Performance of Corporate, Overseas Development Institute.

Witte, J.M., C. Streck and T. Brenner (2003), 'The road from Johannesburg: what future for partnerships in global environmental governance?', in T. Benner, C. Streck, J. Martin Witte (eds), *Progress or Peril? Networks and Partnerships in Global Environmental Governance. The Post-Johannesburg Agenda*, Berlin: Global Public Policy Institute, pp. 59–84.

5. Partnerships for sustainable development in the energy sector: explaining variation in their problem-solving effectiveness

Kacper Szulecki, Philipp Pattberg and Frank Biermann

While previous assessments have highlighted that UNCSD partnerships vary in function, size, goals and organizational structure (Andonova and Levy 2003; Hale and Mauzerall 2004; Biermann et al. 2007b; Appendix), relatively little is known about why partnerships for sustainable development vary in their problem-solving effectiveness. Many partnerships seem to be ineffective and, at times, not even traceable in empirical research, while others are well known and achieve the organizational goals that they have set for themselves. The key question is then what explains differences in effectiveness between the most effective and the least effective partnerships.

This chapter scrutinizes this question with regard to the sub-set of partnerships for sustainable development that focus on energy. Out of the total set of around 340 UNCSD partnerships, 46 are dedicated to sustainable energy, which is primarily understood as the provision of energy from renewable sources or the popularization of means to economize the use of renewable energy. With regard to their primary function, most partnerships in this area seek to contribute to sustainable development through knowledge dissemination and technology transfer (33 per cent), building of institutional capacity and training (22 per cent), technical implementation (17 per cent), knowledge production and innovation (13 per cent), and some other planned functions (15 per cent). Only 8 out of 46 energy partnerships have been established to create new energy infrastructure on the ground, while the majority is engaged in disseminating information and knowledge related to sustainable energy.

This chapter assesses both the effectiveness of partnerships and possible factors that may explain variation in the effectiveness. We assume that variation can be explained either by the internal structure of partnerships, especially the decision-making mechanisms and management structures, or by the character of actors involved. Our empirical restriction to the field of energy policy controls for a number of variables that may explain differences between policy fields and consequently allows us to focus on the two sets of factors that we are studying. Our study combines qualitative and quantitative methods of analysis, thus attempting to move beyond the 'case-study fallacy' that characterizes a large amount of recent research on partnerships (see Chapter 1, this volume). The results of both types of analysis suggest that a high level of institutionalization is necessary for a partnership to function, while a specific tri-partite organizational structure and the involvement of powerful actors can additionally improve the effectiveness and scale of an initiative. The research shows, however, that even these modest institutional features are often absent for many of the UNCSD-registered energy partnerships. Our study thus not only contributes to a better understanding of energy partnerships, but also to a broader assessment of novel governance arrangements beyond the state (for an overview, see Biermann and Pattberg 2008).

In the next section, we introduce the two competing hypotheses that may explain variation in effectiveness of partnerships, along with a brief review of the broader academic literature in which these hypotheses are rooted. We then discuss the methodology used in the qualitative and quantitative analysis. Subsequently, we proceed with our empirical analysis: we first test assumptions derived from the competing hypotheses against statistical data, and then provide an in-depth analysis of ten selected partnerships. The final section summarizes our findings and suggests some avenues for future research. The empirical assessment is based on the Global Sustainability Partnerships Database (see Chapter 1, this volume).

HYPOTHESES AND RESEARCH DESIGN

Within the burgeoning field of study related to multi-stakeholder partnerships, there are essentially two core hypotheses that are brought forward to explain variation in the effectiveness of such initiatives. A first hypothesis, derived from International Political Economy and realist theories in International Relations, points to the power of the actors involved as the main explanatory variable. It posits that partnerships that involve powerful business actors and major industrialized countries perform best. The reasoning behind this hypothesis is that considerable resources are needed to influence the activities of the energy sector worldwide. On this theoretical basis one can hypothesize that the most powerful and influential states will try to dominate specific partnerships to limit access of other actors. Partnerships can consequently be expected to appear in areas that are strongly linked to private business. Hypotheses centring on power can also be linked to neo-Gramscian theory. On this account, we expect powerful industrialized countries and major corporations to dominate effective partnerships, thus exercising hegemony under the cover of development aid and environmental initiatives (Goverde et al. 2000; Reinalda and Verbeek 2001; Arts 2003; Dimitrov 2003; Fuchs 2004).

A competing hypothesis, derived from institutionalist research traditions, posits that internal structures of partnerships influence their effectiveness: in other words, partnership design matters. Variation in effectiveness would then be related to the legal and institutional design as well as the internal organizational structure of a partnership. This argument is related to a large body of literature on intergovernmental regimes and the legalization of world politics (see for instance Mitchell 1994; Barett 1999; Abbott et al. 2000; Koremenos, Lipson and Snidal 2001). Consequently, not the characteristics of the participants but the institutional arrangements in place influence effectiveness. For example, we assume that within an institutionalized and structured context of the partnership, a more process-oriented, deliberative decision-making procedure, combined with network-style governance, enhances effectiveness.

The testing of the relative value of these competing hypotheses requires a concept to measure relative effectiveness of partnerships. Assessing the effectiveness of partnerships is contested because the concept is often under-defined, weakly operationalized and hard to measure. In the area of environmental governance in general, the impact of institutional arrangements on environment quality indicators has to be distinguished against the background noise of a large variety of other factors. Young (2001: 100) emphasized the need for large-n studies and medium-n comparative approaches (e.g. QCA). Yet while research on international regimes has made significant progress in its scope, moving from single cases to large-n analysis of databases (especially see Breitmeier, Young and Zürn 2006), the more recent literature on transnational policy networks and partnerships is still dominated by small-n approaches (Vollmer 2009). Often such studies bring interesting insights; but even though they provide measurements of effectiveness, they often fail to identify reasons for variation in influence (Mitchell 1994). Our work combines large-n research approaches, drawing on the GSPD, with an in-depth analysis of ten carefully selected cases.

The effectiveness of transnational multi-stakeholder partnerships could be measured at three levels: output, outcome, and impact (based on Easton 1965). Impact would measure the actual improvement in the problem area in the form of tangible changes in economic, social or environmental parameters. However, given that transnational multi-stakeholder partnerships are a rather recent phenomenon, we expected little observable effects in terms of outcome – that is changes in behaviour of targeted communities – or even impacts, that is positive changes of target indicators such as reductions in energy consumption. Outcome and impact are especially difficult to measure when it comes to large-*n* research programmes, such as our use of the GSPD, while it is more amenable to in-depth case study research. For these reasons, our focus in assessing the effectiveness of transnational multi-stakeholder partnerships is on their output, that is, their actual activities such as issuing regulations, producing reports, conducting research or organizing meetings. These core functions are similar for a large number of partnerships. Many partnerships provide some funding to target groups; they provide training, information, or technologies to address core areas of sustainable development. Most of these functions have been operationalized and empirically assessed in the GSPD to measure effectiveness in terms of output (see Chapter 1, this volume).

While measurements of output alone suffice for a first analysis, an in-depth study needs to take into account also how far this output is related to specific functions. Only if a partnership is active in a way necessary to fulfil its function, can it be ultimately effective. Within the GSPD, there are 12 types of output for each partnership. These types are linked to specific functions. In order to be able to (potentially) fulfil a function and thus (potentially) have some effects on a given sector, the output of a partnership has to be in line with its functions. The function of a partnership as used here is an abstraction of the partnership goals as interpreted by the researchers of the GSPD. The coding of functions for all UNCSD partnerships was based on information provided to the UNCSD (see also Chapter 1, this volume).

A partnership is seen as partly fulfilling a function if it has at least one type of visible output related to it. Working towards fulfilling a function is, however, not equivalent to making concrete progress against targets and reaching the partnership goals initially set out. Within the context of this research, we define the effectiveness of a partnership as the sum of all its effects measured by observable output (see Biermann et al. 2007b). Strictly speaking, our research assumes that observable output will eventually influence behaviour (outcome) and change target indicators (impact); in this sense, we are measuring the potential effectiveness of partnerships rather than their real impact on sustainable development.

In testing these two conflicting hypotheses outlined above, we employed two complementary methodologies. First, we studied all 46 energy partnerships registered with the UNCSD by analysing the GSPD. It accounts for a number of possible explanatory factors such as actors (number, involvement of powerful states, etc.), design (inclusiveness of membership rules, flexibility, governance mechanisms, task division, institutional features, etc.), leadership (type, organizational leadership capacity) and problem type. We used descriptive statistics to show how certain variables and their combinations correlate with the effectiveness (measured in terms of observable output) of energy partnerships.

Second, we conducted qualitative case studies of a sample of ten partnerships in the energy sector, selecting the five most effective and the five least effective from those partnerships that are operational. The studies focus on different aspects of the partnership's internal organization and assess their impact on the effectiveness. Our research approach is comparable to that of nested analysis proposed by Liebermann (2005). On the background of a large-n statistical study, we chose a sample of cases (divided according to the variation of the dependent variable they represented) and investigated them more closely. The sample selected for qualitative investigation thus covers 20 per cent of the whole energy partnerships population.

The group of five most effective partnerships has been selected based on two variables used in the GSPD: aggregated output and an expert survey that ranks partnerships in a number of functional areas, giving a reliable general description of the partnership's potential influence. The expert survey (see Chapter 1, this volume) measured, among other variables, how often an individual partnership was mentioned by experts as being relevant in their field. This serves as a proxy for the visibility and acknowledged activeness of a partnership in its area. The five most effective partnerships according to these criteria are

- the Global Gas Flaring Reduction Partnership,
- the Methane to Markets partnership,
- the Renewable Energy and Energy Efficiency Partnership,
- the Renewable Energy Policy Network for the 21st Century,
- and the International Solar Energy Society. Considerable differences between these partnerships are observable.

As of 2009, the Renewable Energy and Energy Efficiency Partnership is by far the largest, with more than 250 organizational partners involved, while the Global Gas Flaring Reduction Partnership has only 12 partners. Other important differences, allowing for the observance of variation in the explanatory variables, are also present and will be discussed below.

The group of five least effective (but operational) partnerships in the energy sector includes

- the African Energy Legacy Projects,
- the LPG Challenge partnership,
- the Pacific Islands Energy for Sustainable Development partnership,
- the US Clean Energy Initiative,
- and the International Renewable Energy Alliance.

Among these, two were completely unknown to the experts surveyed, while the US Clean Energy Initiative was mentioned ten times.

QUANTITATIVE ANALYSIS OF TRANSNATIONAL ENERGY PARTNERSHIPS

Non-operational Partnerships

To start with, our analysis of the GSPD revealed that 21 of 46 energy partnerships are entirely inactive, that is, they do not generate any observable output. Five of these 21 partnerships were indeed launched, but stopped working after an agreed period. The remaining 16 non-operational partnerships have either not started yet or were never operational. Among all the UNCSD partnerships, 37 per cent do not generate any output, which suggests that energy-related initiatives are more likely to be non-operational. This is an interesting observation given that the provision of renewable energy is a very important policy goal that attracts much political attention. In the remainder of this section, we try to answer why this dysfunctionality occurs, not only through looking at zero-output initiatives, but more importantly by showing the common characteristics of most successful initiatives. What is the most important factor affecting variation in measurable output? Is it the presence of important governmental and business actors, or rather partnership design and internal governance patterns?

Influence of Inclusion of Important Actors

According to the 'powerful actors' hypothesis, the problem-solving effectiveness of partnerships is related to the power and resources of important partners, who have an interest in the initiative's activities. This should mean that effective partnerships (those with high output levels) are led by powerful states or business actors, while ineffective initiatives should have many small developing states or NGOs as partners (Table 5.1).

Table 5.1   Variables and operationalization

Variable	Operationalization
Involvement of 'powerful actors'	Three variables from the GSPD database have been considered separately as well as together: Involvement of OECD states, EU states and private business.
Level of institutionalization	Several elements are taken into account, such as: own staff, office, signs of corporate identity such as logo.
Steering	Three types of steering are distinguished: hierarchical steering, partial steering and network-type steering.

Our data show that states are indeed reluctant to give away control over energy initiatives to private actors – two-thirds (30) of partnerships in this sector are led by states (16), intergovernmental organizations (8) or UN agencies (6). However, having public actors as main partners does not seem to necessarily improve the effectiveness of partnerships, as about the same percentage of public-led partnerships are found to be non-operational, as compared to those partnerships that are not led by states or intergovernmental bodies (47 per cent). Just under two-thirds of all UNCSD partnerships are public-led, and 44 per cent of these have no signs of output. Thus, energy partnerships are hardly different from the average. Only 16 energy partnerships are led by private organizations, in four cases business and in two cases NGOs. This suggests that there is very little correlation between the type of lead actor in a partnership and its effectiveness measured in output.

Only 7 out of 16 state-led initiatives have output, suggesting that states (no matter if they are powerful or not) are even less effective leaders than international organizations. However, if we only look at the partnerships with a high participation of member states of the Organisation for Economic Cooperation and Development (OECD) (more than four OECD states as partners), we receive a set of seven partnerships. Six of these have visible output, and three belong to the five most effective partnerships (Methane to Markets, Renewable Energy and Energy Efficiency Partnership and Renewable Energy Policy Network for the 21st Century). From the state-led partnerships that have at least one European Union member as partner, all are fully operational. Only 15 of the total 340 UNCSD partnerships meet the same criteria, and all show output. This finding is very interesting and seems to be consistent with the 'powerful actor' hypothesis. The role of EU states may thus be an important factor. On the other hand, partnerships with high OECD representation but no

European Union involvement are largely ineffective. This could suggest that decision-making culture and the specific deliberative decision-making style represented by the continental EU states has an influence on the overall effectiveness of transnational multi-stakeholder partnerships.

A combination of powerful state and business partners is also very common. One example is the Renewable Energy and Energy Efficiency Partnership, which is one of the largest energy partnerships and one of the largest UNCSD partnerships. Some 72 per cent of the energy partnerships with both OECD and private for-profit actors as partners generate output. More than half of these (among them four of the five best performing) show at least six different types of activity, which according to our conceptualization equals a very high potential effectiveness. This correlation is even stronger for the overall sample of all UNCSD partnerships, where over 80 per cent of partnerships with both OECD states and businesses have some observable output (82 per cent if an OECD state is also leading the partnership).

These data indicate merely a positive correlation but not necessarily a causal relation. However, if additionally the partnerships' internal structure is taken into account – i.e. if we only look at the initiatives with network-type steering (non-hierarchical) – we find that 91 per cent of partnerships meeting all these criteria are active. OECD and business involvement plus network-type steering is perhaps a formula for success, but not an explanation. Again, the conclusion can be that based on statistical analysis it is not possible to explain fully the difference in influence, although the correlation observed is quite strong. However, the suggested formula mixes variables from two realms: the one external to the partnership itself, comprising of actors, and the internal structure.

Influence of Number of Actors

Following the hypothesis that the characteristics of the members of partnership matter, one could suggest that larger partnerships are more powerful and should thus perform better. The energy partnerships with visible output are highly diversified. Their size, measured by number of partners, varies from two (Industrial Energy Efficiency Association) to over 250 (Renewable Energy and Energy Efficiency Partnership), giving an average of 46 partners. This makes them on average much bigger initiatives than the group of non-operational partnerships, which have on average less than ten partners. This can suggest that active energy partnerships are more effective because they are on average quite large. It is also likely that they are larger because they attract more partners, and they attract more partners because they have visible output. They may also gain new partners who bring in new resources and in turn enhance output even further. The primary reason for output is not the number of partners, as every partnership at some point had to start with only a handful of stakeholders. Effective energy partnerships rather appear to simply gather more partners (which can be interpreted as getting more attention) than effective partnerships on average, supporting the claim that sustainable energy is now an issue high on the political agenda. Only an analysis of concrete cases in time, showing the growth of specific partnerships, could help in directing the causal arrow one way or the other. That sort of analysis is beyond the scope of large-*n* methods alone, but will be done in this chapter at a later stage.

Influence of Internal Organization

Organizational structures can explain the effectiveness of partnerships both at the most superficial and at deeper levels. In particular, partnerships that are institutionalized in the form of a formal organization with its own staff generate much more output than other partnerships. This does not come as a surprise, since it only means that people who are paid to work for a given initiative are doing their job. However, the finding gains practical significance if one considers that only 10 out of 46 energy partnerships have at least one staff member.

Another relevant factor is also typical for organizations in the strict sense: corporate identity, which is usually associated at the very least with having a brand name and a corporate logo. Only 11 energy partnerships have a corporate identity thus defined, and ten of them are effective according to our measure.

QUALITATIVE ANALYSIS OF TRANSNATIONAL ENERGY PARTNERSHIPS

While quantitative data can provide an overview of the UNCSD partnerships in the energy sector and show general tendencies, there is a need to look into the actual structures of partnerships in order to explain variation in their effectiveness. Therefore, we have complemented our analysis of the GSPD with ten in-depth case studies of transnational multi-stakeholder partnerships in the energy sector. The selection of the ten cases has been described above: we have studied the five most effective and the five least effective energy partnerships that are operational. Five factors appeared as relevant in our analysis: the level of institutionalization; the type of function that partnerships are supposed to fulfil; the possibility of a misfit of functions and output; the influence of internal organization; and the specific institutional context and embeddedness. We will discuss each of these explanatory factors in turn.

Influence of Level of Institutionalization

First, it appears from our analysis that the level of institutionalization makes a difference. To start with, the level of institutionalization[1] of the five least effective partnerships is very low. For example, the African Energy Legacy Projects is a joint venture of energy producers rather than an organization (SADC 2009; SAPP 2009). The initiative is led by the South African private company ESKOM, but even the single company's employee directed to represent the African Energy Legacy Projects is unreachable, or does not work for ESKOM anymore (UNCSD 2009). The LPG Challenge resembled a UNDP project rather than an actual formalized partnership. Its vagueness is made evident by the two different names (also LP Gas Rural Energy Challenge) under which it can be traced, challenging its corporate identity. The Pacific Islands Energy for Sustainable Development is a programme, undertaken to implement a policy document, realized by SOPAC – Pacific Islands Applied Geoscience Commission. The SOPAC (2009) website does not list Pacific Islands Energy for Sustainable Development at all. Additionally, the 'partnership' has recently been subsumed under the larger Renewable Energy and Energy Efficiency Partnership. The first major problem of ineffective partnerships is the lack of institutionalization in form of an independent organization. This results in the unclear structure of most such partnerships. This does not mean that they are grass-root arrangements. Usually they are just proposed initiatives, which have never been fully made operational. Most of them are inactive, but those that claim to be, are also doing very little, perhaps because there is no one to work in the name of a given partnership. Neither the actors' power nor the style of decision-making can have any impact in that case. However, the involvement of OECD and business actors can make a difference by introducing good practices to the workings of such partnerships. One example is the Pacific Islands Energy for Sustainable Development newsletter that has been issued after the signing of a memorandum of understanding with the Renewable Energy and Energy Efficiency Partnership (Pacific Islands Energy for Sustainable Development 2007). Minimal institutionalization, self-reports, website – all this can be achieved with small cost and effort.

Once a formal structure is established and a partnership becomes operational, the style of decision-making can also play a role. In that sense, institutionalization is the basic factor leading to partnerships' effectiveness. All five highly effective partnerships are highly institutionalized, usually in a typical form of international organizations with steering committees and secretariats (Dingwerth and Pattberg 2009).

Ineffective partnerships often also seem to be not institutionalized on purpose, as they often play a role of brands rather than actual organizations. Two partnerships from the group of the least effective energy partnerships – the US Clean Energy Initiative and the International Renewable Energy Alliance – are examples of such brands or labels. Their role is to be an umbrella for other existing partnerships, organizations and programmes, but they themselves have neither staff nor actual resources to perform any functions. The US Clean Energy Initiative (2009) is only a name given to a wide range of US-led programmes and organizations. Although it brings together very powerful actors (US Department of State, Environmental Protection Agency (EPA), USAID, the World Health Organization (WHO), UNDESA, the World Bank, UNDP), it has little actual action capacities. Probably because it is only a brand sticker for numerous other initiatives, it has a very high score in our expert survey.

The International Renewable Energy Alliance is a coalition of four actual renewable energy organizations: the International Geothermal Association, the International Hydropower Association, the International Solar Energy Society, and the World Wind Energy Association (International Renewable Energy Alliance 2009). They are all active and visible in the energy sector, some for more than half a century (as for the International Solar Energy Society), but the advocacy projects bearing the International Renewable Energy Alliance brand are performed by individual member organizations. It is the only one of the least effective operational partnerships with a website and a logo. Nevertheless, it has no visible output of its own. The question is then why such initiatives are established in the first place. Why create a partnership which is meant to do nothing concrete and has no chance of success? To answer these questions, we must first problematize the concept of success. As Marianne Beisheim and Klaus Dingwerth (2008: 6) point out, we first need to ask: success for whom? Success from the perspective of founders or members at large is not necessarily the same as objective success from the perspective of the entire society or the environment. Therefore, what may seem as unacceptable waste of resources and attention – multiplying the number of dysfunctional sustainability initiatives – can well be explained by publicity and synergy profits for the partners. It is definitely better to have a broad portfolio of partnerships in various sectors than none or just a few, even if they are active. This explains, to some extent, the alarming ratio of inactive and ineffective partnerships in the UNCSD register.

Table 5.2   Functions of highly effective and little effective partnerships compared

Function	Number of partnerships performing the function	
	Five most effective energy partnerships	Five least effective among the operational energy partnerships
Knowledge dissemination	3	–
Technology transfer	3	4
Technical implementation	3	2
Participatory management	–	3
Training	2	1
Planning	1	1
Norm-setting	1	–
Lobbying	1	–
Capacity building	–	1

Influence of Type of Function Partnerships are Supposed to Fulfil

The groups of highly effective and non-effective partnerships vary significantly in terms of the functions they are expected to perform (as coded in the GSPD, see Table 5.2).

The most visible difference is the emphasis on participatory management, technology transfer and technical implementation among the less effective partnerships, in contrast with knowledge dissemination as one of the key functions for highly effective ones. Insofar as the laggards do not have any visible signs of output at all, it is not possible to see any function–output fit. What is to be noted, however, is that participatory management and technical implementations are difficult to achieve. None of the five most effective energy partnerships manages to have any influence in this area either. In other words, the third reason explaining ineffective partnerships' failure is the choice of functions and goals that are very difficult to reach. This may account for less effectiveness. As Table 5.2 shows, energy partnerships rarely take up the more difficult functions. Do the most effective partnerships perform that well, in contrast to the laggards? The analysis of the fit between function and output reveals, however, a more complex relationship.

Fit Between Function and Output

Output is not equivalent to problem-solving capacity but rather an indicator for the potential success of a partnership. In order to be considered successful in terms of making progress against certain predefined targets, a partnership is expected to be active in ways fulfilling its functions. Having many types of output is not necessarily conducive to reaching goals, it does add, however, to publicity. On the other hand, fewer types of output concentrated only on function fulfilment can be interpreted as an indicator for potential effectiveness. Output-generating partnerships vary significantly with regard to their function–output fit. Some partnerships have activities, but related to a function that the partnership did not initially plan to perform, while others only produce few types of output, but focused precisely on the actual function to be fulfilled.

The table presents the activities of partnerships in the GSPD categorized according to the three functions coded for each partnership in the database. The fourth column lists output not related to any of the three functions. For each function, the activities of a partnership are shown as a fraction of all the types of output that are aimed at fulfilling this function. The output types not related to function fulfilment are shown as a fraction of the total output types of a given partnership, thus showing what part of its output is not related to the actual goal fulfilment.

The Mediterranean Renewable Energy Program has only three types of output, yet they act towards the fulfilment of two out of three of its functions. An even better example is the Energy for Poverty Eradication and Sustainable Development initiative, which has only one type of output, but it is also (ideally) helping it in reaching its goals in two out of three areas. Among the five most effective energy partnerships are only two partnerships that fulfil all of its functions – Methane to Markets and the Renewable Energy Policy Network for the 21st Century. However, the remaining three champions are performing relatively well and act towards two out of three functions (Table 5.3).

It is important to note that types of output are much diversified in the efforts and resources needed to generate them. The participation in conferences or the organization of a workshop is hardly related to infrastructure construction. Three of the five most effective energy partnerships have 'technical implementation' as their function, but none of them has matching visible output. The African Energy Legacy Projects, one of the laggards, was established to fulfil this function alone and, so far, it fails. Should the African Energy Legacy Projects finally complete the construction of at least one transmission line improving the Pan-African electric grid, it would reach a very important and measurable goal, perhaps its actual impact

Table 5.3   Highly effective partnerships function–output fit and excess activities

P-ship	Function I and related activities	Function II and related activities	Function III and related activities	Excess activities Fraction of total
GGFRP	Knowledge Dissemination 3/4 Training, Workshop, Conference participation	Technical Implementation 0/1 —	Technology Transfer 2/4 Training, Workshop	Research, Standards, Policy, Self-Reports 4/7
Methane to Markets partnership	Planning 3/4 Policy, Workshop, Conference participation	Technology Transfer 2/4 Workshop, Infrastructure and Technology transfer	Training 1/2 Workshop	Advocacy, Self-Reports, Database, New Institutions 4/8
Renewable Energy and Energy Efficiency Partnership	Knowledge Dissemination 3/4 Database, Workshop, Conference participation	Technical Implementation 0/1	Norm Setting 1/1 Standards	Advocacy, Self-Reports, New Institutions 3/7
REN 21	Lobbying 2/2 Policy, Conference Participation	Knowledge Dissemination 2/4 Workshop, Conference Participation	—	Research, Advocacy, New Institutions 3/6
International Solar Energy Society	Training 2/2 Workshop, Training	Technology Transfer 2/4 Training, Workshop	Technical Implementation 0/1	Research, Advocacy, Policy, Conference participation 4/6

would be much more important than all five most effective energy partnerships combined. However, the functions chosen by the five most effective partnerships are usually much more modest. Three of them aim at knowledge dissemination, three at technology transfer, two at training and the remaining functions are planning, lobbying, and norm setting. All of these functions relate to information and the dissemination of know-how.

Another relevant observation is the amount of excess output generated because of activities not related to initially declared functions. If we exclude the possibility that this 'bonus' output is a result of theoretical and methodological shortcomings (the explained subjectivity of function–output fit analysis, meaning that the so called 'excess output' could in fact be perceived by the partnership itself as fulfilling its core functions), the remaining conclusion is that active partnerships are putting effort and resources into irrelevant activities. Irrelevant again from the perspective of the general public, in the sense that the partnership is not working towards goals and impact but rather working just for the sake of it. For all five most effective partnerships, at least half of the performed activities are not meaningfully related to its functions. If we assume that such mode of operation is using many resources, which could have been channelled towards progress against important targets, it turns out that even the most effective energy partnerships are quite inefficient. This last criticism should not divert our attention away from the fact that more than 50 per cent of all UNCSD partnerships are showing hardly any output related to achieving their sustainability targets. Among them, the five most effective energy partnerships analysed here are real 'champions'.

Influence of Internal Organization

An inductive study of the five most effective energy partnerships shows that they have common features at the level of internal organization, which can be seen as increasing effectiveness. While the very low level of institutionalization among the least effective partnerships is the key reason for their dysfunctionality, the energy sector champions are highly institutionalized and have robust organizational structures (Pattberg et al. 2009). This helps them work towards the achievement of their goals, despite the fact that all these initiatives are much diversified (with the exception of the Global Gas Flaring Reduction Partnership). Through our qualitative analysis, two important structural features became visible in the sample of the most effective partnerships that play a role in increasing problem-solving capacity: management structure and the presence of executive and administrative sub-organs.

Management Structure

The first is the management structure, resembling international organizations, in which three elements are present: a general assembly representing all the partners/members, a smaller executive board performing regular activities, and an administrative as well as representative secretariat that keeps the organization running. The second feature is the presence of sub-bodies organized along issue areas or geographic location, allowing for the constant reception of signals from the organization's environment.

All of the five most effective partnerships show elements of this structure.

- The Methane to Markets partnership has a permanent Steering Committee, which comprises of maximum two delegates from each of the partner-states (Methane to Markets 2009). The Steering Committee meets regularly, but the daily administrative activities are implemented by the Administrative Support Group, the partnership's secretariat. Sub-committees act both as lower level executive organs and as focused governance organs. Sub-committees implement the partnership's strategies in the respective sectors (coal, oil and gas, landfill gas and agriculture) and coordinate specific projects.
- The Renewable Energy and Energy Efficiency Partnership maintains a clear task division between the permanent executive body and the general assembly (Pattberg et al. 2009). The Head of the Governing Board (executive) also chairs the annual Meeting of Partners. The organizational backbone of the partnership is the International Secretariat, employing 8–10 permanent staff members. It not only deals with the administrative and coordination issues, but also engages in lobbying activities and public relations (Moscoso-Osterkorn 2005). The Programme Board and Finance Committee are elements of a complex yet transparent decision-making structure, which also involves Regional Secretariats (with permanent Renewable Energy and Energy Efficiency Partnership staff) and Focal Points.
- The Renewable Energy Policy Network for the 21st Century has a similar structure. The Steering Committee in this case is the larger assembly, while the day-to-day executive is the elected standing Bureau (Renewable Energy Policy Network for the 21st Century 2009). Again, the administrative and representative functions are performed by the permanent Secretariat, which is (as in the case of Renewable Energy and Energy Efficiency Partnership) the main carrier of the partnership's corporate identity.

- The International Solar Energy Society, as a transnational NGO with a 54-year track-record, has the most complex structure of the most effective initiatives. It is, however, possible to distinguish the same core organs as in the three initiatives already discussed. In the International Solar Energy Society, the Board of Directors acts as a steering committee, with the Executive Committee as permanent executive body. The International Headquarters in Freiburg is only an alternative name for a typical secretariat. Additional bodies such as the Divisions, Councils and Standing Committees diversify the executive, while Regional Offices and National Sections act as local secretariats and focal points for the organization.
- Only the Global Gas Flaring Reduction partnership is coordinated by a temporary secretariat at the World Bank. A steering committee is currently planned (Global Gas Flaring Reduction Partnership 2009).

Overall, this supports our argument that such tri-partite structure enhances the potential effectiveness of a partnership. The secretariat is a nodal point; that is where the staff dedicated to its day-to-day output is employed. This implies two things: the secretariat is the carrier of the partnership's organizational identity, and therefore is crucial for its effectiveness.

The other key point with regard to organizational structure is the steering committee or board. If we analyse the names of people sitting in the various steering committees and executive boards, we notice a certain overlap among the energy partnerships. The most striking example is Griffin Thompson from the US State Department, who sits in the Steering Committee of the Renewable Energy Policy Network for the 21st Century, the Governing Board of the Renewable Energy and Energy Efficiency Partnership, and another successful partnership, the Global Village Energy Partnership. Piotr Tulej from the European Commission also serves both the Renewable Energy Policy Network for the 21st Century and the Renewable Energy and Energy Efficiency Partnership. Although board members come and go, the fact that certain names appear more than once suggests that these executive bodies are the focal points for expertise. While secretariats guarantee visibility, operational disposition and 'brand' continuity (they are also the driving force of the organization, like any bureaucracy), executive boards are necessary for important decisions leading to goal attainment, partnership's growth and donor credibility. In other words, partnerships that do not adopt this basic tri-partite structure are far less likely to succeed in the long term.

Executive and Administrative Sub-organs

The second decisive feature of successful partnerships in the energy sector is the presence of executive and administrative sub-organs. Methane to Markets has a set of four sectoral subcommittees, representing the methane producing industries, while the Renewable Energy and Energy Efficiency Partnership has eight Regional Secretariats (and corresponding regional steering committees) and two regional focal points. Both these (seemingly different) sets of organs play a very similar role. Methane to Markets draws its relative success from the close link with industry in specific issue areas, while the Renewable Energy and Energy Efficiency Partnership, as emphasized by one of its senior staff members, aims at a regional and local focus: 'In the past a lot of these regional consultations were really one-sided. [. . .] Being bottom-up and driven by your partners in the regions has a significant advantage in terms of ownership by those countries'.[2]

The International Solar Energy Society is situated in-between these two approaches, combining a regionally and nationally focused approach with the issue-oriented perspective. Such lower-level orientation plays an important role in enhancing a partnership's influence. This does not necessarily show in the output, but rather in the actual fulfilment of partnership functions.

Influence of Institutional Embeddedness

One final explanatory factor that has emerged through the qualitative analysis is the way in which a partnership is embedded in already established institutional structures. The Global Gas Flaring Reduction partnership stands out from the rest, as its organizational structure is rooted in a different tradition. The initiative resembles more a project on an intergovernmental organization than a self-standing transnational NGO. It is essentially a programme of the World Bank, headed by a Programme Manager. At first glance, the partnership is almost a twin of the LPG Challenge – also a project of an intergovernmental organization, but hosted by the UNDP. Both are also rather narrow-in-scope sectoral initiatives. Such degree of similarity allows for a fruitful comparison.

While the structure of LPG Challenge was unclear and there seems to be no person responsible for the partnership's activities (or lack thereof), the Global Gas Flaring Reduction Partnership has a permanent staff of ten (all World Bank employees), which is a rather high number compared with the total set of all 340 UNCSD partnerships. A Steering Committee is to be established, until that time the World Bank takes care of the day-to-day administrative activities. While the lack of institutionalization, staff, and resources can be an explanatory variable, it also needs explanation. The LPG Challenge is a development-oriented programme under the United Nations. While energy is its main theme because it deals with liquid petroleum gas (LPG), its goals are in fact related to the improvement of living standards, health and poverty alleviation (UNCSD 2009).

The Global Gas Flaring Reduction Partnership unites a number of very influential and powerful partners, and its activities can have important environmental impact precisely because it is related to one of the most important industries globally: the oil industry. The comparison between these two initiatives supports the 'powerful actor' hypothesis about partnership effectiveness. With private partners like British Petroleum, Exxon Mobil, TotalFinaElf, Statoil, Shell Petroleum, Norsk Hydro and Chevron Texaco, governments of the United States, Norway, the United Kingdom, of members of the Organization of the Petroleum Exporting Countries as well as other oil exporters, and the administrative support of the World Bank, the Global Gas Flaring Reduction Partnership seems to be destined for success. Yet, its effectiveness raises many questions. Despite the potential resources available, it failed to fulfil the most difficult function, which is technical implementation. More than a half of its output is not related to its functions. The Global Gas Flaring Reduction Partnership seems to be a perfect example of the privatization of global environmental governance (Falkner 2003). In the lack of existing international regulation of gas flaring, private actors and interested governments (Norwegian government, which is the main owner of the semi-private oil industry companies Statoil and Norsk Hydro stands somewhere between public and private stakeholders in this case) decided on voluntary regulation for themselves. This can be interpreted either as a positive action and greening of the oil industry, or as green window dressing, which hides cartel-like practices. In either case, the role of powerful public and private actors is considerable, while the impact of internal organization is hard to evaluate.

CONCLUSIONS

Overall, we conclude from our analysis that the involvement of powerful actors is necessary but not sufficient for a partnership's success. As the quantitative analysis has shown, the presence of industrialized countries, along with that of private for-profit partners, is quite strongly correlated with output. The in-depth qualitative analysis suggests that the influential partnerships link many powerful states and businesses. By contrast, most of the least effective partnerships include weaker and poorer African countries (African Energy Legacy Project, LPG Challenge) or small island developing states. However, a more detailed analysis suggests that powerful actors alone are not a sufficient condition for partnership success. First of all, if a partnership serves as a brand rather than an actual organization, it will not be effective even if it has far reaching support from the United States (as the US Clean Energy Initiative) or from influential and established international organizations (as the International Renewable Energy Alliance). In such cases, the powerful partners can influence a partnership's visibility and reputation (as for the US Clean Energy Initiative), but effectiveness as a partnership is not really the direct goal of these initiatives.

Another point emerging from the qualitative analysis is that the level of institutionalization and the internal organizational structure of an initiative matter. Effective partnerships have to be institutionalized into real organizations. If they are, they become operational and can work towards achieving the envisaged goals. Depending on the scale of these goals, the activities of a partnership may require more or fewer resources. If the aim of a partnership is knowledge dissemination, training or advocacy, the resources needed are quite limited. The non-governmental International Solar Energy Society is able to function effectively for over five decades without being co-opted by business actors or powerful states. The same holds for the Renewable Energy Policy Network for the 21st Century, which is primarily a lobbying and advocacy network. However, the more salient an issue area is for governments (for example, oil or energy security), the higher are the chances that powerful state actors will get involved. The example of the Global Gas Flaring Reduction Partnership shows that petroleum-related issues feature prominently on the agenda, attracting powerful actors to voluntary private regulation. The case of the Renewable Energy and Energy Efficiency Partnership suggests that while wealthy and powerful donors are important for the scale of an initiative, it may actually be the bottom-up (be it regional or issue-oriented) approach that explains the influence a partnership can have and the impact it potentially could make.

The decision-making styles and the governance culture might also play a role, but only in the context of a functional partnership. If a partnership is operational and well institutionalized in the form of an organization with functional forums of decision-making, then (and only then) can the factor of deliberation make a difference. Hence, the main policy-conclusion of this chapter is that a partnership, in order to be effective, needs to be institutionalized, preferably in the form of an organization with an executive board that should include the representatives of major stakeholders, and a permanent administrative secretariat, dedicated to the goal and mission of the initiative. The involvement of powerful actors can help by bringing in necessary resources, and is crucial in the case of large-scale partnerships established to perform difficult and costly activities.

Our analysis has also shown the adequacy of an approach that combines quantitative and qualitative methods to assess the effectiveness of partnerships for sustainable development. We have proposed to approach the question of effectiveness by analysing the concrete output of partnerships, using its fit with the partnerships' function as a proxy for potential effectiveness. Future research should engage further with the challenging question of how to gather comparative data on partnership outcome (behavioural change) and partnership impact (problem solving).

Finally, we come back to a central question that underlies much of the current sustainability discourse: are partnerships a major innovation in global governance for sustainable development or rather old wine in new bottles? First, our finding that a partnership should be institutionalized to be functional may seem trivial, but in the context of 340 UNCSD partnerships, it clearly is not. As we have shown, some partnerships are purposefully left as hollow, non-institutionalized brands, while others simply do not have the necessary resources to support a standing administration. Hence, the findings of this study directly challenge claims that partnerships are a positive institutional innovation established to reach the goals of sustainable development. While their broad and general goals are widely accepted, it seems that many partnerships do not offer concrete steps towards achieving international commitments and remain mostly at the level of political rhetoric (see Biermann et al. 2007a).

Only a minority of partnerships is operational and has visible signs of output, which normally correlates with a certain degree of institutionalization and organizational form. The examples of relatively effective partnerships that we investigated show that this organizational form often hardly differs from the standard structure of intergovernmental organizations. Partnerships are regarded as institutional innovations only because they take the form of private–public governance schemes. However, the example of the International Solar Energy Society suggests that as far as NGOs and epistemic communities are concerned, the private sector has already been included in such initiatives for some time. Only direct involvement of business actors seems to be new, but then the question is if this form of innovation is in all cases necessarily positive.

One argument in support of the claim that partnerships improve global governance is that their permanent secretariats – the administrative bureaucratic cores – are usually quite efficient. They employ few professionals who are meticulously monitored by the donors. This helps to save financial resources for other activities than just running the organization. This is an often-mentioned weakness of traditional intergovernmental organizations. In this sense, the closer cooperation with business actors and the diffusion of modern corporate management patterns is indeed a positive innovation.

However, within the overall community of partnerships, where numerous actors are involved in similar activities, we can also observe substantial turf wars. It is quite clear that numerous partnerships with a larger scope are doubling their functions and efforts to some extent. The British and Norwegian governments lead Renewable Energy and Energy Efficiency Partnership, the Italian Mediterranean Renewable Energy Program, the German Renewable Energy Policy Network for the 21st Century, the French ADEME and the US GVEP – all partnerships in the general area of renewable energy, are good examples. Sometimes this leads to cooperation, on other occasions potential areas of intervention are demarcated along the lines of older aid regimes, often of colonial origin. However, resources can also be wasted this way, and this is a conclusion supporting the establishment of an overarching regulatory body in the sustainable development and environmental governance sector (Biermann 2000).

In sum, based on our assessment of sustainable energy partnerships in the overall sample of partnerships for sustainable development, the positive expectations that were placed on multi-stakeholder partnerships by both governments and civil society organizations have hardly been met. If inactive partnerships were erased from the UNCSD database by the United Nations Department of Economic and Social Affairs, the number of partnerships would most likely be halved. However, the political myth of partnerships is still alive. Partnerships that are non-operational remain in the UNCSD database and can even become partners of other partnerships (as happened with the Pacific Islands Energy for Sustainable Development Partnership and Renewable Energy and Energy Efficiency Partnership). This critique may seem unfair to those partnerships that are doing their best to fulfil their goals. However, even when considering success cases such as Renewable Energy and Energy Efficiency Partnership, the promise of effective, fair and equitable global governance through multi-stakeholder partnerships is quite exaggerated.

ACKNOWLEDGEMENTS

This chapter has previously been published in revised form as: Szulecki, Kacper, Philipp Pattberg and Frank Biermann (2011), Explaining variation in the effectiveness of transnational energy partnerships. In *Governance: An International Journal of Policy, Administration, and Institutions* **24**(3), 713–36. We thank the publisher for the kind permission to reproduce the article here.

NOTES

1. For the purpose of this analysis, the level of institutionalization is understood as a combination of 'institutional' variables coded in the GSPD (staff, office, own budget, logo), as well as the results of a qualitative assessment of the ten partnerships analysed. This included evaluation of the relationship between the partnership and the founding partners (i.e. is the partnership institutionalized as a separate organization or is it only a project run within the existing structures of a larger entity), corporate identity and the legal basis on which the partnership operates.
2. Interview with REEEP staff member, April 2008, Vienna.

REFERENCES

Abbott, K.W., R.O. Keohane, A. Moravcsik, A.M. Slaughter and D. Snidal (2000), 'The concept of legalization', *International Organization*, **54**(3), 401–19.
Andonova, L.B. and M.A. Levy (2003), 'Franchising global governance: making sense of the Johannesburg Type II Partnerships', in O.S. Stokke and O.B. Thommessen (eds), *Yearbook of International Co-operation on Environment and Development*, Oxford, UK: Earthscan, pp. 19–31.
Arts, B. (2003), *Non-State Actors in Global Governance. Three Faces of Power*, Köln, Germany: Max-Planck-Institute for the Study of Societies.
Barrett, S. (1999), 'Montreal versus Kyoto: international cooperation and the global environment', in I. Kaul, I. Grunberg and M.A. Stern (eds), *Global Public Goods: International Cooperation in the 21st Century*, Oxford, UK: Oxford University Press, pp. 192–219.
Beisheim, M. and K. Dingwerth (2008), 'Procedural legitimacy and private transnational governance. Are the good ones doing better?', *SFB-Governance Working Paper Series*, **14**, June 2008.
Biermann, F. (2000), 'The case for a world environment organization', *Environment*, **42**(9), 22–31.
Biermann, F. and P. Pattberg (2008), 'Global environmental governance: taking stock, moving forward', *Annual Review of Environment and Resources*, **33**, 277–94.
Biermann, F., S. Chan, A. Mert and P. Pattberg (2007a), 'Partnerships for sustainable development: an appraisal framework', *Global Governance Working Paper*, **31**, October 2007.
Biermann, F., S. Chan, A. Mert and P. Pattberg (2007b), 'Multi-stakeholder partnerships for sustainable development: does the promise hold?' in P. Glasbergen, F. Biermann and A.P.J. Mol (eds), *Partnerships, Governance and Sustainable*

Development. Reflections on Theory and Practice, Cheltenham, UK: Edward Elgar, pp. 239–60.

Breitmeier, H., O.R. Young and M. Zürn (2006), *Analyzing International Environmental Regimes: From Case Study to Database*, Cambridge, MA: MIT Press.

Dingwerth, K. and P. Pattberg (2009), 'World politics and organizational fields: the case of sustainability governance', *European Journal of International Relations*, **15**(4), 707–43.

Dimitrov, R.S. (2003), 'Knowledge, power, and interests in environmental regime formation', *International Studies Quarterly*, **47**(1), 123–50.

Easton, D. (1965), *A Systems Analysis of Political Life*, New York: Wiley.

Falkner, R. (2003), 'Private environmental governance and international relations: exploring the links', *Global Environmental Politics*, **3**(2), 72–87.

Fuchs, D. (2004), Channels and dimensions of business power in global governance, Paper presented at 45th Annual International Studies Association Convention, 17–20 March, Montreal.

Global Gas Flaring Reduction Partnership (2009), The website of the Global Gas Flaring Reduction Partnership, available online at: http://web.worldbank.org/ggfr (retrieval: 30.01.2010).

Goverde, H., P.G. Cerny, M. Haugaard and H.H. Lentner (eds) (2000), *Power in Contemporary Politics. Theories, Practices, Globalizations*, London: Sage.

Hale, T.N. and D.L. Mauzerall (2004), 'Thinking globally and acting locally: can the Johannesburg partnerships coordinate action on sustainable development?', *The Journal of Environment and Development*, **13**(3), 220–39.

International Renewable Energy Alliance (2009), The website of the International Renewable Energy Alliance, available online at: http://www.ren-alliance.org/ (retrieval: 14.01.2010).

Koremenos, B., C. Lipson and D. Snidal (2001), 'The rational design of international institutions', *International Organization*, **55**(4), 761–99.

Lieberman, E. (2005), 'Nested analysis as a mixed-method strategy for comparative research', *American Political Science Review*, **99**(3), 435–52.

Mitchell, R.B. (1994), 'Regime design matters: intentional oil pollution and treaty compliance', *International Organization*, **48**(3), 425–58.

Methane to Markets (2009), The website of the Methane to Markets partnership, available online at: http://www.methanetomarkets.org/ (retrieved on 29.01.2010).

Moscoso-Osterkorn, M. (2005), 'The Renewable Energy and Energy Efficiency Partnership: redefining "natural" resources', Washington, USA: Office of Science and Technology Bridges, Embassy of Austria, 6 December 2005, available at: http://www.ostina.org/content/view/145/290/ (retrieval: 02.02.2009).

Pacific Islands Energy for Sustainable Development Partnership (2007), Pacific Islands Energy for Sustainable Development Partnership Newsletter, **1**, July 2007, SOPAC, available at: http://www.sopac.org (retrieval: 01.12.2009).

Pattberg, P., K. Szulecki, S. Chan and A. Mert (2009), 'Assessing the role and relevance of the Renewable Energy and Energy Efficiency Partnership in global sustainability governance', in D. Vollmer (ed.), *Enhancing the Effectiveness of Sustainability Partnerships*, Washington DC: US National Academies Press, pp. 97–129.

Reinalda, B. and B. Verbeek (2001), 'Theorising power relations between NGOs, inter-governmental organisations and states', in B. Arts, M. Noortmann and

B. Reinalda (eds), *Non-State Actors in International Relations*, Aldershot, UK: Ashgate, pp. 145–59.

Renewable Energy Policy Network for the 21st Century (2009), The website of the Renewable Energy Policy Network for the 21st Century, available at: www.ren21.net (retrieval: 14.01.2010).

Southern African Development Community (SADC) (2009), The website of the Southern African Development Community, available at: http://www.sadc.int/ (retrieval: 01.12.2009).

Southern African Power Pool (SAPP) (2009), The website of the Southern African Power Pool, available at: http://www.sapp.co.zw/ (retrieval: 01.12.2009).

South Pacific Applied Geoscience Commission (SOPAC) (2009), The website of the Pacific Islands Energy for Sustainable Development, available at: http://www.sopac.org/tiki-index.php?page=Introduction (retrieval: 19.01.2010).

United Nations Commission on Sustainable Development (UNCSD) (2009), Partnership for Sustainable Development Database, available online at: http://webapps01.un.org/dsd/partnerships/public/welcome.do, (retrieved on 29 01 2010).

Vollmer, D. (ed) (2009), *Enhancing the Effectiveness of Sustainability Partnerships*, Washington DC: National Academies Press.

Young O. (2001), 'Inferences and indices: evaluating the effectiveness of international environmental regimes', *Global Environmental Politics*, **1**(1), 99–121.

PART III

Partnerships for sustainable development beyond the OECD world

6. Partnerships for sustainable development beyond the OECD world: comparing China and India

Sander Chan

Partnerships for sustainable development, introduced at the 2002 WSSD in Johannesburg, represent a large-scale transposition of partnerships as a governance instrument beyond the OECD context. However, the introduction of partnerships for sustainable development beyond the OECD context does not necessarily entail a convergence of governance approaches and practices among developing countries. To which extent global governance instruments such as partnerships for sustainable development influence domestic governance practices is an open question. This chapter discusses partnerships for sustainable development in China and India. Together, these two countries have been referred to as the 'Asian drivers of global change' (Messner and Humphrey 2006; Kaplinsky and Messner 2008; Humphrey and Messner 2009), implying that they have become more than mere objects of global governance; instead they are increasingly shaping the architecture and the outcomes of global governance. China and India have even been seen as countervailing powers to current processes of globalization (Bhattacharya and Bhattacharya 2006). A transposition of partnerships into these countries, therefore, does not necessarily represent a case of domestic adoption of global governance instruments, and much less an imposition of governance norms by Western governments. Rather, the Asian drivers increasingly have the capacity to adapt global governance instruments to better suit their domestic governance systems or even to challenge the premises and instruments of global governance.

In addition to the policy relevance of analysing Asian drivers in global governance, there are also methodological considerations for a comparative analysis of public–private partnerships in India and China. The Asian drivers share many characteristics: they are the most and second most populous countries in the world; both are emerging world powers; both are leaving behind a past of low development and poverty; both have abandoned planning as the primary method of economic coordination in favour of markets; both experience rapid economic growth. While sharing characteristics, Asian drivers, however, represent very different political systems, featuring different state–society relations and different structures of civil society. A comparison between India and China allows for an assessment of political and institutional contexts as key explanatory factors in the implementation and organization of partnerships for sustainable development beyond the OECD.

In the following section, I discuss global assumptions about governance and partnerships, the distinct drivers and movers in global governance, the influence of global governance on domestic governance, and finally the specific cases of partnerships for sustainable development in China and India. This chapter concludes by assessing the constraints and the potential of partnerships for sustainable development in the Chinese and Indian contexts. The empirical assessment is based on the GSPD (see Chapter 1, this volume).

GLOBAL ASSUMPTIONS ABOUT GOVERNANCE AND PARTNERSHIPS

Industrialized countries have been generally more supportive of adopting partnerships as instruments in global sustainable development. Partnerships in these countries had been part of domestic governance for long. To some degree, the partnerships regime that emerged from the WSSD reflects therefore the preferences, norms and practices of OECD countries. Partnership governance in the OECD area emerged as a result of political, societal and economic developments. The turn towards partnership governance was sometimes part of political campaigns to restructure government, for instance under the 'New Right' governments of the 1980s. A broader public management paradigm emerged throughout the OECD area: the New Public Management, in which partnerships were instrumental (Hood 1991; Savas 2000). Moreover, people throughout the OECD area experienced an extended period of peace and economic growth leading to higher expectations towards public service provision and higher tax-consciousness, demanding budget discipline and more efficient services (cf. Hood and Schuppert 1988: 250–52; Hood 1991). Coupled with a widely shared sentiment that large state-controlled public sectors are inefficient and ineffective, this led to increasing pressure for government reform and the adoption of alternative governance approaches that embody less hierarchical, more participatory and slimmer alternatives to traditional government. Partnerships are one manifestation of this drive towards alternative government, as they complement and at times even substitute government by including non-governmental stakeholders, such as NGOs, business and science organizations in decision-making and policy implementation. As drivers of global governance, OECD countries also shape international institutions and instruments (e.g. Krasner 1991; Büthe and Mattli 2003). Drawing from their experience at home, these OECD countries replicated their norms and practices of governance into global governance; while international organizations such as the UN and the World Bank played intermediating roles in the transposition of these instruments beyond the OECD.

In the case of non-OECD countries, the connection between domestic economic, societal and political developments and the emergence of partnership governance is not always apparent. While partnerships have been advocated by international organizations, and have been introduced through development projects, partnerships do not necessarily become part of domestic governance. In other words: individual partnership projects exist quite isolated from other domestic institutions and policies, and they do not amount to the regular use of partnerships as a means of governance. It is hardly surprising that developing countries expressed worries during the WSSD negotiation process, since partnerships are not mere implementation instruments, but also carriers of governance norms, which are not necessarily compatible with domestic practices. For instance, partnerships for sustainable development assume vibrant civil societies and strong non-governmental actors that can handle assistance funds channelled outside of governmental relations. This alternative channelling of funds and resources was viewed with suspicion by some governments, as they feared Western interference into their societal development. To describe the introduction of partnerships beyond the OECD as a case of 'imposition' by foreign donors and international organizations would, however, be a tenuous generalization. First, facing questions of sustainable development, governments beyond the OECD also look for 'best practices' and alternative governance methods. Moreover, non-governmental actors in developing countries are also learning from, and connecting with, their counterparts abroad. Second, governments do not fear the mere existence of partnerships within their borders, since partnerships per se do not necessarily amount to partnership governance; rather individual partnerships can exist isolated from national institutions and policies. For instance, they can take the form of (short-term) projects with very limited effect in terms of scale and policy reform. Therefore, whether partnerships in developing countries amount to partnership governance will depend on the fit between partnerships and domestic governance, i.e. the compatibility of new global governance instruments, such as partnerships, with domestic governance. For example, an established rule of law creates a stable and contractual environment conducive to the formation of partnerships. Moreover, freedom of association allows for non-governmental actors to form alliances and to actively engage in policy making and implementation. In addition, governments that lack capacity and budget may seek to forge partnerships to leverage resources from third parties.

As partnerships are introduced into the Chinese and Indian contexts, they are also confronted by existing institutions of domestic governance. The compatibility between structural developments, the partnership practice and government reform often found in the OECD context is more ambiguous here. Partnerships have been put forward by international organizations and consultants as an instrument of reform of public service provision, alongside privatization, subcontracting and decentralization. According to some observers, global governance and its instruments suggest an extension of the process of neo-liberalization (beyond the OECD) (Miraftab 2004; Overbeek 2005). However, the transposition of the partnership model as a part of neo-liberal expansion would suggest a close concurrence between social, political and economic developments and the emergence of partnerships. In practice, the role of international organizations, foreign governments and consultants in the introduction of partnerships beyond the OECD can hardly be discounted (Chan 2009). The WSSD process is a case in point. While developing countries were sceptical of the introduction of partnerships as an official outcome of the WSSD, fearing substitution of bi- and multilateral development assistance, industrialized countries, including the United States, the European Union, Canada and Japan along with the World Bank and major corporations, readily suggested partnerships as new and innovative governance instruments. The application of partnerships beyond the OECD may therefore be a projection of the desires and the worldviews of these 'first-mover' actors onto global sustainable development governance, rather than a response to domestic gaps in governance in developing countries. Indeed, many of the UNCSD registered partnerships seem to be predominantly promotional efforts with no apparent demand for them (Andonova and Levy 2003). Partnerships in developing countries may be more responsive to foreign governments, international non-governmental organizations and international organizations than to the governments and citizens of the developing countries they operate in. However, rather than generalizing for all developing countries, it is important to acknowledge that the potential for partnership governance in sustainable development will vary by country and by respective political, societal and economic contexts.

CHINA AND INDIA

China and India represent cases of Asian drivers, but they are also second-movers in global governance (Büthe and Mattli 2003). In global governance, their influence on global institutions used to be rather limited, while they cope with a set of global governance institutions that have historically been shaped by OECD countries. The gap between global governance and domestic governance has widened through distinct historical pathways between the Asian drivers and the OECD. For instance, both India and China have relied on planning and central coordination rather than on market coordination. However, both countries embarked on a far-reaching transition towards market economy, resulting in rapid economic growth and also increasing political influence on the world stage. In the course of these developments, the Asian drivers have become more compatible with governance models employed in the OECD. However, to what extent China and India have adapted their domestic governance of sustainable development to global governance remains an open question. A comparison between the two countries is of interest, since substantial differences continue to exist notwithstanding the fact that they have often been grouped together. For example, the respective governments are increasingly regarded as leaders of the developing world (Payne 2010) and have even been referred to as 'Chindia' (Ramesh 2005). Despite these groupings, as stated above, marked differences between the two Asian drivers are present in terms of civil society development, political freedom and rule of law.

In terms of civil society, there are significant distinctions between China and India, with varying levels of autonomy and influence vis-à-vis the government. India is known to accommodate a vibrant civil society, supported by a long tradition of rule of law introduced under the British colonial rule. Civil society development continued under post-colonial modernization, although suffering setbacks, such as during the emergency rule imposed in 1975 by Prime Minister Indira Gandhi when restrictions were put on civil society. Nonetheless, civil society continued to widen, for instance, through caste solidarity systems. It should be noted that autonomy and influence of civil society organizations are relative notions. For instance, the Indian government exerts strong influence over NGOs and civil society by controlling registration which is necessary for foreign funding of NGOs (Jalali 2008). Recently, Hindu nationalists have animated a more homogeneous Indian political community, disregarding communitarian organization among religious and ethnic minorities. Nonetheless, while not free from political interference and government restrictions, Indian civil society enjoys relative autonomy under a democratic constitution, supported by a relatively stable legal framework for social organization.

In contrast, Chinese civil society is notorious for its constraints. Some even argue that there is no real or mature civil society (Lai 2006). In modern history the Communist Party of China (CPC) has monopolized the social and political spheres, leaving room for only CPC related mass organizations. Prerevolutionary social movements and groups were either absorbed into the CPC and its affiliated organizations, or they were abandoned. Without a doubt, China has come a long way since liberalization started under Deng Xiaoping, despite setbacks in 1989 and again in 1997. While China's civil society is still restricted and the state and the CPC remain entangled in a pervasive party-state, there is room to manoeuvre for social organizations, NGOs and other non-state actors. Since 1978, the grip of the party-state eased, allowing a spectacular growth in numbers of NGOs and social organizations. In 2007, the total number of non-governmental organizations reached nearly 410 000. Some estimates are even much higher (Liu and Wang 2009). However, the numerical rise of NGOs and social organizations is not necessarily matched by growing influence. The autonomy of organizations is restricted by law. Under the dual management system (or *shuangchong guanli tizhi*), NGOs need to obtain official support by a government agency in order to register with the Civil Affairs bureau. This way NGOs are held on a relatively tight leash. Moreover, mobilization and activities across sectors and provinces are often not allowed. This has not only led to a mismatch between the number and the influence of organizations, but also to a lack of resources and operational continuity. In addition, continuously altering regulation has also led to an unstable environment for civil society organizations, complicating, for instance, the formation of partnerships. Some civil society organizations, however, manage to increase their influence and autonomy by taking advantage of their embeddedness within the authoritarian state (Ho 2007; Edmonds and Ho 2008). Case studies have consistently found that 'governmentally organized NGOs' (GONGOs) enjoy greater autonomy and influence than 'grassroots' NGOs (Wu 2002; Lu 2007). However, it seems fair to conclude that civil society in China, and in particular the influence of independent non-state actors is not as strong as in India. While (GO)NGOs, in some cases enjoy autonomy, and even make use of the party-state to increase their influence, their position depends on embeddedness within the party-state and on governmental sponsorship. Positions of these civil society organizations often tend to reflect their supporting government agency's opinions rather than opinions at the grassroots level.

In terms of political freedom, the contrast between India and China is perhaps even greater than in the case of civil society organization. In India, a system of rule of law was introduced by the British. Law served to legitimize colonial rule as the British considered it a step forward from the assumed pre-existing rule of man. While law was not equal for all, and also institutionalized social inequity, rule of law in general led to a persisting 'universal language of law' (Ocko and Gilmartin 2009). A similar historical development is discernible with regard to electoral democracy. Challenged by rising Indian nationalism, the British colonial rulers introduced elections in 1919, to give vent to critical voices while trying to consolidate colonial rule. As India became independent the motives of colonial rule disappeared but the institutions largely remained in place. When building the independent Union, India had a historical experience with rule of law and electoral democracy to draw from.

China has been referred to as a case of 'trapped transition' (Pei 2006), where political liberalization has lagged behind economic liberalization. What evolved instead has been ominously referred to as a 'decentralized predatory state' (ibid). China has consistently been referred to as 'unfree', for instance in the Freedom House Index (Freedom House 2010). That is not to say that there are no practices of political freedom exercise in China, for instance, elections have been common practice at the village level and for local people congresses since the early 1980s. However, the CPC closely watches elections at the local level, and while individual candidature is permitted, alternative party formation is not allowed. It is not uncommon to hear complaints from people having to choose candidates whom they do not know and whose positions are unknown. Therefore, while formal political participation exists, the lack of political pluralism and the lack of real power of elected state organs and representatives render a political system unfree.

Finally, the different legal-constitutional backgrounds and the historical legacies of the Asian drivers matter, notably the interactions between administrative levels and between non-governmental actors and the state. China is not a 'Rechtsstaat', and its governance system is not primarily driven by formal institutions and legal codes. Instead, governance has often been defined in terms of expected outcomes and policy goals under central planning. Policy objectives are set by the central government, and subsequently translated into objectives and quantifiable indicators for lower levels of administration. While planning has also played an important role in India's economic governance, central–local relations are not primarily structured around quantifiable goals. Rather India's federal constitution provides for a legal distinction and division of competences between the Union and the constituent states.

As both Asian countries increasingly become drivers in a (previously) Western shaped system of global governance, the fit between global governance institutions and instruments with domestic political and societal conditions will increasingly become more salient. Clearly discernible differences between China and India lead us to hypothesize on the good-ness of fit between the types of partnerships and partnerships governance on the one hand and the domestic governance contexts of India and China on the other.

GOODNESS OF FIT

Partnerships vary across a number of characteristics (see Appendix), including the number of partners, geographical orientations, constella-tions of partners, functions, internal organizational structures, and dura-tion, among others. Therefore, there are innumerable variations to the tune of partnerships; not every form of partnership will find acceptance in every political and social context. Differences of domestic implementation contexts in China and India with regard to, for instance, civil society and rule of law, will significantly impact on the prevalent types of partnerships and the potential of partnership governance.

Civil society has often been suggested as a precondition for partnership governance. For instance, the presence of activist organizations allows for transnational linking, the brokering of partnerships, and interest representation in the face of cross-border challenges in sustainable devel-opment (e.g. Tarrow 2005). Moreover, civil society renders legitimacy to institutions that suffer a 'democratic deficit', urging partnership arrange-ments with civil society (Mason 2004; Bäckstrand 2006). On the other hand partnerships have also been suggested as instruments that promote the development of civil society. Indeed, the empowered role of business and civil society actors has been a leading objective in the UN partner-ships process. However, the degree to which civil society collaboration with business (and government) has led to empowerment and positive development outcomes has been questioned. Ashman (2001) for instance finds that impacts are more likely where there are clear business interests, while empowerment of citizens can easily be overshadowed by corporate decision-making.

The relative freedom and autonomy of Indian civil society would allow for more partnerships with, as well as among, NGOs and social organiza-tions. The (electoral) democratic legitimization of government in India may motivate government agencies to partner with civil society. In terms of constellation of partners within partnerships, we expect a larger propor-tion of NGOs, social organizations and non-profit organizations in Indian partnerships than in Chinese partnerships. In China, civil society is more constrained; its influence depends on a collaborative attitude towards the party-state. The role of the state, in particular of central government organizations, should therefore not be overlooked. It can be expected that central state agencies take leading roles within partnerships for sustainable development in China. On the other hand, few partnerships are expected to be led and initiated by NGOs and social organizations.

The degree of political freedom we expect to see is reflected in the issues addressed by partnerships. Emancipation and human rights are particularly controversial in the context of the Chinese party-state, whereas India allows for association and advocacy for these causes. More partnerships in India are expected to seek emancipation and empowerment of stakeholders such as women, the poor and ethnic minorities. On the other hand, few Chinese partnerships are expected to address issues related to emancipation, human rights and the empowerment of ethnic minorities.

'Governance by objectives', the strong goal orientation in Chinese central–local relations, as opposed to rule and procedural-based central–local relations under the federal constitution of India, is expected to be reflected in the organization of partnerships. Partnerships in China are not expected to fit into a more institutionalized (legal) environment; rather, they are expected to deliver and to increase output. The relative narrow goal formulation and the functional mindset typical of individual partnership projects would fit this output oriented governance. Also, this form of governance has its historical precedent in 'campaign style' environmental and social policies of pre-1978 China. These campaign policies do not require long-term standing institutionalization of governance functions; instead they take the form of projects. Organization is geared towards attaining certain goals without the need to survive the duration of the campaign and the need for further embedding into a longer term governance structure. It should be mentioned that campaign style governance is steadily replaced by law and law implementation (Van Rooij 2002). However central–local relations still feature a form of governance that is driven by the attainment of objectives. In India, a pluralist governance environment, in combination with a federal constitution, allows for a clear division of competences between different levels of governance and between state and non-state institutions, expectedly leading to a better acceptance of partnership as a governance instrument.

ANALYSIS

The following analysis consists of comparisons at three tiers: comparing the set of partnerships active in India and China with the rest of the world (meta-partnerships analysis); comparing the set of partnerships that are active in India, but not in China, with the set that is active in China, but not in India (inter-partnership analysis), and comparing the set of partnerships that are active in both China and India (intra-partnerships analysis).

The analyses are based upon two sets of data: one from the GSPD, and a smaller and more detailed dataset on partnerships in China and India. The GSPD allows for a comparison between partnerships that are active in China and India and partnerships in the rest of the world. This allows us to reach a better understanding of the global process of partnership governance, and to the roles of China and India in this process.

Within the sample, there are partnerships that are both active in China and India, and those that are active in China or India. The former allows for an intra-partnership comparative analysis and the latter permits an inter-partnership analysis between Chinese and Indian partnerships. The intra-partnership analysis allows us to learn about how, within the same partnerships, organization is differentiated and adapted to the different implementation contexts of India and China; while the inter-partnership analysis allows for an assessment of which types of partnership are active in respectively China and India.

Meta-partnership Analysis

Both the database of the UNCSD and the GSPD take partnerships for sustainable development as units of analysis. They therefore contain limited information on the partnerships' countries of implementation. Moreover, in the GSPD, achievements of partnerships have not been detailed per country of implementation. With these restrictions, the analysis at this level is still of interest because it indicates how partnerships for sustainable development in China and India are representative of, or different from, the global partnerships process.

At the global level, partnerships have been regarded as implementation instruments. In this regard, India and China are important as countries of implementation. According to the UNCSD registry, 64 partnerships (or 19.4 per cent) of all partnerships for sustainable development are (partly) implemented in India, while 55 partnerships (16.7 per cent) of all partnerships are (partly) implemented in China. In the expert survey conducted for this research (see Chapter 1), held at two consecutive meetings of the UNCSD, partnerships that were active in India and China were among the most recognized (Figure 6.1). While 36.7 per cent of all partnerships registered with the UNCSD were unknown, even by experts, figures were much lower for partnerships that were implementing in China and India (respectively: 27.2 per cent and 18.8 per cent).

Partnerships implemented in China and India are not only among the most recognized, they are also relatively effective. Data on outputs and

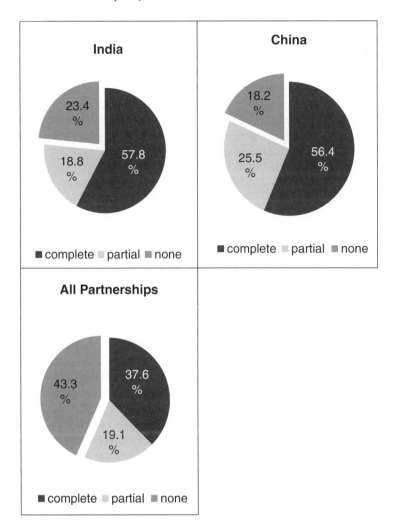

Figure 6.1   Function–output fit

functions were matched in the GSPD, resulting in an effectiveness indicator, the so-called 'function–output fit'. The logic was that for a partnership to fulfil a certain function it should at least produce output. For instance, a training partnership should at least produce a curriculum or organize seminars. According to this logic, the function–output fit was much higher than average for partnerships that were implementing in China and/or India (Figure 6.1). Respectively, 81.9 per cent and 76.6 per cent of the partnerships active in China and India had a function–output fit or a partial fit; comparing favourably to only 56.7 per cent on average. This suggests that, in terms of effectiveness of implementation of international sustainable development agreements through partnerships, both China and India serve as relatively favourable implementation contexts. The comparatively strong performance may be accounted for by relatively developed infrastructures and stable governments in these countries.

It should be mentioned that registered partnerships usually have a global or regional focus, therefore output is not necessarily achieved in China and India, but within other countries of implementation. Moreover, output is a necessary indicator for effectiveness, but insufficient for impact (changes in sustainable development indicators) or outcome (behavioral changes). The meta-partnership analysis renders an impression of China and India as important countries of implementation. Partnerships in these countries are not only among the most widely recognized, but also among the most effective (in terms of output).

Inter-partnership Analysis

There are few differences in terms of number of registered partnerships implemented in respectively India and China. Of the UNCSD registered partnerships, 24 report implementation activities in India but not in China. The number of partnerships for sustainable development reporting implementation in China but not in India is the same. However, a review of the status of each of these partnerships shows that five of the partnerships in China (16.7 per cent) are not active, that is, these partnerships produced no output in China. Only one partnership in India is not active. Therefore, respectively, 19 and 23 partnerships are implementing activities in China and India. These sets of partnerships form the basis of an inter-partnership comparative analysis that allows for an assessment of which types of partnerships are more prevalent in China and India.

In terms of geographic focus, a large share of both the India and China sets has a global focus. Partnerships often comprise of international and transnational initiatives that are initiated and implemented across different continents. In China, 45 per cent of the partnerships have a global geographic focus, while another 45 per cent of the partnerships have a regional focus (Asia; Asia–Pacific; East Asia; South-East Asia). Only one partnership is exclusively focused on implementation in China, the 'Sino-Italian Cooperation Programme for Environmental Protection'. More partnerships in India tend to have a global focus (82.6 per cent), while there are also a few partnerships exclusively focusing on implementation in India (17.4 per cent). This suggests that partnerships for sustainable development in the case of China is a regional strategy, integrating and

Table 6.1   Types of partnerships hosted in India and China

	India	China
Policy, policy–science interface	5	11
Science, research and training	3	2
Technical implementation	7	3
Clearing house, database knowledge platform (gathering information)	5	3
Advocacy	7	1
Industry	2	0

harmonizing regional implementation, while it is not a reform strategy within the domestic context. On the other hand, partnerships in India do not aim at a regional coordination and harmonization, which is likely due to India's precarious and tense regional environment. Rather, many partnerships in India are part of global networks, seeking to implement international and global aspects of sustainable development. Moreover, more partnerships in India have a domestic focus, which indicates a role for partnerships within India's domestic sustainable development governance.

I distinguished partnerships in the domains of 'policy', 'advocacy', 'clearing house', 'science and research', 'industry association' and 'technical implementation'. The Chinese and Indian sets of partnership show marked differences with respect to the types of partnerships they host (Table 6.1). Both policy and advocacy partnerships aim at policy change, however in the former, government agencies are partners, while in the latter they are not. Policy partnerships are directly involved in decision-making, while advocacy partnerships need to attract the attention of policy makers and they also can take a more antagonist position towards government agencies. In India, the institutional and legal conditions for advocacy partnerships are more favourable. The scope for antagonism vis-à-vis the government and for independent organization without involvement by government agencies is greater in India, resulting in a higher number of advocacy partnerships in this country, while a majority of partnerships in China are policy partnerships, often providing a science–policy interface. The underrepresentation of advocacy networks can be attributed to the fact that in the Chinese legal and political context, the room for NGOs and independent opposition is limited. To gain influence, NGOs prefer to partner with government agencies. This has also been institutionalized by the registration requirement for NGOs to find sponsorship with a government partner. Government agencies therefore

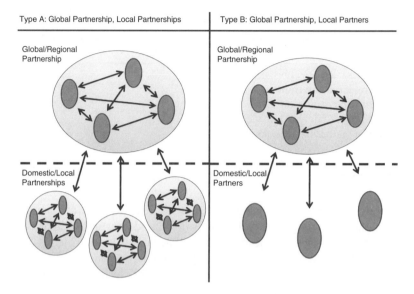

Figure 6.2   Organizational types of global partnerships

become *ex ante* partners in partnerships, complicating the formation of advocacy networks.

Another marked difference is the number of technical implementation partnerships active in India and China. This form of partnership requires a strong local presence. The lack of experience with this type of organization coupled with the reticence from the side of local authorities to allow for concurrent infrastructure and installation provision is an obstacle in China. In India, there are more technical implementation partnerships. Technical implementation partnerships indicate a better compatibility and acceptance of partnership as a domestic governance instrument, as they require partnerships at the local level, rather than global or regional partnerships.

In terms of organizational structures of partnerships we distinguish two types (Figure 6.2). Type A consists of partnerships at the global or regional level, which are also organized as partnerships domestically. Type B concerns global or regional partnerships, often initiated by international organizations that are not organized as partnerships domestically; rather, they take the form of a project under a single national partner.

Among the partnerships that are active in India, the type-A organization is more prevalent than in China. Of the partnerships under review, 42.1 per cent belong to this type. In China, only 10 per cent of the cases analysed form partnerships domestically. In the light of these findings, the partnership process in China should not be regarded as a transposition of partnership governance. Rather, partnerships for sustainable development in China connect individual organizations with global and regional partners. Moreover, no global or regional partnership is led by partners from China, with the exception of the bilateral Sino-Italian Cooperation Programme for Environmental Protection. Partnerships for sustainable development in China often take the form of a bilateral cooperation between government partners and foreign partners rather than a local partnership among governmental and non-governmental stakeholders. In this light it is not surprising that central governmental institutions are strongly represented among Chinese partners; they take the domestic lead in 10 partnerships. Only one partnership lists a domestic NGO as the Chinese partner (the Shangri-la Institute in the Earth Charter Youth Initiative). In the case of India, global partnerships are often domestically organized as partnerships. This does not necessarily imply that partnership governance has been transposed into the Indian context, because this would suggest that there was no partnership governance prior to the WSSD process. More likely, the roles of non-governmental actors have been acknowledged for a long time in India, allowing for partnership governance or at least creating a better goodness-of-fit with the global partnerships process. Among partnerships for sustainable development we find evidence of a more proactive role of Indian NGOs and business in initiating (global and domestic) partnerships. For instance, the Electricity Governance Initiative is a global partnership initiated by Prayas Energy Group, an Indian non-governmental non-profit trust. Also, Indian partners played a leading role in the Southern Business Challenge, an international developing country business network promoting sustainable development. A comparatively high number of partnerships exclusively focus on implementation within India (17.4 per cent), often building local partnerships. Within the Indian local partnerships (under global and regional partnerships), NGOs make up 37.5 per cent of all domestic partners, local government partners represent 25 per cent, central government 8.5 per cent, business 12.5 per cent and research and science institutions 8.3 per cent of all partners. Such figures are not available for the set of partnerships in China since very few build local partnerships.

Finally, we compare the issue areas that partnerships in China and India address (Figure 6.3). Some partnerships address multiple issue areas – especially those implemented in India – in which case more than one issue area was assigned to the partnerships.

The limitations put on empowerment in China's relatively restricted (civil) society are clearly observable in the pattern of issue areas that partnerships engage in. Only one partnership, Education for Rural People,

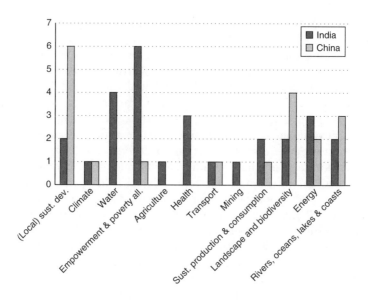

Figure 6.3   Issue areas addressed by partnerships

addressed empowerment, human rights and poverty alleviation as primary issue areas, while six of the partnerships in India (26.1 per cent) addressed these issues, often with a focus on minorities (e.g. the urban poor and women). On the other hand, partnerships in China are more concerned with broader issues like (local) sustainable development, but also landscape and biodiversity.

Intra-partnership Analysis

In this section we look at 29 partnerships that implement activities both in China and India. Most of these partnerships are policy partnerships (45 per cent), research and science partnerships (21 per cent) and clearing house partnerships (14 per cent). While such partnerships include one or a few partners from China and India, they do not require strong local presence. These partnerships may be hosted by a donor government partner, an international organization or with (international) NGOs and they rarely adapt their institutional organization to local circumstances. Through these partnerships Indian and Chinese partners draw experience and resources from foreign partners and vice versa. However, a number of partnerships are active on-the-ground. They need an actual domestic presence in the form of a local partnership: a local office, staff, etc. In terms of differences between implementation partnerships in China and India it is most meaningful to focus on this subset of partnerships. There are eight partnerships for sustainable development involved in on-the-ground implementation in both China and India. Six of these have further differentiated their organization by introducing local/domestic partnerships and organizations. A closer look at such differentiated partnership organizations allows for a better assessment of how and to which extent partnerships adapt to specific domestic political, economic and social contexts.

The total number of partners in India's local partnership organizations is slightly higher as compared to China: 21.8 partners on average in India compared to an average of 18.8 partners in China. However, this small difference would be considerably greater if we discount the CEPF, since this partnership has been active in China for a longer time and has actually finalized its projects in this country. In India, CEPF activities are still ongoing and Indian locations are only part of larger regional biodiversity hotspots that also include Sri Lanka, Nepal and Bhutan. Excluding the CEPF, the result would be an average of 11.1 partners in Chinese partnership networks and 17.7 partners in Indian partnership networks.

Non-profit organizations play a greater role in the local implementation by partnerships in India compared to partnerships in China. A total of 45.3 per cent of Indian partners are domestic non-profit organizations, including NGOs, industrial associations, faith-based organizations and forums, while only 15.6 per cent of Chinese partners belong to this category. The participation of government agencies is considerably higher in China than in India. Local government organizations represent 11.9 per cent of the partners in Indian partnership networks, while 21.6 per cent of partners in Chinese networks are local government agencies. The role of central government agencies (such as ministries, planning bureaus and implementation agencies) is greater in Chinese domestic partnership networks than in India (respectively: 17.6 per cent and 10.1 per cent). Also research, academia and think-tanks are strongly represented among Chinese partners (20.3 per cent), whereas only 8.3 per cent of Indian partners belong to this category.

While the constellation of partners confirms a stronger civil society presence in India, and a greater role for government agencies in China, it is important to take into account who takes the lead in the implementation and coordination of domestic networks. In China, central government agencies often take up leading roles in domestic partnership networks. For instance, the National Development and Reform Commission – China's planning agency under the State Council which is higher in rank than ministries – fulfils leading roles in the Global Methane Initiative (formerly called Methane to Markets) and in the Partnership Promoting an Energy-Efficient Public Sector (PEPS). However, the leading roles of domestic non-profit organizations cannot be discounted. Most of these are so-called Governmentally Organized NGOs (GONGOs), partners that are difficult to categorize, as their activities include research and training, while they are also directly related to government agencies. Leadership in Indian partnership networks is less often in the hands of central government agencies, while local government agencies are better represented. For instance, while PEPS' activities in China are coordinated through central government agencies, in India, the Maharastra State and the Maharastra Energy Development Agency (MEDA) act as lead partners. While the proportion of leading non-profit organizations in India's domestic partnership network is slightly lower, they do not include GONGOs. In general, we observe that among partnerships active in both China and India, the diversity of (lead) partners is greater in India than in China. In China, a few partners are contributing to a number of partnerships. Most notable partners include the National Reform and Development Commission, the Chinese Academy of Sciences and their affiliates. In India, partnership activities are more often led by local and state governments, business and NGOs.

The duration of activities under the same partnerships in India is significantly shorter than in China. Within the set of partnerships that are active in both China and India, the average durations of partnership activities are respectively 7.6 and 5.3 years. This suggests that it takes significantly more time for the same partnership to start up similar activities in India than in China. This is partly explained by the higher number of partners in the average Indian partnership networks, which requires more coordination and a longer consensus seeking process.

CONCLUSIONS

Partnerships for sustainable development represented a large-scale transposition of partnerships into developing and emerging countries. However, this general trend did not lead to the domestic institutionalization of partnerships as a form of sustainable development governance in China and India. In China, global and regional partnerships do not seem to amount to domestic partnership governance, since they take the form of rather isolated projects. They rarely build local Partnerships and the role of government organizations, in particular central state agencies, remains central, while the role of civil society remains fairly limited. In India, rather than introducing partnership governance, Partnerships for Sustainable Development better fit into the existing governance system: global partnerships mimic global multi-stakeholder participatory patterns at the local level; non-state actors and civil society take leading and coordinating roles in many partnerships; and a number of partnerships are focusing exclusively on implementing aspects of sustainable development within India.

Importantly, the concrete application of partnerships in India and China is not a mere projection of the governance norms and practices from the OECD area. Rather, in a global implementation context, partnerships for sustainable development in China and India play an important role. Not only are there many partnerships being implemented in these countries, but they are also relatively successful at the output level, compared to partnerships elsewhere.

Comparative analyses (between and within partnerships) allowed for an assessment of the political and institutional context as factors in the transposition and organization of partnerships in developing countries. They confirm that the potential for partnership governance in sustainable development varies from country to country with regard to political, societal and economic contexts. In China, where formal political participation exists but there is a lack of political pluralism and real influence for citizens, the potential for partnerships on the basis of equality between governmental and non-governmental partners is rather limited. In India, in contrast, the relative freedom and autonomy of civil society allows for more partnership initiatives that include NGOs and social organizations. Within the same partnership, differences in organization can be observed depending on whether activities take place in China or India. In spite of the global reach and universal goal formulations of these partnerships, we observe considerable adaptation at the domestic level. In China, global (and regional) partnerships tend to involve fewer partners, while few local partnership networks are set up. Rather than transposing partnership governance to China, the partnership process serves to connect individual (mostly government) organizations in China with global and regional partners. In India, global partnerships involve many partners, including a diverse set of governmental and NGOs, forming local networks. Therefore, partnerships for sustainable development do not only connect Indian partners to counterparts around the world, they also introduce partnership networks in India. In terms of geographical scope, partnerships in China are more often part of regional strategies than in India, aiming at the integration and harmonization of regional implementation, rather than at domestic reform. The Chinese type of domestic organization of partnerships seems to be congruent with an objective-oriented type of governance, seeking immediate goal attainment, rather than long-term institutionalization of partnership governance. This type of domestic organization is also characterized by a comparatively short preparation time for domestic activities.

Partnerships in India do not aim at regional coordination and harmonization. Rather, many partnerships for sustainable development in India are part of global networks, seeking to implement international and global sustainable development agreements. In addition, many partnerships in India have a domestic focus, indicating a domestic role for partnerships for sustainable development in the implementation and in the reform of domestic policies and institutions. The Indian type of domestic organization of partnerships takes a much longer time to develop: more partners from more sectors need to reach an agreement. This process, however, does not only lead to output, but also to domestic and local partnerships. The impacts, in terms of institutional reform, are therefore deeper in India than in China.

These analyses of partnerships for sustainable development in China and India are momentary assessments. They predict limited potential for partnership governance in China, and greater compatibility of domestic governance with partnerships in India. However, in the long-term it is difficult to assess whether, for instance, China will become a more suitable place for partnership governance. This will depend on domestic reform at large, rather than reform in the relatively limited area of sustainable development. Also, as Chinese partners – particularly within the central government bureaucracy – gain more experience with partnerships, they also obtain transnational capacity, the ability to work across sectoral and cultural boundaries, which is conducive to the development of domestic partnership governance in the long term.

REFERENCES

Andonova, L.B. and M.A. Levy (2003), 'Franchising global governance: making sense of the Johannesburg Type II Partnerships', in O.S. Stokke and O.B. Thommessen (eds), *Yearbook of International Co-operation on Environment and Development*, Oxford, UK: Earthscan, pp. 19–31.

Ashman, D. (2001), 'Civil society collaboration with business: bringing empowerment back', *World Development*, **29**(7), 1097–113.

Bäckstrand, K. (2006), 'Multi-stakeholder partnerships for sustainable development: rethinking legitimacy, accountability and effectiveness', *European Environment*, **16**(5), 290–306.

Bhattacharya, S.K. and B.N. Bhattacharya (2006), 'Free trade agreement between People's Republic of China and India: likely impact and its implications to Asian Economic Community', *ADB Institute Discussion Paper*, **59**, November 2006.

Büthe, T. and W. Mattli (2003), 'Setting international standards: technological rationality or primacy of power?', *World Politics*, **56**(1), 1–42.

Chan, S. (2009), 'Partnerships for sustainable development in China: adaptation of a global governance instrument', *European Journal of East Asian Studies*, **8**(1), 121–34.

Edmonds, R.L. and P. Ho (eds) (2008), *Embedded Environmentalism: Limitations and Constraints of a Social Movement in China*, New York: Routledge.

Freedom House (2010), Country Report on China, Freedom House, available at: http://www.freedomhouse.org/template.cfm?page=22&year=2010&country=7801, (retrieval: 06.04.2010).

Ho, P. (2007), 'Embedded activism and political change in a semi-authoritarian context', *China Information*, **21**(2), 187–209.

Hood, C. (1991), 'A public management for all seasons?', *Public Administration*, **69**(1), 3–19.

Hood, C. and G.F. Schuppert (1988), *Delivering Public Services in Western Europe*, London: Sage.

Humphrey, J. and D. Messner (2009), 'China and India as emerging global governance actors: challenges for developing and developed countries', *IDS Bulletin*, **37**(1), 107–14.

Jalali, R. (2008), 'International funding of NGOs in India: bringing the state back', *Voluntas*, **19**, 161–88.

Kaplinsky, R. and D. Messner (2008), 'The impact of Asian drivers on the developing world', *World Development*, **36**(2), 197–209.

Krasner, S. (1991), 'Global communications and national power: life on the Pareto Frontier', *World Politics*, **43**(3), 336–66.

Lai, H. (2006), 'Religious policies in post-totalitarian China: maintaining political monopoly over a reviving society', *Journal of Chinese Political Science*, **11**(1), 55–77.

Lu, Y. (2007), 'The autonomy of Chinese NGOs: a new perspective', *China: An International Journal*, **5**(2), 173–203.

Mason, M. (2004), 'Representing transnational interests: new opportunities for non-governmental access to the World Trade Organization', *Environmental Politics*, **13**(3), 566–89.

Messner, D. and J. Humphrey (2006), 'China and India in the global governance arena', *IDS Bulletin*, **37**(1), 107–14.

Miraftab, F. (2004), 'Public–private partnerships. The Trojan horse of neo-liberal development?', *Journal of Planning Education and Research*, **24**(1), 89–101.

Ocko, J.K. and D. Gilmartin (2009), 'State, sovereignty, and the people: a comparison of the "rule of law" in China and India', *The Journal of Asian Studies*, **68**(01), 55–100.

Overbeek, H. (2005), 'Class, hegemony and global governance: a historical materialist perspective. Contending perspectives on global governance', in A. Ba and M. Hoffmann (eds), *Coherence, Contestation, and World Order*, London: Routledge, pp. 39–56.

Payne, A. (2010), 'How many Gs are there in "global governance" after the crisis? The perspectives of the "marginal majority" of the world's states', *International Affairs*, **86**(3), 729–40.

Pei, M. (2006), *China's Trapped Transition: The Limits of Developmental Autocracy*, Cambridge, UK: Harvard University Press.

Ramesh, J. (2005), *Making Sense of Chindia: Reflections on China and India*, New Delhi: India Research Press.

Savas, E.S. (2000), *Privatization and Public–Private Partnerships*, New York: Chatham House.

Tarrow, S. (2005), *The New Transnational Activism*, New York: Cambridge University Press.
Van Rooij, B. (2002), 'Implementing Chinese environmental law through enforcement, the Shiwuxiao and Shuang Ge Dabiao campaigns', in J. Chen, J.M. Otto and Y. Li (eds), *Implementation of Law in the People's Republic of China*, Den Haag: Kluwer Law International, pp. 149–78.
Wu, F. (2002), 'New partners or old brothers? GONGOs in transnational environmental advocacy in China', *ECSP China Environment Series*, **5**, 45–58.

7. Africa's involvement in partnerships for sustainable development: holy grail or business as usual?

Daniel Compagnon

Multi-stakeholder partnerships for sustainable development were launched at the WSSD in Johannesburg in September 2002 as a new mechanism to implement the various commitments under Agenda 21 and the Millennium Development Goals that UN member states had previously failed to fulfil. Both the UN Secretariat and the great powers were happy to deflect criticisms on their past record, and transfer their responsibilities to non-state actors, if only to avoid a complete summit failure (Andonova and Levy 2003: 21–2), while transferring to the private sector a substantial share of multilateral environmental agreements' implementation costs (Hale and Mauzerall 2004). Safe access to water, energy supply, poverty alleviation and food security became primary targets in the Johannesburg Plan of Implementation. It seemed as if the Johannesburg Plan also offered a way for Southern actors to obtain what, in their view, had been denied to them at the Monterrey Summit in March 2002, when Western powers refused to increase substantially their development aid beyond a mere extension of debt reduction programmes. Consequently, the founding consensus underlying the main summit outcome, partnerships for sustainable development, is politically ambiguous and contested (see Chapter 2). Partnerships registered with the UNCSD were presented as a unique opportunity for African countries. The continent is lagging behind in terms of economic development, and Sub-Saharan Africa more specifically is the poorest region of the world with the largest share of people living on less than $1 per day. At the same time, the region is burdened with numerous environmental problems (AMCEN/UNEP 2006: 4–8). It was quite logical to assume that Africa would become a primary target and an active participant in the newly founded partnerships. However, it is OECD countries that attract the bulk of partnerships when it comes to implementation (while Africa ranges second on par with non-OECD Asia; see Chapter 4).

I focus hereafter on Sub-Saharan African countries involved in partnerships for sustainable development. Although Africa as a continent is not more heterogeneous than Asia or Latin America, it is very fragmented politically. Admittedly there is one regional organization that includes all African states, the African Union (successor to the Organization of African Unity formed in 1963), and historically, the Sahara used to be a bridge between the Sahel and North Africa rather than a barrier between them, especially before the nineteenth century. Nevertheless, the Arab countries of North Africa are distinct for cultural reasons and are connected to the outside world in many ways, different from those of 'black Africa'. Therefore, the analysis will exclude the five member countries of the Arab Maghreb Union (UMA) and Egypt, which is geographically African, but politically and culturally part of the Middle East. Besides, and since this chapter is concerned with the potential impact of limited statehood on the relative effectiveness of partnerships for sustainable development, it makes sense to focus on the weakest and most impoverished African states. Out of 48 least developed countries (LDCs), 33 are African and 32 Sub-Saharan – Mauretania being both partly Sahelian by its geography and its economy, but still a member of UMA. So, to a certain extent it is relevant to separate Sub-Saharan Africa from North Africa, in order to understand what specificity the continent may have in the broader picture of UNCSD partnerships.

This chapter will use data drawn from the GSPD in order to explore some of the characteristics of Sub-Saharan African partnerships. However, the database does not provide a detailed picture of African partnerships as such. There are actually very few partnerships initiated and led by an African partner, be it a governmental or non-governmental partner. However, the database provides us with information on partnerships with at least one African country as a country of implementation. Most of these will have countries of implementation also outside Africa and a non-African lead partner. Therefore, these partnerships are not in essence African per se. However, they can provide a glimpse on the variations introduced by the participation of Sub-Saharan African partners in global sustainability partnerships. This, of course, should not lead us to neglect the important issue of actual ownership – or the lack thereof – by African actors.

Some of the data referred to hereafter relates to partnerships with at least one African country of implementation, and sometimes more specifically to Sub-Saharan African countries of implementation. For the sake of fluidity in writing, I will refer to them respectively as African and Sub-Saharan African partnerships. This chapter answers the following questions: (1) What is the significance and implications of state participation in Sub-Saharan African partnerships? (2) What is the relative effectiveness of these partnerships? (3) Do partnerships for sustainable development contribute to filling the participation and implementation gaps in sustainable development regimes? Given that the partnership literature tends to ignore the political context of partnership implementation and its impact on effectiveness/efficiency, I will discuss the nature of the 'post-colonial state' in Africa – understood as a deviant form of modern statehood (Sørensen 2001: 83–6) – that will have a strong bearing on the future of partnerships. The empirical assessment is based on the GSPD (see Chapter 1).

ACTOR PREDOMINANCE AND ITS IMPLICATIONS

African partnerships have a higher number of partners on average (33.6), compared to the average number of partners in the overall partnerships sample (24.8), and this trend is even more pronounced in Sub-Saharan Africa (37). There are also important variations from one partnership to another. This could be explained by the global nature of these partnerships: partnerships that implement their activities in Sub-Saharan Africa are more often global in scope (67 per cent) than the average. They are less often regional (28 per cent) or local (5 per cent) (Figure 7.1). Outside Africa, the proportion of partnerships with a regional focus is considerably higher: 55 per cent of partnerships that *do not* implement in Africa have a regional or sub-regional geographical focus.

It seems that Sub-Saharan African countries, when given the chance, have a tendency to jump on the bandwagon of broader partnerships, yet lacking the resources or the political will to initiate partnerships on their own, which could address more specifically their national policy priorities. The globality of the partnerships in which Sub-Saharan African countries are involved raises issues of effectiveness and governance. First of all, the

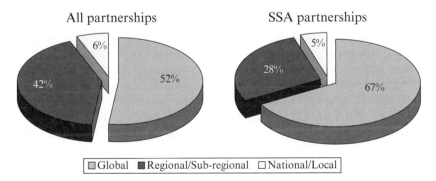

Figure 7.1   Geographical scope

more partners at the global level, the higher the risk of some of them being 'sleeping partners' or free riders. Besides it is unlikely that implementation will take place everywhere at the same pace and Africa is likely to trail behind. Second, the governance of such partnerships is likely to be more complex, creating a context for imbalance between more powerful actors from OECD countries and resource-less African actors. Further in-depth case studies would be necessary to support this hypothesis.

Few partnerships for sustainable development focus on Africa as a region or on sub-regions within Africa. For the most part, partnerships that implement in at least one African country are global partnerships, in which African actors are only marginal players. This marginalization reproduces similar patterns found in other forms of transnational environmental governance, such as in CDM projects (De Lopez et al. 2009) or norm-setting regimes (Clapp 1998), and at a deeper level mirrors the marginalization of African actors in the global political economy (Collier 1995; Shaw 1995, 2000). Among those African partnerships that have a regional or sub-regional geographical scope, Southern Africa and the SADC are more often targeted than other sub-regions. This might have to do with the fact that the strongest regional power in Sub-Saharan Africa, South Africa, is involved in more partnerships than any other African country. However, we should not jump to hasty conclusions about a possible 'shadow of hierarchy' in partnership formation. The reason for this overrepresentation could very well be that the WSSD took place in Johannesburg, attracting a lot of interest for South Africa from would-be partners and encouraging Pretoria's government to take a proactive stance (see also Chapter 3). To a certain extent, the same observation applies to Indonesia, which held the PrepCom IV of the WSSD in Bali.

Not all partnerships in the GSPD sample have state partners, as partnerships as a governance innovation were meant to increase the participation of the private sector. Against this background, African governments show real interest for partnerships for sustainable development. Among partnerships implementing in continental Africa, 54 per cent have African state partners. This rate is lower for South American and non-OECD Asian partnerships for states within their regions: 38 per cent and 42 per cent, respectively (Figure 7.2).

When selecting Sub-Saharan African states specifically, the rate goes up to 56 per cent. Only OECD countries have a higher rate of state involvement: 67 per cent of partnerships implemented in the OECD have at least one OECD state as partner. This cannot be for the same reasons as for Africa. Rather, it could be linked to the characteristics of partnerships' activities in Western countries and the use of partnerships by governments

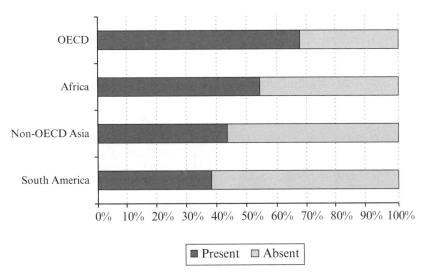

Figure 7.2   Presence of state partners in partnerships implementing in their region

to implement public policy, in the wake of the neo-liberal inspired 'retreat of the state' (Strange 1996; Mazouz 2009).

Partnerships implemented in Africa, as a whole, have the highest average number of states *from* the region among their partners compared to other regions in the world (Figure 7.3). For once the number is higher when including Northern Africa and Egypt in the sample, than just Sub-Saharan Africa. These findings suggest that African states are keener to take part in partnerships than state actors in other parts of the developing world. This might be because they expect the partnerships to provide them with additional resources they can no longer obtain from traditional channels, as bilateral and several multilateral development aid budgets have declined since the late 1990s. Alternatively or in parallel, African states – many of which suffer at various degrees from authoritarian rule – want to get involved to keep an eye on the development projects taking place in their countries, and in particular the external actors (governmental or non-governmental) implementing them. One of the characteristics of governmental elites in Africa, in the context of the post-colonial state, is a disproportionate emphasis on formal sovereignty – 'negative sovereignty' as defined by Robert Jackson (1990) – and their resistance to anything near an infringement on such a valued symbolic resource (Clapham 1996). Another possibility, which does not necessarily contradict the first interpretation, is the use of the partnership mechanism to consolidate traditional bilateral

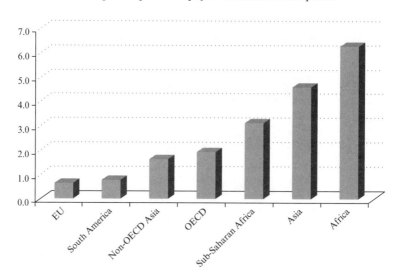

Figure 7.3　Average number of state partners from the region of implementation

cooperation between OECD and African countries – hence the necessary involvement of states.

In addition, many partnerships with state partners are endorsed by a majority of African states. There is a tendency of regional organizations such as the African Union, the SADC and the COMESA, to become partners to several global partnerships – especially those seen as politically important. In such cases, all AU member countries are listed as state partners and that increases the average. In doing so, African state elites behave towards global partnerships as they do towards regional organizations (Sidaway and Gibb 1998) and regional environmental governance mechanisms (Compagnon, Florémont and Lamaud 2011), i.e. using every opportunity to foster their 'negative sovereignty' to use the term coined by Robert Jackson.

Despite the significant state participation, partnerships implementing in Sub-Saharan Africa are significantly less often led by state partners or by international organizations outside the UN system. They are mostly led by UN agencies, as shown in Figure 7.4.

The implication is that African states, although often involved as partners, do not initiate these partnerships and do not assume responsibility for (and bear the transaction costs of) coordination and day-to-day management. This situation can be ascribed to various factors: (1) the lack of institutional and financial capacity of 'weak states' especially in Least Developed Countries (LDCs); (2) the preference of most African governments for

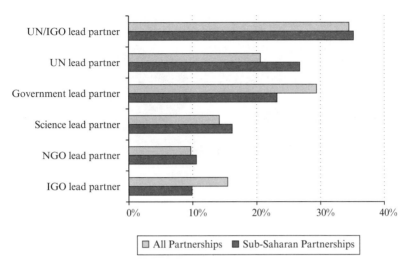

Figure 7.4   Presence of at least one lead partner from the listed sectors

traditional aid circuits – bilateral or multilateral – and their scepticism towards the partnership mechanism; (3) the eagerness of UN agencies to enter into partnerships, a policy framework to which the whole UN apparatus is committed and a means to re-legitimate their action on the ground, which is often criticized by development and environmental NGOs. This would fit with Liliana Andonova's perspective of international organizations as 'entrepreneurs of collaborative governance' (Andonova 2010: 29, 31–2).

Although some partnerships focus on capacity building and the transfer of institutional models, their governance structures tend to mirror LDCs' deficiencies. No wonder that more institutionally developed, middle-income economies in the developing world are more attractive to Northern partners, and are more often involved in partnerships than the poorest countries. Hence, according to the GSPD database, out of 330 registered partnerships, 27 involve the Chinese government, 26 the Brazilian government, 21 the Indian government, but only 8 partnerships involve the government of Burkina Faso, one of the poorest countries in the world. According to another survey, Haiti and Somalia do not participate in any of 231 partnerships studied, whereas Thailand and the Philippines each participate in about 20 partnerships (Andonova and Levy 2003: 28). Fragile states are involved more often when an international organization leads the partnership and makes a deliberate effort to include them.

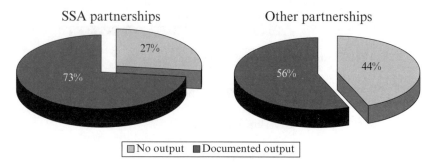

Figure 7.5   Proportion of partnerships with and without Africa output in Sub-Saharan Africa and worldwide

PARTNERSHIPS' INFLUENCE IN SUB-SAHARAN AFRICA

The information obtainable from the GSPD does not allow us to measure the effectiveness of registered partnerships directly, not to mention their ultimate effectiveness in promoting sustainable development. That would require an in-depth analysis of their impact on the ground that is outside the scope of this book. However, there is data available on their outputs – according to Oran Young's typology (Young 1999, 2002) the first level of effectiveness – in terms of organizing formal activities, training people, setting up offices and administrative structures, as well as reporting. Partnerships that implement in a Sub-Saharan country of implementation have a higher rate of output than the average (Figure 7.5). The same is true for African partnerships as a whole, but it is more pronounced when focusing on countries in the South of the Sahara.

This is a rather unexpected result, since Africa carries a dramatic image of social disorder (Kaplan 1994); of weak (Migdal 1988) and neo-patrimonial states (Médard 1982, 1991; Clapham 1985; Bratton and Van de Walle 1994); prone to ineffective multilateral environmental agreements implementation (Blaikie and Simo 1998; Gray 2003), and of a continent where most countries fall into a 'bad governance trap' that prevents any effective policy (Collier 2007) to the extent that 'an increasing number of individual nation-states are no longer able to provide localized order and an adequate degree of environmental management within their own borders' (Hurrell 1994: 147). Thomas Risse (2005: 64) proposed the notion of 'areas of limited statehood' to underline the lack of authority of these governments over at least part of their territory, their dependence on the international system and the UN agencies, and their limited capacity to

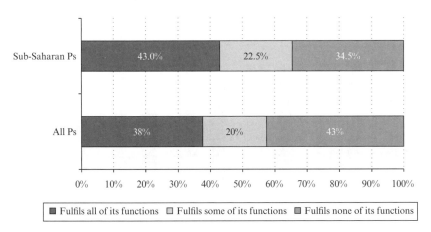

Figure 7.6   Function fulfilment in partnerships from Sub-Saharan Africa and worldwide

implement policies. In such context, we could expect the UNCSD partnerships implementing in Sub-Saharan Africa to perform rather badly.

A possible explanation of this apparent paradox is the role of the UN agencies. UNCSD partnerships with African countries of implementation tend to report their activities better. Many of the partnerships involving African countries are led by a UN agency as mentioned above, and these UN-led partnerships in Africa tend to report better than the average. However, when checked against all UNCSD partnerships, UN-led partnerships over the world are not prone to better reporting than partnerships led by other actors. They do so only in an African – especially Sub-Saharan African countries – context, either because the lead actor tends to keep its African partners in closer check through reporting procedures, or because the lead actor wants to defeat the assumption that African partnerships are likely to be less effective than others. The UN agencies involved, thus, make sure there is indeed something to report on. Although the database itself cannot tell us the definite answer, the interpretation of this variable suggests a political construct behind this apparently objective, technocratic assessment. Outputs are not necessarily what they look like.

Partnerships claim to fulfil a number of functions – the rationale for their creation – and they have some outputs that are likely to serve at least as partial fulfilment of these functions, hence the database measurement of a 'function–output fit' – a proxy for a measurement of actual effectiveness (for more details see Chapter 1). Surprisingly perhaps, partnerships involving African countries do not have a lesser function–output fit record than the average.

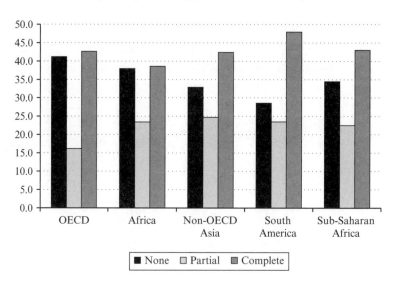

Figure 7.7   Function fulfilment in various regions

It is even higher if we select Sub-Saharan African countries only: 65.5 per cent of relevant partnerships fulfil some or all of their stated functions, against 58 per cent in the total sample (Figure 7.6). When we compare the continent to other regions of the world, Africa as a whole is doing better, although the highest percentage of partnerships fulfilling all their functions is found in South America (Figure 7.7).

Does it mean that contrary to many observers' expectations, partnerships for sustainable development are effectively used as a conduit for the fulfilment of their legitimate activities? In such cases, the plurality of partners and the rules established in their covenant provide perhaps sufficient safeguards against the capture of resources for other purposes. However, we should interpret this data conservatively: function–output fit is based on the optimistic assumption that the outputs that might fulfil the function actually do, when the nominal check of the existence of a report does not say anything about its actual contents, and the organization of a workshop does not say anything about the outcome of this activity. After all, only a little over 40 per cent of Sub-Saharan African partnerships perform all the tasks they claim to do.

However, if we want still to explain the largely counterintuitive result of higher function–output fit in Sub-Saharan African partnerships, we should remember that they are, more often than the average, led by UN agencies, and in general, UN-led partnerships tend to have a higher function–output fit rate than others, except NGO-led partnerships (Figure 7.8). This means

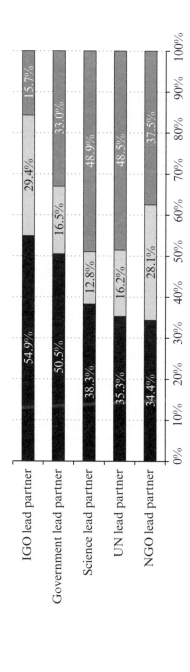

Figure 7.8   Function–output fit according to the lead partner for all partnerships

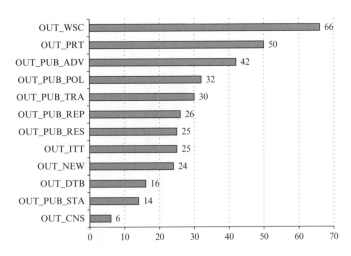

Output code	Explanation
OUT_PUB	Publications (research, advocacy, standards, training, policy and reports): documents found on the Internet and at partnership meetings pertaining to:
_RES	*Research: Any publication by the partnership (not by individual partners) documenting academic research, data-gathering for implementation and policy, and action research.*
_ADV	*Advocacy and Public awareness-raising: Any publication by the partnership (not by individual partners) arguing in favour of the partnership cause with a wider audience than policy-makers (public); campaign material, newsletters, petitions, and promotion material (posters, leaflets, brochures).*
_STA	*Standards: Any publication by the partnership (not by individual partners) setting out policy and/or procedural standards (except internal operating procedures) for application to a sustainable development issue.*
_TRA	*Training: Any publication by the partnership (not by individual partners) aimed at training, including best practice manuals; and instruction materials.*
_POL	*Policy: Any publication by the partnership (not by individual partners) arguing for specific policies (whether regional, national, or trans-national) with policy-makers (public) to regulate and manage sustainable development issues.*
_REP	*Self-Reports: Any publication by the partnership (not by individual partners) pertaining transparency and accountability towards the partners, stakeholders and wider audiences (such as annual reports, and evaluations of the partnership).*
OUT_DTB	Database and systematically organised retrievable information (except databases of self-reports).

Output code	Explanation
OUT_WSC	Workshops/seminars/conferences including training seminars, exhibitions, stakeholder consulting events and courses organized by the partnership (excluding events organised during the 2002 WSSD).
OUT_ITT	Infrastructure and technology transfer: Construction or improvement of new and existing physical facilities as well as the application and transfer of new technologies (including the exchange of grassroot innovations).
OUT_CNS	Consultancy service (excludes implementation).
OUT_PRT	Conference and workshop participation (excluding conferences and workshops organized by the partnership or the UN CSD, WSSD processes).
OUT_NEW	New institutions, organizations and new partnerships.

Figure 7.9   Dominant forms of outputs in Sub-Saharan Africa partnerships

that the apparent effectiveness of Sub-Saharan African partnerships could be, in part, the result of a strong UN involvement in their implementation.

Another explanation would focus on the partnerships' limited ambition levels, thus making the subsequent fulfilment of the latter much easier with attainable outputs. It is difficult to validate this hypothesis without a qualitative analysis of specific partnerships. However, the nature of the outputs produced provides us with some clues. As shown in Figure 7.9, the dominant form of output is, first, the organization of workshops and conferences, followed immediately by the participation in workshops and conferences organized by other organizations and partnerships. Sub-Saharan African partnerships produce this type of output significantly more often than partnerships in other regions. It is congruent with the other strong output, i.e. 'publications' especially of policy and training documents that are likely to be used in similar workshops.

It is of course perfectly legitimate to promote the dissemination of information and the training of people to improve their capacity in sustainable development issues. However, it is hard to see how this trend departs from traditional forms of development aid in LDCs, and in particular what has been coined as the popular 'workshop industry' in some developing countries that sees participants as the main driver behind a stream of 'training', 'planning' and 'assessment' meetings. If partnership governance is meant to overcome bureaucratic red tape and apathy associated with traditional development aid channels, the practical activities deployed on the ground look unpromisingly familiar. The relatively high level of outputs and the observed fit between functions and actual outputs noted above would then appear largely fictitious.

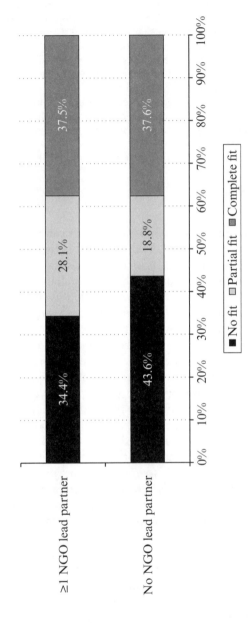

Figure 7.10   Function–output with and without an NGO as lead partner

State-led partnerships   Other partnerships

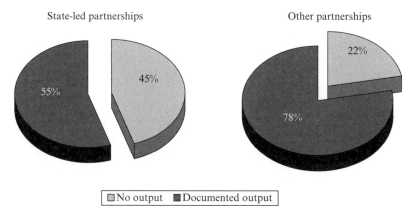

□ No output   ■ Documented output

Figure 7.11   Partnership output in Sub-Saharan partnerships with and without a state as lead partner

The state involvement in partnerships does not promote effectiveness as opposed to the role of non-state actors. UNCSD partnerships that have at least one NGO among their lead partners have a higher function–output fit than those without – the 'no fit' rates rises from 34.4 per cent to 43.6 per cent (Figure 7.10).

State-led partnerships implementing in Sub-Saharan Africa have lower outputs (our proxy for effectiveness) than the average: 45 per cent of these partnerships have no outputs (Figure 7.11), compared to 27.5 per cent for all UNCSD partnerships.

Partnerships with government or government agencies as lead partners also have a lesser function-output fit (Figure 7.12), and the fit between function and output further decreases in cases where the said partnerships have a non-OECD state as lead partner.

The relative lack of outputs from state-led partnerships and the lack of fulfilment of their stated objectives can certainly be related to the structural defects of many weak/fragile states, a dominant phenomenon in Sub-Saharan African as mentioned above. Whether this correlation between state involvement and poor effectiveness is a genuine causal link can be established only through a detailed analysis of each Sub-Saharan African partnership, a task beyond this chapter.

However, among state-led partnerships implementing in Africa, only 26 per cent are led by non-OECD states while 74 per cent are led by OECD states (Figure 7.13). Therefore, we need to be cautious when attributing to the African state solely the responsibility for the relative lack of effectiveness of partnerships implemented in Africa.

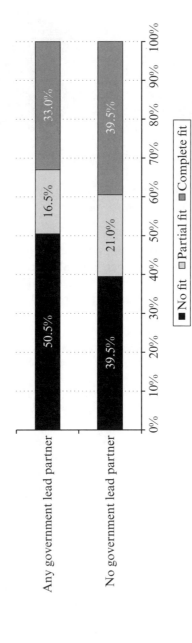

Figure 7.12   Function output fit with and without a government agency as lead partner

SSA partnerships

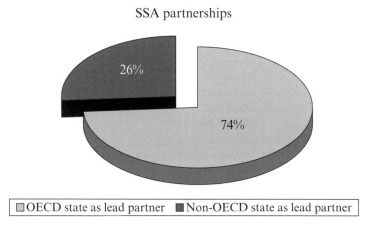

OECD state as lead partner   Non-OECD state as lead partner

Figure 7.13   Proportion of OECD and non-OECD lead partners in Sub-Saharan partnerships

FILLING THE IMPLEMENTATION AND PARTICIPATION GAPS

Public–private partnerships are intended to address the deficits of intergovernmental politics by integrating into a common policy network NGOs, businesses and state bureaucracies (Reinicke 1998, Reinicke and Deng 2000, Streck 2004). The question remains whether transnational partnerships, broadly defined as 'institutionalized transboundary interactions between public and private actors, which aim at the provision of public goods' (Schäferhoff, Campe and Kaan 2007), achieve even to a limited degree what they are intended to. Multi-stakeholder partnerships are supposed to: facilitate knowledge dissemination and social learning; 'set non-binding norms'; build management capacities and 'close the "participation gap" in global politics' (Andonova and Levy 2003: 20, 25), therefore contributing to a democratization of global environmental governance (Bäckstrand 2006). The normative discourse on multi-stakeholder partnerships must be confronted, however, to the political realities on the ground.

Partnerships implementing in Sub-Saharan Africa do not necessarily differ from others in terms of the issue area they focus on (Figure 7.14). The only issue areas that are significantly more popular in Sub-Saharan African partnerships are poverty, agriculture and energy. Disaster management is significantly less popular compared to the world average. The concentration on such issues reflects some of the Millennium Development Goals, but one would expect to see also water, sanitation and health

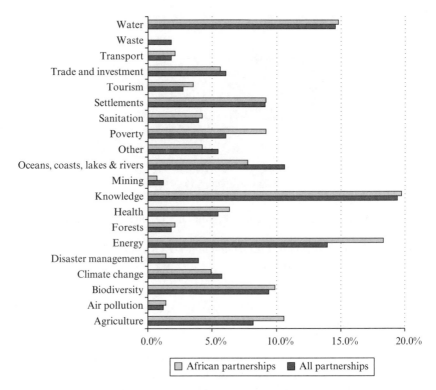

Figure 7.14   Proportions of UNCSD partnerships according to issue areas in Africa and worldwide

appear more prominently on the list. Although HIV-AIDS and other major health issues are taken care of in other forums (UNAIDS and other, non-UNCSD partnerships in WHO), it is interesting to note that these UN partnerships formed in the wake of the Johannesburg Summit do not always reflect the priority concerns of African LDCs as they were listed in the Johannesburg Plan of Action. This insufficient focus on African priority concerns echoes the global nature of Sub-Saharan African partnerships and the fact that partners outside the continent steer a majority of them. They were not set up to address primarily African countries' policy priorities but rather to address sustainability in a broader sense. This raises suspicions that UNCSD partnerships 'do not necessarily match the priorities set out in the multilateral process' (Hale and Mauzerall 2004: 234) and do not contribute effectively to the implementation of multilateral environmental agreements.

Formal registration with the UNCSD being based on wide and

loosely defined criteria, partnerships do not necessarily correspond to new projects. For instance, most of registered partnerships involving the Japanese government look suspiciously like some hasty repackaging of traditional bilateral aid programmes. Another case in point is the Nile Basin Initiative reclassified as a partnership for sustainable development around the Johannesburg Summit, although it began already in the late 1990s and is basically an intergovernmental cooperation mechanism. Some WSSD partnerships hardly fit in any definition of sustainable development. For example, one partnership operating in Africa is led by Eskom, the South African electricity utility. It aims at connecting the countries' power networks in Southern Africa to facilitate sub-continental electricity trading, in other words, working to enhance South African electricity exports. Partnerships for sustainable development may also serve to greenwash transnational corporations (TNCs) targeted by NGO campaigns by diverting public attention from their standard practices that damage the environment – the oil industry being a case in point.

Another way of looking at the potential implementation of international sustainability regimes is to focus on outputs and outcomes. The database gives us information only on the former. Although a significant number of African partnerships produce some Infrastructure and Technology Transfer (ITT) outputs, and they tend to do so above the average of all partnerships in our sample, the main industry remains still, as noted above, the workshops and conferences. Albeit the partnership ideology suggests that they are more efficient in overcoming deadlocks and producing practical results (Reinicke and Witte 2005), the picture that emerges from the data suggests a more modest and indirect contribution to the actual implementation of sustainable development projects.

Most partnerships do not directly contribute to a more sustainable environmental management, on their own admission, according to one survey (OECD 2006: 24):

> 28 per cent of partnerships considered themselves to provide clear, direct environmental benefits [. . .] The figure of 28 per cent producing clear, direct environmental benefits seems to be an overestimate. From the description of the partnerships available in the UNCSD database, it would seem that in several cases a more appropriate response in line with the intention of the question would have been 'one step upstream' – it likely that of the 32 partnerships only three or four had direct environmental impact with the rest facilitating impact further down the line.

It does not seem to be very different when focusing on Sub-Saharan African partnerships.

Partnerships for sustainable development are also seen as a means to supplement defective regional cooperation. For instance, the Congo Basin Forest Partnership (CBFP), launched in Johannesburg with the support of the South African government, is seen as the main conduit for implementing the 1999 Yaoundé Declaration on the Congo Basin Forest and the subsequent 2005 'Plan de Convergence' of the Central Africa Forests Commission, COMIFAC. In addition to the latter's ten member states, the CBFP includes several prominent donor countries,[1] intergovernmental organizations, international NGOs and private companies. An obvious admission that the COMIFAC governance process is unlikely to succeed without significant external input, due to the shortcomings of the African states involved, the CBFP works as a transmission belt between donors and COMIFAC member states while providing a forum for policy assessment and knowledge dissemination. It supports capacity-building efforts within COMIFAC and member states, and can develop innovative funding mechanisms involving the corporate sector.[2] Although the CBFP is credited with increasing the funding available and the actors' coordination for forest conservation in Central Africa, it stands accused also of not involving local civil society and 'taking over basic tasks of African governments, like managing protected areas, instead of investing in processes that will enable African governments to do these tasks themselves' (Visseren-Hamakers and Glasbergen 2007: 415). Besides, the CBFP framework does not allow some core but sensitive issues in forest conservation, such as corruption in the granting of logging rights and the defective control of illegal logging to be tackled effectively.

Expectations that UNCSD partnerships would alleviate the participation deficit in global sustainability governance by allowing a wider involvement of non-state actors are not supported also by the data available. Only 12 per cent of Sub-Saharan Africa partnerships – compared to 16 per cent for all partnerships – have no state partners, whether African or otherwise. This might mirror a relatively weak African civil society and its frequent subordination to state authorities – especially the famous governmental NGOs – so that, even when local NGOs get involved, the state is not far away.

Looking at membership rather than leading actors as we did previously, we still find an overrepresentation of state actors in Sub-Saharan African partnerships (Figure 7.15), a finding consistent with some empirical case studies (Stewart and Gray 2006). What is interesting, though, is the hierarchy with 'scientific institutions and networks' and 'subnational and municipal governments' coming rather strongly after 'national governments' and 'NGOs', and before 'industry and business' and 'IGOs'. This is a significant variation from the hierarchy observed in UNCSD

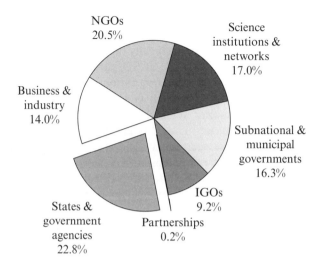

NGOs
20.5%

Science
institutions &
networks
17.0%

Business &
industry
14.0%

Subnational &
municipal
governments
16.3%

IGOs
9.2%

States &
government
agencies
22.8%

Partnerships
0.2%

Figure 7.15   Actor distribution in Sub-Saharan partnerships

partnerships as a whole (for comparison: Biermann et al. 2007: 254, Figure 11.5), indicating a better-balanced participation in partnerships involving Sub-Saharan Africa. It is perhaps a side effect of UN agencies' leadership noted above.

However, Africa does not perform better than other regions in terms of involving marginalized groups such as youth and children, women, indigenous people, workers and farmers. Among all UNCSD partnerships registered by December 2006, less than 1 per cent had marginalized groups as partners (Biermann et al. 2007: 253). According to a previous survey, only 6 per cent of the partnerships reviewed were really multi-stakeholder (Andonova and Levy 2003: 23), i.e. involving all the categories of stakeholders, including local communities, which are most likely to be left out. Social agents endowed with resources (both material and symbolic), including middle-class based local NGOs, are often favoured. In addition, there is a discrepancy between the multi-stakeholder rhetoric emphasizing greater participation and the actual partnership management on the ground. According to a comparative study, the participation rhetoric is used mainly to legitimize top-down oriented projects and thus guarantee a smoother implementation (Kerebel 2007: 335–73). It is a technique to foster project acceptance by local communities – very much like 'participation' in traditional development projects. It betrays a top-down approach, not significantly departing from traditional aid practices, and of a supply-side, donor-driven process (Andonova and Levy 2003: 23, 26).

CONCLUSIONS

African partnerships, and more specifically the Sub-Saharan African ones, do not differ radically from other UNCSD partnerships the world over, especially in terms of focus. A greater variation could have been expected given the specific needs of the continent as well as its marginalized position in the global political economy. Where a variation occurs – involvement of the state, more significant outputs and larger participation – it underlines the characters of both state and non-state actors on the continent.

Sustainable development partnerships were tasked to 'compensate for weak institutions or institutional deficits across levels of governance' (Andonova and Levy 2003: 20). However, they are not designed to overcome the policy implementation difficulties arising from public governance characteristics in most Third World countries, especially African LDCs. Altogether sustainable partnerships do not bring about a radical transformation of development aid patterns, and the shift towards participatory governance that is part of the partnership discourse seems more rhetorical than real. The fact that some of these partnerships still have limited outputs, or no outputs at all – let alone outcomes – suggests that part of this phenomenon is fuzzy and does not necessarily qualify as governance.

As part of a wider movement involving private actors in global environmental politics (Dingwerth 2007; Pattberg 2007a), creating some 'hybrid' forms of governance (Falkner 2003; Börzel and Risse 2005; Andonova 2010), thus allegedly contributing to a transnational governance of sustainable development (Pattberg 2007b; Biermann and Pattberg 2008), UNCSD partnerships attracted a growing academic attention since 2002, and enjoyed widespread popularity among policy makers. However, they are not the magic wand for overcoming Africa's development and governance conundrums, contrary to some expectations (on Madagascar, see Brinkerhoff 2007). Partnerships for sustainable development in Africa are largely what the states make of them – to mimic Alexander Wendt's well-known phrase about international anarchy (Wendt 1992) – and their development as a policy instrument should not distract our attention from the persistent challenge of state reform on the continent.

ACKNOWLEDGEMENTS

This chapter originated from a three-month stay as a guest researcher at the Institute for Environmental Studies, VU University Amsterdam, in late 2006, which was funded by the EU Commission through the GARNET network of excellence. I am grateful to my colleagues at IVM, especially within the GSPD partnerships database project, Frank Biermann, Philipp Pattberg, Sander Chan and Ayşem Mert, for welcoming me into their team, and sharing with me their data and ideas. I am particularly indebted to Ayşem Mert for her quantitative analysis of the database and her help with data interpretation on Sub-Saharan Africa.

NOTES

1. Originally a US initiative, it was facilitated by the US from 2003 to 2004, then by France, from 2005 to 2007, and now by Germany, since 2008. Canada took over in 2010. See http://www.pfbc-cbfp.org/home.html.
2. The CBFP facilitated in 2007 the creation of a Foundation for the Sustainable Financing of the Sangha Tri-National Trans-boundary Forest Complex, a private entity under British law, with a board of directors where international non-governmental organizations and donors sit alongside representatives of the three Central African states involved. See http://www.pfbc-cbfp.org/home.html.

REFERENCES

Andonova, L.B. (2010), 'Public–private partnerships for the earth politics and patterns of hybrid authority in the Multilateral System', *Global Environmental Politics*, **10**(2), 25–53.

Andonova, L.B. and M.A. Levy (2003), 'Franchising global governance: making sense of the Johannesburg Type II Partnerships', in O.S. Stokke and O.B. Thommessen (eds), *Yearbook of International Co-operation on Environment and Development*, Oxford, UK: Earthscan, pp. 19–31.

AMCEN/UNEP (African Ministerial Conference on the Environment/United Nations Environment Programme) (2006), *Africa Environment Outlook 2*, Nairobi: AMCEN/UNEP.

Bäckstrand, K. (2006), 'Democratizing global environmental governance? Stakeholder democracy after the World Summit on Sustainable Development', *European Journal of International Relations*, **12**(4), 467–98.

Biermann, F., S. Chan, A. Mert and P. Pattberg (2007), 'Multi-stakeholder partnerships for sustainable development: does the promise hold?', in P. Glasbergen, F. Biermann and A.P.J. Mol (eds.), *Partnerships, Governance and Sustainable Development. Reflections on Theory and Practice*, Cheltenham, UK: Edward Elgar, pp. 239–60.

Biermann, F. and P. Pattberg (2008), 'Global environmental governance: taking stock, moving forward', *Annual Review of Environment and Resources*, **33**, 277–940.

Blaikie, P. and J. Mope Simo (1998), 'Cameroon's environmental accords: signed, sealed, but undelivered' in E. Brown Weiss and H.K. Jacobson, *Engaging Countries. Strengthening Compliance with International Environmental Accords*, Cambridge, MA: MIT Press, pp. 437–74.

Börzel, T.A. and T. Risse (2005), 'Public–private partnerships: effective and legitimate tools of international governance?', in E. Grande and L.W. Pauly (eds),

Complex Sovereignty: Reconstructing Political Authority in the Twenty First Century, Toronto: Toronto University Press, pp. 195–216.

Bratton, M. and N. van de Walle (1994), 'Neo-patrimonial regimes and political transition in Africa', *World Politics*, **47**, 453–89.

Brinkerhoff, D.W. (2007), 'Enabling environmental partnerships: the role of good governance in Madagascar's forest sector' in P. Glasbergen, F. Biermann, and A.P.J. Mol (eds), *Partnerships, Governance and Sustainable Development. Reflections on Theory and Practice*, Cheltenham, UK: Edward Elgar, pp. 93–114.

Clapham, C. (1985), *Third World Politics: An Introduction*, London: Croom Helm.

Clapham, C. (1996), *Africa and the International System: The Politics of State Survival*, Cambridge, UK: Cambridge University Press.

Clapp, J. (1998), 'The privatization of global environmental governance: ISO 14000 and the developing world, *Global Governance*, **4**(3), 295–316.

Collier, P. (1995), 'The marginalization of Africa', *International Labour Review*, **134**(4–5), 541–57.

Collier, P. (2007), *The Bottom Billion: Why the Poorest Countries are Failing and What Can Be Done about It*, Oxford, UK: Oxford University Press.

Compagnon, D., F. Florémont and I. Lamaud (2011), 'Sub-Saharan Africa: Fragmented environmental governance without regional integration', in S. Breslin and L. Elliott (eds), *Comparative Environmental Regionalism*, Oxford, UK: Routledge, pp. 92–112.

De Lopez, T., T. Ponlok, K. Iyadomi, S. Santos and B. McIntosh (2009), 'Clean Development Mechanism and least developed countries: changing the rules for greater participation', *The Journal of Environment and Development*, **18**(4), 436–52.

Dingwerth, K. (2007), *The New Transnationalism. Transnational Governance and Democratic Legitimacy*, Houndsmills, UK: Palgrave Macmillan.

Falkner, R. (2003), 'Private environmental governance and international relations: Exploring the links', *Global Environmental Politics*, **3**(2), 72–87.

Gray, K.R. (2003), 'Multilateral environmental agreements in Africa: efforts and problems in implementation', *International Environmental Agreements: Politics, Law and Economics*, **3**, 97–135.

Hale, T.N. and D.L. Mauzerall (2004), 'Thinking globally and acting locally: can the Johannesburg partnerships coordinate action on sustainable development?', *Journal of Environment and Development*, **13**(3), 220–39.

Hurrell, A. (1994), 'A crisis of ecological viability? Global environmental change and the nation state', *Political Studies*, **42**, 146–65.

Jackson, R.H. (1990), *Quasi-states: Sovereignty, International Relations and the Third World*, Cambridge, UK: Cambridge University Press.

Kaplan, R. (1994), 'The coming anarchy: how scarcity, crime, overpopulation, tribalism and disease are rapidly destroying the social fabric of our planet', *The Atlantic Monthly*, **73**(2), 44–76.

Kerebel, C. (2007), *Les Partenariats Multi-acteurs: Entre Discours et Pratiques, quelle Contribution au Développement Durable? Quatre études de cas dans le secteur de l'énergie*', unpublished PhD dissertation in Political Science, Sciences Po Paris.

Mazouz, B. (2009), 'Les aspects pratiques des partenariats public-privé: de la rhétorique néolibérale aux enjeux, défis et risques de gestion des PPP', *Revue française d'administration publique*, **130**, 215–32.

Médard, J.F. (1982), 'The underdeveloped state in tropical Africa: political clientelism or neo-patrimonialism?' in C. Clapham (ed), *Private Patronage and*

Public Power: Political Clientelism in the Modern State, London: Francis Pinter, pp. 162–81.

Médard, J.F. (1991), 'L'Etat néo-patrimonial en Afrique noire', in J.F. Médard (ed), *Etats d'Afrique Noire: Formations, Mécanismes et Crise*, Paris: Karthala.

Migdal, J.S. (1988), *Strong Societies and Weak States: State–Society Relations and State Capabilities in the Third World*, Princeton, NJ: Princeton University Press.

OECD (2006), 'Evaluating the effectiveness and the efficiency of partnerships', paper presented at the workshop: 'Evaluating the Effectiveness and Efficiency of Partnerships', Paris: OECD Environment Directorate, ENV/EPOC15, 12 September 2006.

Pattberg, P. (2007a), *Private Institutions and Global Governance: The New Politics of Environmental Sustainability*, Cheltenham, UK: Edward Elgar.

Pattberg, P. (2007b), 'Partnerships for sustainability: an analysis of transnational environmental regimes' in P. Glasbergen, F. Biermann, and A.P.J. Mol (eds), *Partnerships, Governance and Sustainable Development. Reflections on Theory and Practice*, Cheltenham, UK: Edward Elgar, pp. 173–93.

Reinicke, W.H. (1998), *Global Public Policy: Governing without Government?*, Washington DC: Brookings Institution.

Reinicke, W.H. and F.M. Deng (eds) (2000), *Critical Choices. The United Nations Networks and the Future of Global Governance*, Toronto, Canada: International Development Research Council.

Risse, T. (2005), 'Two-thirds of the world: governance in areas of limited statehood is a global problem', *Transnationale Politik (Transatlantic Edition)*, **6**(4) (Winter), 64–9.

Schäferhoff, M., S. Campe and C. Kaan (2007), 'Transnational public–private partnerships in international relations: Making sense of concepts, research frameworks and results', *SFB-Governance Working Paper Series*, **6**, August 2007, available at: http://www.sfb-governance.de/en/publikationen, (retrieval: 06.04.2011).

Shaw, T.M. (1995), 'Africa in the global political economy at the end of the Millennium: what implications for politics and policies', *Africa Today: The Politics of Economic Integration in Africa*, **42**(4), 7–30.

Shaw, T.M. (2000), 'Africa in the global political economy: globalization, regionalization or marginalization?', in B. Hettne, A. Inotai, and O. Sunkel (eds), *The New Regionalism and the Future of Security and Development*, London: Macmillan Press.

Sidaway, J. and R. Gibb (1998), 'SADC, COMESA, SACU: contradictory formats for regional integration in Southern Africa?' in D. Simon (ed), *South Africa in Southern Africa: Reconfiguring the Region*, Oxford, UK: James Currey, pp. 164–84.

Sørensen, G. (2001), *Changes in Statehood: The Transformation of International Relations*, Houndmills, UK: Palgrave.

Stewart, A. and T. Gray (2006), 'The authenticity of "type two" multistakeholder partnerships for water and sanitation in Africa: when is a stakeholder a partner?', *Environmental Politics*, **15**(3), 362–78.

Strange, S. (1996), *The Retreat of the State: The Diffusion of Power in the World Economy*, Cambridge, UK: Cambridge University Press.

Streck, C. (2004), 'New partnerships in global environmental policy: the Clean Development Mechanism, *Journal of Environment and Development*, **13**(3), 295–322.

Visseren-Hamakers, I.J. and P. Glasbergen (2007), 'Partnerships in forest govern-
ance', *Global Environmental Change*, **17**(3–4), 408–19.
Wendt, A. (1992), 'Anarchy is what states make of it: the social construction of
power politics', *International Organization*, **88**(2), 391–425.
Young, O.R. (ed) (1999), *The Effectiveness of International Environmental Regimes:
Causal Connections and Behavioural Mechanisms*, Cambridge, MA: MIT Press.
Young, O.R. (2002), 'Evaluating the success of international environmental
regimes: where are we now?, *Global Environmental Change*, **12**, 73–7.

PART IV

Legitimacy of partnerships for sustainable development

8. Are partnerships for sustainable development democratic and legitimate?

Karin Bäckstrand

The aim of this chapter is to examine critically whether transnational public–private partnerships can be regarded as democratic and legitimate. The empirical focus in this chapter is on the partnerships for sustainable development adopted at the WSSD, which are framed as voluntary multi-stakeholder partnerships for sustainable development under the auspices of UNCSD. The question on the democratic credentials of partnerships for sustainable development taps into larger debates in International Relations on the 'democratic deficits' of international organizations and global governance arrangements and how to make these more accountable, transparent and inclusive. The language of democracy has gained currency in debates on the reform of global institutions and efforts to counter the democratic deficit in the European Union (Moravscik 2004). Democratic values, such as participation, representation, deliberation, inclusion and accountability are parts and parcel of the mainstream rhetoric of multilateral institutions and global governance mechanisms. Critics of the utopian cosmopolitan agenda to democratize global governance along statist lines argue that democratic theory has to be adjusted to fit real-world international institutions in a non-ideal world beyond the nation states. Consequently, democracy has to be rethought in the era of 'new multilateralism', represented by the emergence of transnational networked governance. Moreover, a recurrent argument is that democracy is only one source of legitimacy. The relationship between democracy and global public–private partnerships cannot be isolated from questions of environmental performance, effectiveness, societal effects or output legitimacy of public–private partnerships. If partnerships for sustainable development do not live up to the high standards of democratic and procedural legitimacy in democratic theory, output legitimacy, effectiveness or problem-solving capacity is an alternative source of legitimacy. Drawing on the scholarship on global democracy beyond the nation state, this chapter attempts to answer the principal question whether partnerships for sustainable development can be regarded as democratic. If they cannot be considered democratic in terms of democratic principles, is it sufficient that they are legitimate or effective? This chapter contrasts research on global democracy claiming that global partnerships will not approximate democracy with literature rethinking the notion of democracy in the light of new forms of transnational governance. The contested debate on the democratic governance of partnerships for sustainable development illustrates a gap between normative theories of democracy and calls for a recalibration of theories of democracy to fit real world institutions in a non-ideal world (Moravscik 2004: 336; Keohane 2011).

Transnational public–private partnerships for sustainable development have been framed as new modes of governance that potentially can reduce the three deficits of global governance, namely the implementation, governance and legitimacy deficits (Haas 2004). They have been celebrated by international multilateral agencies as a panacea for solving global challenges such as climate change mitigation, development and hunger (Miraftab 2004). Partnerships for sustainable development have 'evolved from a novelty in the multilateral system to a quite common practice' from 'being business UNusual' to 'becoming business as usual' (Bull and McNeill 2010: 103–104). They are presented as win–win solutions that can increase the democratic credentials of global governance and simultaneously strengthen environmental performance and effectiveness. In the IR scholarship, transnational public–private partnerships are seen as a response to market and state failure, shaped by a functional need to supply better governance (Buchanan and Keohane 2005). On this account, the emergence of transnational public–private partnerships is a response to state failure, governance gaps and inadequacies of interstate bargaining. According to principal-agent theory, governance functions such as agenda setting, monitoring, verification, enforcement and service provision can be outsourced to partnerships by governments and multilateral agencies.

Partnerships are frequently highlighted as innovative and new forms of public–private collaboration, which hold the promise of more effective and legitimate governance (Benner, Streck and Witte 2003; Benner, Reinicke and Witte 2004). While the primary rationale for partnerships is their purported effectiveness and performance, they are also framed as democratically legitimate tools that can promote values associated with democratic governance, such as, accountability, representation, transparency and participation. Accordingly, the policy rhetoric does not only stress partnerships as 'implementation mechanisms' but also as democratic innovations toward 'participatory multilateralism' in terms of multi-stakeholder dialogue between civil society, government and business (UN 2010). '"Partnerships" as a term is rapidly becoming the new mantra shaping the UN discourse on global politics' (Martens 2007: 4). Partnerships are underpinned by discourses of participatory democracy, stakeholder inclusion and sustainable development (Mert 2009). In conjunction with the rise of a legitimacy discourse on partnerships, the scholarly literature on the democratic credentials and legitimacy of partnerships has expanded. Contemporary research includes comparisons on the democratic credibility of transnational public–private partnerships across different policy fields (Bexell and Mörth 2010) and conceptual work on how to analyze the legitimacy and effectiveness of partnerships (Börzel and Risse 2005; Glasbergen 2011; Schäfferhoff, Campe and Kaan 2009; Meadowcroft 2007). Almost a decade of research has critically examined the legitimacy and effectiveness of the Johannesburg partnerships, which currently list 348 partnerships in the UNCSD database (Andonova and Levy 2003; Hale and Mauzerall 2004; Bäckstrand 2006; Biermann et al. 2007; Pattberg 2010; Szulecki, Pattberg and Biermann 2011).

However, the research on the legitimacy of partnerships for environment and sustainable development is still fragmented and lacks systematic comparative studies between different types of partnerships (multilateral, private–private) and across different policy fields (health, environment, security, development). Most studies of partnerships are single case studies or quantitative studies of the Johannesburg partnerships (Biermann et al. 2007: 240). Moreover, there is a methodological problem of selection bias towards successful public–private partnerships.

First, any assessment of whether partnerships are democratic depends on which definition and standard of democracy one applies. The answer to the question whether transnational partnerships (and other forms of transnational public–private governance mechanisms) are democratic, will vary depending on if you apply theories of cosmopolitan (Held 1995), participatory, deliberative (Dryzek 2000, 2010), multi-stakeholder (MacDonald 2008) or liberal institutionalist democracy (Keohane 2011). This chapter advances three arguments related to the democratic legitimacy of partnerships. The first argument, which is derived from democratic theory and international relations (IR) theories on realism and critical political economy, claims that transnational public–private partnerships as new instruments of transnational governance do neither conform to normative principles of democracy nor contribute to the democratization of global governance. A second perspective, which is more optimistic with regard to the democratic credentials of transnational public–private partnerships, stems from IR theories on liberal-institutionalism and global deliberative democracy. While partnerships certainly do not live up to high standards of democratic polity as outlined by traditional democratic theory revolving around the nation-state, they can become global arenas for enhancing democratic values, such as participation, accountability, representation and deliberation. A third argument is that while transnational public–private partnerships may not be democratic as such, they can be legitimate, as output legitimacy (effectiveness) can compensate lack of input legitimacy (procedural values) (see Chapter 9).

This chapter proceeds as follows. In order to evaluate whether partnerships for sustainable development are democratic or legitimate, we first have to grasp the nature of partnerships. The first section presents the sceptical arguments to whether transnational public–private partnerships can be regarded as democratic in terms of living up to basic principles of democracy. The second section examines scholarly work calling for a re-conceptualization of democratic theory to enable an assessment of the democratic legitimacy of transnational public–private governance. The final section examines the arguments of a body of work stressing that there are other sources of legitimacy than democracy, such as output legitimacy or effectiveness. Whether partnerships are legitimate and democratic is an open-ended issue depending on the results from empirical inquiry.[1]

ARE TRANSNATIONAL PUBLIC–PRIVATE PARTNERSHIPS DEMOCRATIC?

The issue of the democratic legitimacy of transnational public–private partnerships is embedded in broader debates in IR on the prospects for global democracy. While cosmopolitan scholars argue that global democracy is necessary to adequately respond to collective action problems such as global environmental threats, sceptics question if it is possible, or even desirable to democratize the global order (Dahl 1999; Cerny 2009). Dahl is the most outspoken critic of the prospect of democratizing global governance arrangements, which he views as neither desirable nor feasible. Communitarians argue that transnational democracy is not possible because of the lack of coherent global constituency or *demos* in the politically, socially and culturally divided community of 193 states. Realists claim that the dynamics of realpolitik, international anarchy and sovereign power are structural features preventing the emergence of global democracy. Critical perspectives are deeply sceptical of the idea of global democracy because of the ways in which power inequalities permeate international institutions and mask power relationships (McGrew 2002). Global democracy is simply shorthand for neo-liberal market economy, liberal democracy and Western hegemony that operates through the language of 'good governance' and civil society participation (O'Brien et al. 2002).

The critical political economy perspective regards transnational public–private partnerships as neo-liberal instruments that shift power away from multilateral institutions to the corporate sector and thereby reinforce market environmentalism (Levy and Newell 2002). On this account, transnational public–private partnerships are likely to become a form of privatization under neo-liberal policies of decentralization. The rollback of the state is a challenge to creating equitable and inclusive partnerships in situations of limited statehood (Miraftab 2004). The turn towards partnerships reinforces marketization, privatization and commodification of global governance, leading to market multilateralism (Martens 2007: 4). The neo-Gramscian critique targets the neo-liberal environmental order, manifested as the global carbon market and the rise of corporate driven public–private partnerships (Matthews and Paterson 2005). Partnerships reflect trends of new public management, a hollowing out of the state, rise of the corporate sector, fragmentation of global governance and the retreat of state responsibility in environmental affairs. Utting and Zammit (2009) highlight the importance of reflecting critically on the mainstream discourse in multilateral agencies and parts of academic research to associate transnational public–private partnerships with good governance (collaboration, trust, participation, responsibility). The idealizing of the partnerships concept risks diverting attention from asymmetrical power relations, the struggle for hegemony, participation deficits and trade-off between diverging partnership goals to questions of effectiveness and efficiency. In sum, these different perspectives arrive at the same conclusion: transnational public–private partnerships cannot be democratic or approximate democratic governance. Democratic theorists argue that transnational public–private partnerships as non-electoral mechanisms cannot live up to normative principles of democratic governance. The realists argue that the sovereignty-based power structures of the international system are incompatible with ideals of global democratic governance through mechanisms such as transnational public–private partnerships. The critical economy perspective claims that agendas of privatization, marketization and neo-liberal hegemony underline the normative partnership 'feel good' discourse of good governance and democratic participation. In conclusion, the partnership phenomenon has little in common with democracy, democratic governance and democratic legitimacy.

DO TRANSNATIONAL PUBLIC–PRIVATE PARTNERSHIPS PROMOTE DEMOCRATIC VALUES?

A recurrent argument in a growing literature on democracy beyond the nation-state is that democratic state-centred legitimacy is not appropriate for evaluating non-electoral, non-territorial governance arrangements, such as partnerships for sustainable development. It is less applicable to global multi-sectoral networks that consist of governments, business, civil society and multilateral agencies. The meaning of democratic legitimacy in the context of complex transnational environmental governance, defined by overlapping public and private authorities, is contested among scholars. There is a growing body of work arguing that we have to rethink notions of democracy, legitimacy, accountability and participation along non-statist lines as we analyse multiple sites of networked public–private governance (Scholte 2011). Keohane (2011) argues that no global institution or governance arrangements would meet the high threshold of liberal democracy derived from domestic politics. It would be inappropriate to impose the high threshold of conformity to democratic ideals developed in the context of the nation-state to global governance practices. Consequently, in assessing the legitimacy of transnational governance, 'the threshold of acceptability that is appropriate to use should be lower than in a well-ordered society' (Keohane 2011: 100). Because of the inherently undeveloped and flawed nature of global governance, legitimacy is a matter of degree: 'we do not merely assess whether it [global governance] is legitimate, but how far above and below the threshold of legitimacy it falls' (Keohane 2011: 101). The scholarship on democracy beyond the nation-state (Grant and Keohane 2005; Dingwerth 2007; Keohane 2011) has outlined democratic values that are central to evaluate the legitimacy of global governance. Democratic legitimacy, which rests on values of participation, inclusion, transparency and accountability, is only one source of legitimacy that is closely associated with domestic models of electoral democracy (Grant and Keohane 2005).

The perspective of normative legitimacy is derived from norms, values and principles of liberal democracy and a 'right to rule'. An institution, governance system or political order is legitimate if it is based on values, such as transparency, rule of law, accountability, fairness, inclusion, participation, representation and deliberation. This can be contrasted with empirical, social or political legitimacy (Bernstein 2011). Legitimacy in this vein is defined as the acceptance of a particular social order, rule, norm or institution by a set of actors or by a specific community (Hurd 1999) and concerns 'authority granted by the political community to its institutions and structures' (Payne and Samhat 2004: 1). Compliance with rules and norms occurs if actors perceive the social and political order as acceptable and an institution or a rule is legitimate if it is widely believed to be legitimate (Buchanan and Keohane 2006: 405). However, the literature assessing the democratic legitimacy of the Johannesburg partnerships and other transnational public–private partnerships rests on a conception of normative legitimacy, where inclusion, accountability and deliberation are used as criteria or indicators of democratic legitimacy.

To what extent do the Johannesburg partnerships incorporate democratic values? Previous empirical studies of the democratic legitimacy of partnerships for sustainable development frequently highlight participation, accountability, transparency and deliberative quality as indicators of input legitimacy. This overlaps with Dingwerth's (2007) study of democratic legitimacy in transnational governance that highlights (1) participation and inclusion; (2) democratic control and accountability; and (3) argumentative practice and deliberative quality.

First, *participation* and *inclusion* by individuals and societal groups is a core element of democratic theory and practice. To what extent are those subject to a decision represented in the policy-making process? Are there equal opportunities to participate? In what phases of the policy process are actors (agenda setting, policy making, implementation) participating and is participation symbolic or real? In transnational public–private partnerships, non-electoral and group-based participation is central. Where transnational constituencies are affected by decisions, the model of stakeholder democracy has been institutionalized, which entails representation, deliberation and participation of non-state actors, such as NGOs and business (Nanz and Steffek 2004; Bäckstrand 2006). There are several studies of patterns of participation of different types of public and private actors in the Johannesburg partnerships. What type of actors (governments, intergovernmental organizations, business, NGOs, etc.) predominates and what is the geographical representation (global, national, regional, local)? Regarding the Johannesburg partnerships, three dimensions of participation can be highlighted: (1) geographical representation of Northern and Southern partners and lead actors; (2) participation of non-state actors; and (3) representation of what are frequently referred to as 'marginalized' stakeholders, such as women, youth, children and indigenous people. The Johannesburg partnerships demonstrate a geographical imbalance as Northern actors predominate. Of the registered partnerships, 60 per cent have industrialized country partners, while only 17 per cent are led by a developing country (Hale and Mauzerall 2004: 30, Biermann et al. 2007). In 70 per cent of the partnerships led by an industrialized country, another OECD country is the country of implementation. This is even higher for the subset of 19 climate partnerships (where the primary focus is on climate change), where 80 per cent is implemented in OECD countries (Pattberg 2010: 282). Hence, industrialized countries are overrepresented as countries of implementation in climate partnerships. Relatively few partnerships are directed to neglected regions with high poverty and environmental pressures. Large developing countries, such as South Africa and Indonesia that hosted the preparatory meetings of the 2002 Johannesburg summit, are more frequent as partners. In this respect, the Johannesburg partnerships represent a coalition of willing between industrialized countries and a few large developing countries, as Andonova and Levy (2003) argue.

Public actors dominate the Johannesburg partnerships while NGOs and business actors have a more marginal presence. A general pattern for the Johannesburg partnerships is that governments or international agencies often are the lead partners. Governments lead almost 25 per cent of the Johannesburg partnerships, followed by UN agencies leading approximately 17 per cent. However, among climate partnerships, 83 per cent of partnerships involve governments, 62 per cent UN agencies and 61 per cent other intergovernmental organizations (United Nations 2010: 11). In climate partnerships, state membership is even higher (90 per cent) compared to the Johannesburg average. Furthermore, only 8 per cent of partnerships are led by NGOs, while business actors lead only 3 per cent. Furthermore, there has been a 30 per cent decline of NGO-led partnerships between 2003 and 2007 (Biermann 2007). Private sector involvement is lower than expected, since business actors choose their own partnerships with less formalized reporting mechanisms and the financing of partnerships by private sectors has been minimal (Mert 2009: 7).

Concerning actors from the nine major groups defined by the UN, participation is low and particularly so when it comes to marginalized groups. Only 1 per cent of the partnerships involve women's groups, youth, trade unions, indigenous people and farmers (United Nations 2010: 11). The more institutionalized major groups were better represented. NGOs are involved in 30 per cent of the partnerships, 38 per cent business, 18 per cent science and technology communities and 8 per cent local authorities (United Nations 2010: 11). This pattern reveals that partnerships are geared towards well-established non-state actors such as large NGOs, the scientific community and business from primarily the Northern hemisphere. Local actors, least developed countries, Southern grassroots movements and marginalized groups are represented to a lesser degree.

To sum up, the Johannesburg partnerships have skewed representation. They are dominated by state and intergovernmental actors from the North or large developing countries with the most advanced capacity, which will reap the benefits of partnerships rather than those with the largest needs.

Partnerships mirror rather than transform existing patterns of power, inclusion and exclusion between North and South, profit and non-profit sectors, public and private authority and professional NGOs and local grass root movements.

Accountability means that those who govern are subject to control and held accountable, hence those in positions of influence should be responsive to the interests of their constituencies. Accountability 'implies that some actors have the right to hold other actors accountable to a set of standards, to judge whether they have fulfilled their responsibilities in light of these standards, and to impose sanctions if they determine that these responsibilities have not been met' (Grant and Keohane 2005: 29). Accountability depends on the availability of sanctions available when actions or decisions are contrary to the values and preferences of principals. The ultimate sanction is if an agent is removed from its position because of a failure to comply, deliver promises or implement goals. Transparency and access to information is a precondition of accountability as the latter depends on information about the performance of partnerships and the monitoring of goal achievement.

The Johannesburg partnerships lack formal mechanisms for accountability. The absence of a single principal in these multi-sectoral partnerships raises the question: to whom should partnerships be accountable? There is no centralized agency overseeing goal attainment in partnerships for sustainable development and there is no formalized supervision, monitoring and implementation review of partnerships and they completely lack coercive elements (see Chapter 2). The Bali guidelines, which were an outcome of the preparatory process that led to the 2002 Johannesburg summit, did not grant the UNCSD secretariat, which is the responsible body, the power to enforce reviewing and reporting of partnerships activities (Mert 2009: 6). Instead, a small partnership team was set up at the UNCSD, and this team can only screen partnerships that apply for registration. Due to this lack of formal accountability, transparency has been emphasized in the context of Johannesburg partnerships. There are three indicators of transparency of the Johannesburg partnerships: a website, a reporting system and a monitoring mechanism (Hale and Mauzerall 2004: 227).

What is the transparency record for the Johannesburg partnerships? A website of all partnerships was set up in 2004 under the UNCSD and has been updated and amended in 2006 and 2007. Only a third of the partnerships fulfil all three indicators of transparency and around half lack mechanisms for monitoring effectiveness and progress of partnerships (Hale and Mauzerall 2004: 228). Systematic monitoring of the progress of partnerships remains a challenge because monitoring is based on voluntary reports compiled by the partnerships themselves (United Nations

2010: 23). Of the registered partnerships, only 20 per cent have submitted updates on progress, which concern organizational activities, coordination activities and implementation activities. Only 1 per cent of the partnerships reported that they met their stated goal (Andonova and Levy 2003: 22). The weak accountability mechanisms of the Johannesburg partnerships are due to the unclear and vague guidelines as well as lack of mandatory reporting requirements. No Johannesburg partnership has been removed from the registry because of insufficient performance. 'Partnerships fairs' with showcases of Johannesburg partnerships have instead become a new practice at the annual UNCSD sessions as a way of information sharing.

Deliberation concerns whether public–private partnerships rest on 'deliberative rationality' such as inclusiveness, unconstrained dialogue, and free and public reason among equal individuals? What is the quality of the deliberation and does it allow for 'arguing' rather than 'bargaining' (Risse 2004)? If the deliberation is limited to negotiations between narrow sets of elites it will compromise the deliberative quality. Coercion and power asymmetries between actors are believed to distort communication and rational discourse. A key question is to what extent is the deliberative process open to competing discourses and arguments from citizens as well as elites (Dryzek 2010). Deliberative theorists suggest that reciprocity assures that arguments of different participants are included and treated in an impartial and respectful manner.

To what extent do the Johannesburg partnerships live up to the deliberative democracy ideals, such as communicative rationality, unconstrained dialogue and free and public reason? Whether public–private partnerships actually promote a venue for deliberation largely depends on the partnership function. In partnerships whose primary function is rule implementation, such as the Johannesburg, the room for deliberation and problem solving is more limited compared to partnerships for rule making, agenda setting or service provision. Deliberative processes tend to be cosmetic and symbolic and are often added-on or serve to legitimize decisions already made.

Deliberative quality also depends on the context of deliberation. Previous studies have analysed mega-summitry deliberation *about* partnerships by various public and private actors at the UNCSD annual sessions rather than deliberation *within* public–private partnerships. The Johannesburg partnerships clearly have a more institutionalized model for deliberation about partnerships through 'partnerships fairs' and multistakeholder deliberations between the nine major groups (Bäckstrand 2006). Finally, the quality of deliberation is adversely affected by barriers to participation, such as power asymmetries between partners and the lack of competing and alternative voices from citizens and marginalized actors. The bias of representation and participation in the Johannesburg partnerships toward Northern states, large developing countries, professional NGOs, climate change capitalists and multilateral bureaucracies at the expense of LDCs, local grass root movements, women and indigenous people limits free and authentic discursive contest between equals.

ARE TRANSNATIONAL PUBLIC–PRIVATE PARTNERSHIPS EFFECTIVE AND THEREFORE LEGITIMATE?

Even with a lower threshold of acceptability of democratic standards, the previous section has demonstrated that the democratic legitimacy record of partnerships for sustainable development is mixed at best and low at worst. Participation is skewed toward powerful actors, accountability mechanisms are weak and the deliberative processes within partnerships are limited. However, in the light of escalating global environmental change that threatens to erode the capacity of ecosystems to harbour human and non-human life, a recurrent argument is that the effectiveness of partnerships for sustainable development is an important source of legitimacy alongside democratic values. The key rationale for partnerships in the policy discourse is that these are better equipped to reverse the environmental crisis, compared to traditional regulation. Accordingly, overall legitimacy rests on combining effective environmental problem solving with accountable, inclusive and transparent procedures. The issue of legitimacy in global governance is approached by separating input and output legitimacy, which is an approach derived from the literature on EU governance (Scharpf 1999, 2006). As outlined in the previous section, input legitimacy stems from procedural logic where the participatory quality of the decision-making process in terms of deliberative quality, participation and accountability is in focus. Output legitimacy is associated with a consequential logic and effectiveness, and relates to if governance arrangements contribute to collective problem solving. Accordingly, if transnational public–private partnerships had strong democratic procedural legitimacy (robust accountability and transparency mechanisms, wide inclusion of stakeholders, venues for deliberation), while failing to solve pressing environmental problems (greenhouse gas emissions, deforestation rates, water shortage and loss of biological diversity), the legitimacy of these governance arrangements would be called in question. A high degree of effectiveness or environmental performance, in terms of reducing collective problems such as environmental threats, can compensate for low input legitimacy. The consideration of effectiveness as a source of legitimacy reflects decades of debates in green political theory on how to balance process (procedural legitimacy) versus substantive sustainable outcomes (effectiveness) in tackling global environmental threats (Smith 2003).

To measure environmental effectiveness in terms of environmental impacts, such as reduced greenhouse gas emissions and sustainable development benefits, is methodologically challenging. For this reason, political scientists have been focusing on the institutional effectiveness, which is a precondition for environmental effectiveness. Chapter 5 provides a detailed assessment of the problem-solving effectiveness of energy partnerships within the Johannesburg partnership database. The level of institutionalization is singled out as a critical factor for implementation. Paradoxically, the Johannesburg partnerships that most closely resemble international organizations in terms of decision-making processes and governance structure (for example having established a Secretariat with staff, Executive Body and General Assembly) were more effective. Inactive or 'low activity' partnerships without visible activities, such as knowledge dissemination and implementation and without organizational structure in place, are the most ineffective. The weak institutional effectiveness in terms of implementation review and mechanisms for reporting, monitoring and accountability make an evaluation of the environmental effectiveness of Johannesburg partnerships very difficult.

As will be argued below, the environmental effectiveness of Johannesburg partnerships cannot be assessed as quantitative goals and system for monitoring and implementation review are lacking. Glasbergen (2011) has outlined a 'ladder of partnership activity' as a method to investigate the societal impact of partnerships for sustainability. Partnerships are seen as a collaborative arrangement between market, government and civil society actors that can be evaluated according to a ladder of activity. In their early phases, partnerships are focused on internal interactions, such as building trust, creating collaborative advantage and constituting a rule system. Higher up the ladder of activity as partnerships mature, the focus is on the external interaction, such as changing the market and changing the political order. However, the Johannesburg partnerships are far from the 'highest' stage on the ladder of activity, which concern the impact of governance of society and the transformation of the political order. Rather than being innovative mechanisms that redefine discourses and practices of sustainability governance, they are geared toward internal dimensions, such as building trust among partners and seeking new partners and funding. For this reason the Johannesburg partnerships reinforce current power imbalances rather than transforming them (Bäckstrand 2006).

The United Nations Environment Programme (UNEP) Executive Director described the 2002 Johannesburg conference as a summit for 'implementation, accountability and partnership' (Bäckstrand 2006: 297). The overall rationale for the summit was that the implementation gap in sustainable development could be reduced by results-based and outcome-oriented partnerships. However, several studies have demonstrated a low performance of Johannesburg partnerships (Biermann et al. 2007; Pattberg 2010). 'Partnerships are most frequent in those areas that are already heavily institutionalized and regulated. They are predominantly not concerned with implementation, but rather with further institution building' (Biermann et al. 2007: 259). Partnerships lack capacity as a majority of them are unfunded and seek funding. More than 80 per cent of the partnerships are seeking additional funding for their activities (United Nations 2010: 13). The Johannesburg Summit failed to mobilize new and additional resources in terms of official development assistance. Less than a third of Johannesburg partnerships focus on direct environmental impact. Instead they are process-oriented, by building capacity, increasing awareness and strengthening means of implementation. Many partnerships primarily aim at building more partnerships or further institution-alization with very little direct environmental impact despite their claimed goal of implementation of sustainable development goals (OECD 2006). The result is many ad hoc partnerships, which are fragmented and decoupled from goals and targets in intergovernmental agreements and regimes. Approximately half of the UNCSD partnerships are not operational and active (Kylsäter 2011; Szulecki, Pattberg and Biermann 2011). In sum, the Johannesburg partnerships contain few clear quantitative goals that can be used as a yardstick for measuring their performance. They revolve around capacity building functions rather than outcome-oriented activities to achieve multilaterally agreed targets for natural resource protection. The weak institutional effectiveness, in terms of implementation review and mechanism for reporting, monitoring and control, precludes an analysis of environmental effectiveness of Johannesburg partnerships. However, the 'political myth of multistakeholder partnerships is still kept afloat' (Szulecki, Pattberg and Biermann 2011) and reproduced in regular UN reports on partnership activities (United Nations 2010).

CONCLUSIONS

The chapter has attempted to answer the principal question whether global public–private partnerships can be regarded as democratic. The multi-sectoral partnerships for environment adopted at the 2002 World Summit on Sustainable Development are used as an empirical illustration. I have contrasted the scholarship on global democracy claiming that partnerships do not conform to core normative principles of democratic governance with research rethinking the notion of democracy in the light of new forms of non-electoral and non-territorial transnational governance. If we do not rethink the concepts of democracy and democratic legitimacy beyond the conceptual prison of state-centric democratic theory, any empirical assessment of the democratic credentials of partnerships is in vain. However, if democratic legitimacy can be re-conceptualized to fit to the 'real-world institutions', an empirical research agenda for critically assessing the democratic values of transnational public–private partnerships is possible.

A central argument highlighted in this chapter is that partnerships can be considered democratically legitimate if they fulfil core *democratic values*, such as participation, accountability, transparency, deliberation. Furthermore, this chapter has considered perspectives arguing that even if public–private partnerships cannot be considered democratic in a traditional sense of electoral democracy, it is sufficient that they are effective for their overall legitimacy. A conclusion from almost a decade of research on the Johannesburg partnerships is that their democratic credentials are weak in terms of incorporation of core democratic values. The Johannesburg partnerships consolidate rather than transform asymmetrical patterns of participation between North and South, established and 'marginalized groups' and state and non-state actors. Furthermore, the accountability mechanisms are weak and the deliberative potential of the partnerships are limited. A problem in conducting empirical research on the Johannesburg partnerships is that they are not amiable to evaluation: they are institutionally underdeveloped and many of them do not live up to basic criteria of transnational public–private partnerships (hybrid interaction, institutionalization, provision of public goods) outlined in the academic literature. A majority of the Johannesburg partnerships are not active or operative, they do not have a website and they lack internal governance structure and funding.

However, the Johannesburg partnerships do not justify fears among its critics arguing that partnerships reinforce neo-liberal market environmentalism and privatization. The findings of the critical political economy research on UN-business partnerships are not applicable to the Johannesburg partnerships, which are dominated by public actors. Business participation is remarkably low since industry prefers to operate outside the UN, which it regards as inefficient and overly bureaucratic. The Johannesburg partnerships do not reflect trends of privatization and free market environmentalism but signify the continued power of intergovernmental organizations that have found new tasks in being facilitators and administrators of voluntary public–private partnerships.

A recurrent argument in the debate on partnerships is that questions of environmental performance, effectiveness, societal effects or output legitimacy are intertwined with the democratic legitimacy of partnerships. If transnational public–private partnerships do not fulfil procedural legitimacy, effectiveness or problem-solving capacity is an alternative source of legitimacy. However, the effectiveness of the Johannesburg partnerships is difficult to ascertain. Due to the methodological challenges, few studies have taken stock of the environmental effectiveness of these partnerships. Institutional effectiveness, that is institutional design and governance structures are preconditions for environmental effectiveness (see Chapter 5). As discussed above, the Johannesburg partnerships are quite ad hoc, fragmented and institutionally underdeveloped. About half of the partnerships in the database are not active and operative any longer. Their mechanisms for compliance, monitoring, enforcement and implementation – which are decisive for environmental performance – are weak. The partnerships rely on voluntary action and the UNCSD has no mandate to review, monitor, supervise or enforce implementation. Environmental effectiveness is not even possible to evaluate given the absence of quantitative goals and targets in the Johannesburg partnerships. There are no benchmarks or yardsticks for goal attainment and environmental performance. In sum, the institutional performance of the Johannesburg partnerships is low, which makes the environmental effectiveness difficult to evaluate and demonstrate. Hence, due to the weak institutional and environmental effectiveness the overall legitimacy of the Johannesburg partnerships can be questioned. The argument that output legitimacy can compensate for weak input legitimacy does not hold in the case of WSSD partnerships.

The *legitimizing function* of the Johannesburg partnerships appears to be a more salient and predominant feature compared to the legitimacy of partnerships in themselves. The discourse of participation, democracy, effectiveness, flexibility and performance of the Johannesburg partnerships has accompanied transnational public–private partnerships from the start. In conclusion, the heightened rhetoric of the promise of transnational public–private partnerships as a governance innovation for sustainability does not match the realities.

NOTE

1. There are many multi-sectoral environmental partnerships in different multilateral settings and beyond UN. However, it is beyond the scope of this chapter to examine the plethora of partnerships for environment and sustainable development beyond the Johannesburg partnerships under the UNCSD. The environmental and energy partnerships under the United Nations Fund for International Partnerships (UNFIP)

(Andonova 2010) are examples of partnerships in another multilateral setting. Second, projects under the Kyoto Protocol's Clean Development Mechanism (CDM) have been framed as public–private partnerships (Streck 2004). Third, while this chapter focuses exclusively on public–private partnerships for sustainable development, there are a plethora of private–private partnerships, transgovernmental partnerships and international sub-regional partnerships between cities and municipalities (Bäckstrand 2008).

REFERENCES

Andonova, L. (2010), 'Public–private partnerships for the Earth: politics and patterns of hybrid authority in the multilateral system', *Global Environmental Politics*, **10**(2), 25–53.

Andonova, L.B. and M.A. Levy (2003), 'Franchising global governance: making sense of the Johannesburg Type II Partnerships', in O.S. Stokke and O.B. Thommessen (eds), *Yearbook of International Co-operation on Environment and Development*, Oxford: Earthscan, pp. 19–31.

Bäckstrand, K. (2006), 'Multi-stakeholder partnerships for sustainable development: rethinking legitimacy, accountability and effectiveness', *European Environment*, **16**, 290–306.

Bäckstrand, K. (2008), 'Accountability of networked climate governance: the rise of transnational climate partnerships', *Global Environmental Politics*, **8**(3), 74–104.

Benner, T., W. Reinicke and J.M. Witte (2004), 'Multisectoral networks in global governance: towards a pluralistic system of accountability', *Government and Opposition*, **39**(2), 191–210.

Benner, T., C. Streck and J.M. Witte (eds) (2003), *Progress or Peril? Networks and Partnerships in Global Environmental Governance. The Post-Johannesburg Agenda*, Berlin: Global Public Policy Institute.

Bernstein, S. (2011), 'Legitimacy in intergovernmental and non-state global governance', *Review of International Political Economy*, **18**(1), 17–51.

Bexell, M. and U. Mörth (eds) (2010), *Democracy and Public–Private Partnerships in Global Governance*, Houndsmills, UK: Palgrave McMillan.

Biermann, F., S. Chan, A. Mert and P. Pattberg (2007), 'Multi-stakeholder partnerships for sustainable development: does the promise hold?', in P. Glasbergen, F. Biermann and A.P.J. Mol (eds), *Partnerships, Governance and Sustainable Development. Reflections on Theory and Practice*, Cheltenham, UK: Edward Elgar Publishing, pp. 239–60.

Börzel, T.A. and T. Risse (2005), 'Public–private partnerships: effective and legitimate tools of transnational governance?', in E. Grande and L.W. Pauly (eds), *Complex Sovereignty. Reconstituting Political Authority in the Twenty-first Century*, Toronto: University of Toronto Press, pp. 195–216.

Buchanan, A. and R.O. Keohane (2006), 'The legitimacy of global governance institutions', *Ethics and International Affairs*, **20**(4), 405–37.

Bull, B. and D. McNeill (2007), *Development Issues in Global Governance. Public-Private Partnerships and Market Multilateralism*, New York: Routledge.

Bull, B. and D. McNeill (2010), 'From business UNusual to business as usual: the future legitimacy of public–private partnerships with multilateral organizations' in M. Bexell and U. Mörth (eds), *Democracy and Public-Private Partnerships in Global Governance*, Houndsmills, UK: Palgrave McMillan, pp. 103–122.

Cerny, P. (2009), 'Some pitfalls of democratisation in a globalising world. Thoughts from the 2008 Millennium Conference', *Millennium*, 37(3), 767–90.

Dahl, R.A. (1999), 'Can international organizations be democratic?', in I. Shapiro and C. Hacker-Gordon (eds), *Democracy's Edges*, Cambridge, UK: Cambridge University Press.

Dingwerth, K. (2007), *The New Transnationalism. Transnational Governance and Democratic Legitimacy*, Houndmills, UK: Palgrave Macmillan

Dryzek, J. (2000), *Deliberative Democracy and Beyond. Liberals, Critics, Contestations*, Oxford, UK: Oxford University Press.

Dryzek, J. (2010), *Foundations and Frontiers of Deliberative Governance*, Oxford, UK: Oxford University Press.

Glasbergen, P. (2011), 'Understanding partnerships for sustainable development analytically: the ladder of partnership activity as a methodological tool,' *Environmental Policy and Governance*, 21, 1–13.

Grant, R. and R.O. Keohane (2005), 'Accountability and abuses of power in world politics', *American Political Science Review*, 99(1), 29–43.

Haas, P.M. (2004), 'Addressing the global governance deficit', *Global Environmental Politics*, 4(4), 1–15.

Hale, T.N. and D.L. Mauzerall (2004), 'Thinking globally and acting locally: can the Johannesburg partnerships coordinate action on sustainable development?', *Journal of Environment and Development*, 13(3), 220–39.

Held, D. (1995), *Democracy and the Global Order. From the Modern State to Cosmopolitan Governance*, Stanford, CA: Stanford University Press.

Hurd, I. (1999), 'Legitimacy and authority in international politics', *International Organization*, 53(2), 379–80.

Keohane, R.O. (2011), 'Global governance and legitimacy', *Review of International Political Economy*, 18(1), 99–109.

Kylsäter, M. (2011), *Is There Really a Deficit? Evaluating the Legitimacy of Transnational Public–Private Partnerships*, Masters thesis, Lund University, Department of Political Science.

Levy, D. and P. Newell (2002), *The Business of Global Environmental Governance*, Cambridge, MA: MIT Press.

MacDonald, T. (2008), *Global Stakeholder Democracy. Power and Representation Beyond Liberal States*, Oxford, UK: Oxford University Press.

Martens, J. (2007), 'Multistakeholder partnerships. Future models of multilateralism?', *Occasional Papers*, 29, January 2007, Berlin: Friedrich-Ebert-Stiftung.

Matthews, K. and M. Paterson (2005), 'Boom or bust? The economic engine behind the drive for climate change policy', *Global Change, Peace & Security*, 17(1), 59–75.

McGrew, A. (2002), 'From global governance to good governance: theories and prospects of democratizing the global polity', in M. Ougaard and R. Higgot (eds), *Towards a Global Polity*, London: Routledge.

Meadowcroft, J. (2007), 'Democracy and accountability: the challenge for cross-sectoral partnerships' in P. Glasbergen, F. Biermann and A.P.J. Mol (eds), *Partnerships, Governance and Sustainable Development. Reflections on Theory and Practice*, Cheltenham, UK: Edward Elgar Publishing, pp. 194–213.

Mert, A. (2009), 'Partnerships for sustainable development as discursive practice. Shifts in discourses on environment and democracy', *Forest Policy and Economics*, **11**(2), 109–22.

Miraftab, F. (2004), 'Public–private partnerships. The Trojan horse of neo-liberal development?', *Journal of Planning and Environmental Research*, **24**, 89–101.

Moravscik, A. (2004), 'Is there a "democratic deficit" in world politics? A framework for analysis', *Government and Opposition*, **29**, 336–63.

Nanz, P. and J. Steffek (2004), 'Global governance, participation and the public sphere', *Government and Opposition*, **39**(2), 314–34.

O'Brien, R., A.M. Goetz, J.A. Scholte and M. Williams (2002), *Contesting Governance. Multilateral Institutions and Global Social Movements*, Cambridge, UK: Cambridge University Press.

OECD (2006), *Evaluating the Effectiveness and Efficiency of Partnerships*, Paris: OECD.

Pattberg, P. (2010), 'Public–private partnerships in global climate governance', *Wiley Interdisciplinary Reviews: Climate Change*, **1**, 279–87.

Payne, R.A. and N. Samhat (2004), *Democratizing Global Politics. Discourse, Norms, International Regimes and Political Community*, New York: State University of New York Press.

Scharpf, F.W. (1999), *Governing in Europe. Effective and Democratic?*, Oxford, UK: Oxford University Press.

Scharpf, F.W. (2006), *Problem Solving Effectiveness and Democratic Accountability in the European Union*, Political Science Series, Vienna: Institute for Advanced Studies.

Schäferhoff, M., S. Campe and C. Kaan (2009), 'Transnational public–private partnerships in International Relations. Making sense of concepts, research frameworks and results', *International Studies Review*, **11**, 451–74.

Scholte, J.A. (2011), 'Towards greater legitimacy in global governance', *Review of International Political Economy*, **18**(1), 110–20.

Smith, G. (2003), *Deliberative Democracy and the Environment*, London: Routledge.

Streck, C. (2004), 'New partnerships in global environmental policy: the Clean Development Mechanism', *The Journal of Environment and Development*, **13**, 295–322.

Szulecki, K., P. Pattberg and F. Biermann (2011), 'Explaining variation in the effectiveness of transnational energy partnerships', *Governance: An International Journal of Policy, Administration, and Institutions*, **24**(3), 713–36.

United Nations (2010), Partnerships for sustainable development: Report of the Secretary General. E/CN.17/2010/13, Commission on Sustainable Development, Eighteenth Session, 3–15 May 2010, New York: Department of Economic and Social Affairs.

Utting, P. and A. Zammit (2009), 'United Nations–business partnerships: good intentions, contradictory agendas', *Journal of Business Ethics*, **90**(Supplement 1), 29–56.

9. Partnerships for sustainable development in the water sector: privatization, participation and legitimacy

Eleni Dellas

Public–private partnerships, along with private regulatory initiatives, market-based governance and similar mechanisms, have been presented as an opportunity to address the pressing problems of global environmental change (Benner, Reinicke and Witte 2004: 194–5). First, they are seen as an opportunity to increase the legitimacy of global environmental governance by involving more stakeholders in decision-making and implementation, thus increasing ownership and empowerment. Second, they are promoted as tools to effectively implement solutions, for example with respect to Agenda 21 and the Millennium Development Goals (United Nations 2002).

Public–private partnerships were encouraged by intergovernmental agreement at the WSSD in 2002. However, like other novel governance mechanisms in this field, partnerships for sustainable development prompt new questions regarding their ability to live up to these expectations: they have also been criticized as a second-best solution that governments and intergovernmental organizations encourage merely because they do not want to or cannot agree on binding agreements, an opportunity for companies to green- or blue-wash their image, and a tool that continues to exclude many marginalized groups rather than including them in the partnership process (on these points, see for example Hale and Mauzerall 2004; Bäckstrand 2006b; Biermann et al. 2007b). This highlights the need for inquiries into the effectiveness and legitimacy of partnerships.

One area where the discussion about whether or not partnerships are able to address such issues has been most intense, is the sector that prompted the greatest number of partnership initiations around the Johannesburg Summit: water. Partnerships involved with the provision of drinking water are framed as providing both challenges or opportunities for more effective and legitimate water governance.

Some of the key debates in the broader discussion on global water governance focus on whether private sector involvement and community participation in partnerships can help achieve water provision that is affordable and accessible to all, but also responsive to stakeholder needs (Hall and Lobina 2006; Bakker 2008). The drinking water partnerships initiated around the WSSD and registered with the United Nations Commission on Sustainable Development (UNCSD) in particular are at the core of another argument linking effective water provision to several other issues, highlighting that water 'is not only the most basic of needs but is also at the centre of sustainable development and essential for poverty eradication. . .Without progress on water, reaching other Millennium Development Goals will be difficult, if not impossible' (United Nations 2002: 96–7). In other words, partnerships are seen as influencing the input and output legitimacy of water governance. These concepts, proposed by Scharpf (1999), refer to both the acceptance and justification of governance processes (input legitimacy), and their perceived problem-solving effectiveness (output legitimacy).

The concept of input legitimacy rests on the idea that recognition of governance processes is affected by their 'fit' with accepted democratic norms (Beisheim and Dingwerth 2008). Thus, studies of input legitimacy examine issues such as the representation and participation of stakeholders, the exercise of democratic control through accountability and transparency, and/or discursive quality (Scharpf 1999; Risse 2004; Dingwerth 2007). Conversely, output legitimacy, or effectiveness, holds that authority can be justified on the basis of performance (Scharpf 1999; Bernstein 2005: 9). This latter dimension is occasionally emphasized as a source of acceptance for private and hybrid governance mechanisms, which face problems in replicating the input legitimacy mechanisms of the state (partnerships, for example, lack a clearly defined constituency to which they are democratically accountable) (Risse 2004). This chapter examines to what extent the drinking water partnerships initiated after the WSSD deliver on hopes of more legitimate and effective water access.

Overall, the potential of public–private partnerships to contribute to these goals has been evaluated critically not only in the case of water partnerships, but also in the broader literature on partnerships. Private sector involvement, for example, may lead to efficiency gains but is also often portrayed as lacking output legitimacy for potentially excluding those that cannot afford to pay for the service provided, and ignoring less profitable neighbourhoods and regions (Swyngedouw 2005a, b). Authors have also cautioned us to examine if, and under what conditions, private sector involvement can provide a legitimate and effective contribution to development (Kolk, van Tulder and Kostwinder 2008; Reed and Reed

2009). Furthermore, private sector involvement is often presented as lacking accountability (as private corporations are accountable to shareholders, rather than constituencies) and less representative and participatory (Bakker 2008). Considering these criticisms, the aim of this chapter is to examine the implications of private sector involvement in the UNCSD partnerships for their input and output legitimacy, especially as the water sector is characterized by many different models of private sector involvement, suggesting that UNCSD water partnerships may reflect a different approach to the 'traditional' examples of public–private partnerships in the water sector.

The chapter is structured as follows: in the next section, the relevant discussions on private sector involvement and issues such as stakeholder participation in the water sector are outlined. It identifies several aspects of input and output legitimacy that have received particular attention with respect to private sector involvement in the water governance. First, with respect to output legitimacy the focus will be on contributing to the drinking water issues identified as urgent in UN documents, in particular 'to halve, by 2015, the proportion of the population without sustainable access to safe drinking-water and sanitation' (Target 7.C, Millennium Development Goals). Secondly, with respect to input legitimacy, the key focus is on participation. After a short overview of the UNCSD water partnerships, information accessible through the database of the UNCSD and the GSPD is used to examine key arguments on input and output legitimacy of water partnerships. This is complemented by a more detailed examination of three partnerships, using evaluations, self-reports, project descriptions and other data available to provide insights on their activities.

DEBATES ON PRIVATIZATION AND PARTICIPATION IN THE WATER SECTOR

Private Sector Involvement in Water Governance

In recent years, a shift from binding regulation and governmental action to market-driven, private, voluntary or flexible initiatives addressing various issues in global environmental governance has often been pointed out (Cashore 2002; Benner, Reinicke and Witte 2004; Lederer 2011). In the context of water governance, 'the legitimation of such market mechanisms has. . .made private sector participation in the water supply and sanitation sector more acceptable' (Finger 2005: 276). However, it has been equally controversial, facing legitimacy crises and public rejection (Hall, Lobina and de la Motte 2005; Swyngedouw 2005a).

Of course, private sector involvement in water services can take many different forms, for example, depending on the division of ownership, operation and investment among private and public actors. Some examples are service contracts, leasing, build–operate–transfer, and complete privatization (Finger and Allouche 2002: 31; Prasad 2006). The lines are furthermore blurred by the existence of public water companies that are commercialized and examples of private sector involvement occurring without liberalization, de-regulation or commercialization (Bakker 2003: 331). The WSSD water partnerships are similarly diverse in the extent and type of private sector involvement. However, perhaps because of the explicit framing of WSSD partnerships as tools to mobilize stakeholder participation, their activities and governance processes are in some ways also different from other examples of private sector involvement. Debates on private sector involvement in water services are often framed as a conflict between the efficiency gains of treating water as an economic good, and ensuring water access for the poor (Bakker 2007; Casey, Kahn and Rivas 2006). Those favouring private sector involvement point out improvements in management, increased infrastructure investment, incentives for water conservation in addition to increased efficiency (Bakker 2007: 423; Casey, Kahn and Rivas 2006). Furthermore, profitable water pricing may not contradict equitable access, as 'higher water rates allow utilities to extend services to those currently not served and those currently forced to purchase water from vendors at very high prices' (Rogers, de Silva and Bhatia 2002: 2). These arguments thus focus on the output legitimacy side, highlighting that private sector involvement can overcome issues of state failure, water scarcity and lacking finances, and thus improve performance.

While increasing private sector involvement in the water sector was a response to challenges to the legitimacy of public water providers (Bakker 2003: 331), this trend is not uncontested. First, water provision tends to lack competition (duplicate water supply networks, for example, are not feasible) (Seppälä, Hukka and Katko 2001: 43), therefore the efficiency gains and lower prices that can make water affordable may not materialize. Thus, price increases may also be a consequence of private sector involvement, with repercussions for water access by marginalized groups (Houghton 2002: 796; Robbins 2003).

Second, a focus on commercial viability may encourage public–private partnerships to predominantly implement in stable, high-income urban areas, while less profitable poor or rural areas are avoided (Swyngedouw 2005a: 95; Hall and Lobina 2006: 5), leaving water provision there to NGOs or the state (Finger 2005: 296). This argument not only challenges the claim that private involvement can help combat water-related poverty, furthermore such cherry-picking of the most profitable areas could undermine the ability of state actors to establish financially sustainable water services (Finger 2005: 297).

Third, accountability to local affected communities may be limited. Business partners are accountable to their shareholders, while they are not perceived as democratically accountable to the communities where they implement (Hall and Lobina 2006: 3–6; Steffek 2010: 48). In this perspective the input legitimacy of water governance involving private actors is incomplete, as companies are only responsive to some, but not all stakeholders.

This line of argumentation consequently represents an anti-privatization stance, and hesitance about private sector involvement in water and sanitation services (Swyngedouw 2005b; Bakker 2007: 423). However, while experiences in several countries illustrate that private, commercially oriented water services can be difficult to reconcile with affordable access for all in both rural and urban, industrial and industrializing country settings (Casey, Kahn and Rivas 2006; Bakker 2007; Otero et al. 2011), other examples demonstrate that it can function well in similar settings (Galiani, Gertler and Schargrodsky 2002; Parker and Kirkpatrick 2005). Conversely, public water utilities have also encountered inefficiency, irresponsiveness to local demands, lack of transparency and a long-term deficiency in both revenue and investment (UNDP 2006). These observations suggest that private sector involvement is neither inherently less capable of servicing the poor, less accountable and less successful at extending overall water access (and thus less legitimate) than public water utilities; nor is it inevitably more efficient and effective than these. Thus, the possibilities and conditions for legitimate and effective private sector involvement in the water sector therefore need to be re-examined.

Stakeholder Participation in Water Governance

The issue of participation also warrants attention regarding its broader implications for legitimate water governance, in particular as partnerships have been presented as opportunities to mobilize community participation (United Nations 2002). In difference to private sector involvement, the broader discussion on public–private partnerships perceives involvement by NGOs and other civil society partners as particularly conducive to stakeholder participation (e.g. Bexell, Tallberg and Uhlin 2010). Conversely, business partners are considered to contribute less in terms of improving the democratic quality of partnerships, but by improving efficiency, providing expertise, knowledge, or funding (e.g. Hale and Mauzerall 2004; Kolk, van Tulder and Kostwinder 2008).

Adequate stakeholder participation has been identified as a source of legitimacy for public–private partnerships because they lack conventional mechanisms of legitimation such as election by democratic means (Benner, Reinicke and Witte 2004; Bäckstrand 2006a; Beisheim and Dingwerth 2008). Agenda 21 emphasizes the importance of including stakeholders representing different interests, sectors and areas, and in particular the "major groups".[1] In the context of the Johannesburg Summit, participation by different sectors and in particular local communities was linked to ownership, empowerment, improved implementation, and transparency, among other things; and furthermore emphasized specifically in relation to water governance (United Nations 2002: 97). Thus, it is no surprise that UNCSD partnerships consistently refer to participatory mechanisms in their project plans. Furthermore, this emphasis on partnerships as participation mechanisms makes a strong case for assessing to what extent they live up to these expectations.

However, the assumption that community participation enhances water governance has also been challenged. A key observation is that the partners themselves may not necessarily live up to the democratic credentials expected of partnerships (Bexell, Tallberg and Uhlin 2010). For example, decision-making is limited to a small group of actors (such as management and large shareholders), rather than involving a broader range of affected stakeholders (Bexell, Tallberg and Uhlin 2010). Bakker (2008) identifies several further points of concern. First, community participation does not necessarily make partnerships more accountable or equally representative of all interests (Bakker 2008: 245). This trend is well established among UNCSD partnerships, with several studies showing that UNCSD partnerships tend to lack participation by some stakeholder groups, in particular traditionally marginalized groups (Andonova and Levy 2003; Bäckstrand 2006b; Biermann et al. 2007a). Other discussions regarding legitimacy of global environmental governance highlight a different dimension of imbalanced participation: often there is a distinction between formal 'partners' and informal 'stakeholders', where the latter are involved less extensively (Stewart and Gray 2006; Schouten and Glasbergen 2011).

Second, community participation may come at the cost of efficiency and effectiveness (Bakker 2008: 245). This reflects an ongoing discussion regarding feedback and trade-offs between input and output legitimacy: while more participation, transparency and accountability may improve local acceptance and lead to better results, legitimacy mechanisms may also be costly and time-consuming (Biermann et al. 2007a; Bexell, Tallberg and Uhlin 2010; Beisheim and Dingwerth 2008).

Third,

> the term 'partnerships' may be used as a euphemism for devolving water supply to informal providers and leaving poor, peri-urban, and rural communities to

their own devices. . .or for using volunteer community labour or concessionary finance as a means of subsidising otherwise unprofitable private-sector water management (Houghton 2002: 796; Bakker 2008: 245–6).

Lastly, while well-implemented community participation measures can have numerous benefits, tackling problems regarding lacking financial sustainability, inequitable access, and unsustainable use requires more than introducing community participation measures (Bakker 2008: 246).

This discussion indicates several areas of contention regarding private sector involvement in water services. First, private sector involvement can be linked to output legitimacy: as the discussion above indicated, it is associated with water that is sold commercially, but not necessarily at a price that is affordable to all. This potentially limits the success of partnerships in contributing to the Millennium Development Goals of reducing poverty and the number of people without access to safe drinking water. The extent to which partnerships contribute to such targets may also be affected by business actors' interest in commercial viability, which may encourage avoidance of less profitable, poor areas.

Second, the discussion on participation in partnerships can be linked to issues of input legitimacy: even partnerships with significant local community participation may lack equal representation of interests; or community participation may be limited to contributions in labour, financing or materials rather than involvement in decision-making. Furthermore, private partners are argued to be accountable primarily to their shareholders, rather than stakeholders. The following sections will examine to what extent commercially oriented UNCSD water partnerships reflect the debates concerning private sector involvement and community participation. In particular, it will focus on demonstrating to what extent the concerns regarding the governance processes and problem-solving effectiveness apply to UNCSD water partnerships.

OVERVIEW OF UNCSD WATER PARTNERSHIPS

Information accessible through the UNCSD database[2] and the GSPD (see Chapter 1) provides useful information for a general overview of the 348 partnerships currently registered with the UNCSD. Among these 348 partnerships, 81 consider water as a primary theme (UNCSD Database 2010). Of these water partnerships, roughly one quarter are involved in the implementation of various types of drinking water infrastructure (such as rainwater harvesting, hand-pumps, desalination stations, and piped water schemes), while the rest are involved in activities such as capacity building or research, or focus on issues not directly related to drinking water, such as freshwater pollution. Business involvement is generally low (active in 35.4 per cent of water partnerships), while in contrast NGOs are involved in 60.6 per cent and national governments or state agencies are involved in every single UNCSD water partnership. This does not mean that examining the implications of private sector involvement in these partnerships is insignificant: on a global scale the majority of water provision still remains public, yet the occasionally serious backlash against private sector involvement indicates that it is still often controversial. Thus, the data in the GSPD and UNCSD databases can also be used to provide insights on the extent to which UNCSD drinking water partnerships are able to contribute to the input and output legitimacy of global water governance.

Selection of Cases

From these drinking water partnerships, three were selected for a more in-depth, qualitative examination of the claims outlined in the previous section regarding private sector involvement and stakeholder participation in the water sector. First, Agua Para Todos (Water for All) is a partnership working to implement improved and affordable water distribution systems in Cochabamba, Bolivia. Second, PROASNE (Projeto Água Subterrânea no Nordeste do Brasil/Northeastern Brazil Groundwater Project) is a partnership involved in transferring various water-related technologies (as diverse as airborne geophysical exploration for water, and solar desalination stations) to drought-prone regions in Northeastern Brazil (PROASNE 2005a). Third, WSUP (Water and Sanitation for the Urban Poor) is the largest of the three partnerships with respect to number of projects: it focuses on providing improved and affordable water and sanitation services to urban poor communities in several African and Asian countries. While all these partnerships engage in a variety of activities, the focus in this chapter is on their drinking water related projects.

These three partnerships stood out as superficially most similar to the private sector involvement models discussed in the broader literature on water governance. First, they included more business partners than other water infrastructure partnerships, in some cases including major global water companies (e.g. Thames Water was a founding partner of WSUP), while many other partnerships included only civil society organizations, NGOs and aid agencies. Second, the technologies implemented by these partnerships were different: while some partnerships implemented low-cost technologies such as rainwater harvesting that are less suitable for commodification, the partnerships examined here also (though not exclusively) implemented medium- or large-scale, costly technologies that cannot easily be maintained without expert advice and are often associated with long-term service provision, such as piped water. And, last, these partnerships may use their projects explicitly as commercial opportunities, or an opportunity for advertising a technology and attracting further customers in the region (e.g. PROASNE 2005a). A further consideration was that in difference to some other water partnerships, the information available on these cases was most substantial.

Throughout the discussion of findings in the following section, the partnership databases are used to provide some initial, quantitative insights on water partnerships. However, the focus is on available information on the three cases of Agua Para Todos, PROASNE and WSUP. Available documents such as reports, internal and external evaluations, project descriptions and other materials were used to provide more insights on their partnership activities.

PRIVATE SECTOR INVOLVEMENT IN UNCSD WATER PARTNERSHIPS

As outlined earlier, some observers see private sector involvement in the water sector as benefiting mainly business interests, while ultimately failing to improve water access, undermining development goals, and failing to address local concerns. The negative implications associated with private sector involvement will be examined in the context of UNCSD partnerships in the following section. First, as discussed above, private sector involvement is associated with water that is sold commercially, but not necessarily affordable to all. Second, public–private partnerships will tend to implement in areas where commercial viability is more likely, avoiding the more unprofitable, low-income areas or informal settlements. And, third, participation by local communities may be limited. Ultimately, a failure to address such issues would mean that the partnerships suffer both from a lack of output and input legitimacy. However, the UNCSD water partnerships seem to at least partially reconcile a market-oriented approach with the Johannesburg Summit messages of participation and meeting the Millennium Development Goal targets.

Quantitative Overview: Private Sector Involvement and Partnership Activities

Two indicators of potential for partnership performance are whether partnerships actually produce any output, and to what extent this output is relevant to their goals. While a positive outcome on these two indicators is

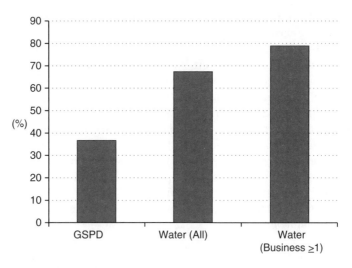

Figure 9.1   Percentage of partnerships producing output

not equivalent to high performance or output legitimacy, they are prerequisites for any partnership influence to occur at all.

Less than 40 per cent of all UNCSD partnerships actually produce any output at all. Water partnerships, however, are far more likely to produce output (67.4 per cent), while water partnerships with at least one business partner are even more likely to produce output (78.9 per cent) (Figure 9.1), and those water partnerships without private sector involvement are less likely to produce output (59.3 per cent). Additionally, water partnerships with at least one business partner are also more likely to engage in activities that fit their objectives (73.7 per cent) (Figure 9.2), compared to water partnerships overall (58.7 per cent), while more than half of the water partnerships with no private sector involvement engage in no activities fitting their objectives at all.

What explains this disparity in output and function–output fit? One possible reason might be that water partnerships with private sector involvement engage in activities where producing output is easier. Thus, one would expect that partnerships engaged in activities such as knowledge dissemination, information management, campaigning or lobbying are more successful at producing output and engaging in activities that fit their functions, than partnerships engaged in technology transfer, which is more complex and costly and may thus lead to lower output. For example, among water partnerships with the function of knowledge dissemination, a comparatively high 87.5 per cent produce output, and the function–output

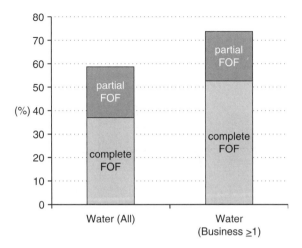

Figure 9.2   Percentage of partnerships with complete or partial function–output fit

fit is also high (88.5 per cent have at least a partial function–output fit). At the same time, both output and function–output fit is generally lower among water partnerships engaged in technology transfer projects such as drinking water infrastructure implementation. However, even among such lower output functions, water partnerships with private sector involvement are more likely to produce output and have a higher function–output fit than partnerships without.

Another possible reason for this disparity in output and function–output fit may be that water partnerships with at least one business partner have more resources, and therefore more means to produce output. While the data for availability of financial resources is incomplete for many partnerships and therefore not examined here, water partnerships with at least one business partner are more likely to have personal computers, office space, staff and other resources than the average water partnership (see Figure 9.3). Conversely, water partnerships with no private sector involvement are more likely to be lacking in all of these areas. In some cases, the division is particularly stark, with for example only water partnerships with private sector involvement having 'other resources'.[3]

Such clear trends in output, function–output fit and resource availability cannot be identified for any other partners in water partnerships, such as NGOs or OECD states, suggesting that the participation of these actors has no significant impact on the resource availability of water partnerships.

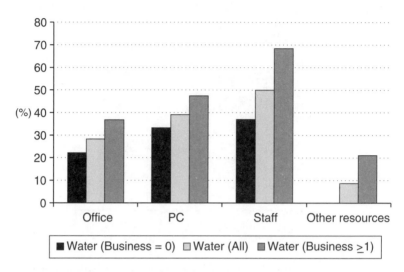

Figure 9.3   Percentage of partnerships with resources available

Furthermore, the observation that partnerships with private sector involvement tend to have more resources indicates a need to reconsider the ability of private partners in supporting the partnership process through resources. Thus, several studies have highlighted that the low overall private sector involvement in the UNCSD partnerships suggests that there is little new, additional and multi-sectoral funding and other resources channelled into these partnerships (Hale and Mauzerall 2004; Biermann et al. 2007a). At the same time, the findings above highlight that while private sector involvement may be low in these partnerships, business does mobilize resources more effectively. Nonetheless, from the figures above it is still not clear whether the funding provided by both business and other actors for partnerships is new and additional, or simply funding from existing projects that has been rededicated. However, the higher function–output fit among partnerships with private sector involvement suggests that they may also be using their resources more efficiently, channelling them towards performing their functions, rather than redundant activities.

What do the findings outlined in the previous paragraphs suggest for the output legitimacy of water partnerships with private sector involvement? While they do seem to have strong prerequisites for output legitimacy, it is important to note that high output and high function–output fit are not equivalent to making progress, meeting targets, or making a notable contribution to problem-solving. Similarly, while water partnerships with business involvement tend to have more resources available, this does not mean that these resources are always used to produce impacts where improvements in water access are needed most.

Output Legitimacy: Reconciling Profitability and Affordability?

The previous paragraphs have established that water partnerships with private sector involvement produce output and have resources. However, as indicated earlier, the literature on private sector involvement in the water sector suggests that the activities of water partnerships may not necessarily be suitable for addressing the problem of lacking water access for the poor, since this contradicts their focus on profitability.

A closer look at the three partnerships examined here shows how these tensions are (not) addressed on the ground. Thus, all three partnerships provide water as a service with a price, yet also sought measures to reduce the financial burden for the intended customers of the water services. The literature on private sector involvement in water services identifies ways to implement financially sustainable services that acknowledge social issues (Finger 2005: 284). Among the most commonly discussed approaches are bloc-tariff pricing systems: the first price level provides a basic water amount for free, while increasing prices for higher consumption levels cross-subsidize the initial, free level (Cleaver et al. 2005; Finger 2005). The UNCSD partnerships examined here use such mechanisms and more: they implement income-generating activities for the unemployed poor so they can afford the service, or identify ways to reduce the cost of infrastructure implementation, maintenance and service provision.

First, partnerships use innovative tariff structures for pro-poor water pricing. One example is Agua Para Todos. Its approach included identifying ways to modify service provision so that users could choose between a very low water fee and a slightly higher one: the lower fee was charged if water was collected from shared neighbourhood storage tanks, while the higher fee applied only for users who chose to receive household water connections (Heid 2006). WSUP, a partnership which works together with public or private local suppliers to help them provide improved, pro-poor water and sanitation access also considers using alternative tariff structures in its project sites, such as bloc tariffs (WSUP 2004, 2009). While WSUP partners do not expect a profit from their investments in project design and implementation, they do anticipate full cost recovery through the services they offer to each water and sanitation project (WSUP 2010).

Second, the partnerships may use income-generating activities to ensure that more consumers could afford their services. For instance, PROASNE funded community projects such as a tilapia fishery and sewing cooperative (PROASNE 2005a, b: 13). These activities seem to have been quite successful at generating a sustainable income source for the participating families: for example, while the basic fishing equipment was provided by the donors, the participants could afford to invest in additional equipment themselves after one season (PROASNE 2005b).

Third, partnerships identified measures to reduce the financial burden of the service, technology implementation and/or infrastructure they provide. For example, Agua Para Todos addressed such concerns by enabling users to lower the price of installation by laying the pipes themselves (Heid 2006). Local communities provided the remaining necessary funding themselves, and access to micro-credits was facilitated by the partnership, which included two non-profit microcredit foundations among its partners (Heid 2006; Agua Para Todos 2007). However, the partnership had to search for other solutions after recognizing that access to funding remained a problem, as communities interested in participation in the project could not always provide the required guarantees for obtaining a credit, or potential users could not provide proof of ownership for their houses (Agua Para Todos 2007).

In terms of output legitimacy, the fact that these partnerships specifically focus on addressing potential tensions between a commercial approach and affordability may contribute to their ability to extend water access to poor consumers. However, output legitimacy may also be undermined by the fact that these strategies rely on voluntary labour and providing different standards of service (e.g. shared connections vs. individual household connections), as this suggests that successfully extending water access to new areas may also involve providing lower quality service to the areas of implementation. Indeed, other studies have suggested that this may lead to a dichotomy of commercially oriented, efficient partnerships, and those that present '"community" water supply as an alternative to private-sector provision' (Bakker 2008: 236). This indicates that even if water partnerships with private sector involvement have more resources, produce more output and have a higher function–output fit, we must still take a closer look on what the implications of their activities are for target communities.

Output Legitimacy: Focusing on Commercially Viable Areas?

As noted above, high output or high function–output fit cannot simply be equated with effectiveness, although they may be considered prerequisites. A further indication of whether partnerships are contributing to problem-solving is where partnerships implement. Several possible patterns of partnership distribution can be expected. For example, if the activities of partnerships in the water sector contribute towards reaching the Millennium Development Goal target of halving the proportion of the population without sustainable access to safe drinking water and sanitation by 2015, then we could expect partnerships implementing water infrastructure to implement in the regions with the lowest levels of sustainable access – the regions with the greatest need. Alternatively, partnerships might be concentrated in regions where they are more likely to have an impact, for example, in regions with well-established markets, stable governments and good infrastructure.

Recent data shows that while all regions globally have seen increases in the number of households with improved water access, the quality of these improvements differs widely within and between regions. Thus, while in 'East Asia, Latin America and Caribbean and Northern Africa progress was exclusively the result of increases in piped connections on premises', in Sub-Saharan Africa and South Asia improvements were of lesser quality than in the other regions, primarily involving shared water access at a distance from the home rather than piped connections on premises (WHO/UNICEF 2010: 25). Additionally, there is a clear rural–urban disparity, such that the 'rural population without access to an improved drinking-water source is over five times greater than that in urban areas', which is again most evident in Sub-Saharan Africa, but to some extent also Asia and Latin America (WHO/UNICEF 2010: 19).

The GSPD dataset indicates no immediate trend regarding the regions where UNCSD water partnerships implement. Thus, water partnerships are almost equally likely to implement in African countries, OECD countries and non-OECD Asian countries (52.0 to 53.6 per cent of water partnerships implement in these regions), and notably less likely to implement in other regions, such as Latin America (26.1 per cent).[4] However, if we focus only on water partnerships that engage in technology transfer, a very clear trend emerges: only one third of technology transfer partnerships with private sector involvement implement in Africa (33.3 per cent), while two thirds implement in OECD countries (66.7 per cent). For water partnerships engaged in technology transfer without private sector involvement the numbers are almost reversed. For all technology transfer water partnerships, the likelihood of implementing in non-OECD Asia or Latin America is particularly low.

While the data does not indicate a clear trend of water partnerships focusing on regions with greater need, or where their activities are more likely to have an impact, the dichotomy between partnerships implementing drinking water infrastructure that do or do not have private sector involvement is clear. While UNCSD water partnerships working on implementing drinking water infrastructure with no private sector involvement implement where progress has been least, those with private sector involvement focus on regions where stable governments and well-established markets are more likely. A further pull factor for partnerships with private sector involvement might be that these areas are also more likely to be profitable. This observation provides further support for the argument that partnerships in the water sector tend to be differentiated into commercially oriented partnerships that implement in regions that are more profitable, and non-commercial partnerships that use volunteer work to implement projects in the poorest, and least profitable regions (Bakker 2008).

In addition to disparities in water access improvements between regions, such imbalances may also exist within regions. In particular, as was highlighted in the literature review, there is a concern that rural, isolated areas may not be benefiting from much attention by partnerships, in particular commercially oriented partnerships with private sector involvement. As indicated earlier, the general trend indeed suggests that rural areas are benefiting less from improved drinking water access, although improvements in urban areas can also not keep up with population growth there (WHO/UNICEF 2010: 19).

However, the GSPD dataset does not code partnerships according to whether they implement in rural or urban regions, so data to support or undermine this observation is difficult to obtain. Nonetheless, looking at the focus of implementation of the three partnerships of PROASNE, Agua Para Todos and WSUP more closely indicates that this observation has some validity, but at the same time may also be somewhat of an oversimplification. For example, PROASNE focused on rural, isolated areas in Brazil (PROASNE 2005a). However, the fact that PROASNE often implemented rather expensive technologies in these poor areas may be an indication why many of its drinking water technologies were not replicated beyond the trial implementation areas (Maurice and Dumont 2003).

The other two partnerships, Agua Para Todos and WSUP, deliberately focused on poor urban areas (WSUP 2004; Agua Para Todos 2007). Often, these partnerships try to address the particular problems of providing water services to urban poor areas, such as taking 'the poorest communities "over the hump" of infrastructure funding, after which they become self-supporting' (WSUP 2004: 1, 2009).

As these observations suggest, UNCSD water partnerships with private sector involvement may face difficulties in addressing concerns of poorer rural areas. Thus, neither Agua Para Todos nor WSUP focuses on rural areas, although they do claim to focus on poor urban areas with a clear lack of investment in water infrastructure, and while PROASNE does engage in efforts in isolated rural areas, it was not entirely successful in combining a focus on poor rural regions with commercial viability.

Thus, in terms of output legitimacy, while these partnerships may avoid the criticism that private sector involvement encourages partnerships to focus exclusively on wealthier urban areas for the sake of commercial viability, they also fail to successfully implement in poorer, isolated rural regions.

Input Legitimacy: Participation of Partners and Stakeholders?

Participation and representation are also often argued to be marginalized with private sector involvement in water services. As was outlined earlier, studies of UNCSD partnerships point to an overall imbalance of participation by different actors. Such a lack of diversity among the formal partners does not mean that local communities are not involved in water partnerships, they may, for example, still be consulted and involved in decision-making and implementation despite lacking formal partner status. However, it is also important to note that such participation is also not necessarily substantial: as one study of two other water partnerships indicated, 'there is a tacit and, at times, explicit distinction made between partners (who make decisions) and stakeholders (on whose behalf the decisions are made, but who are merely informed, and/or consulted)', while the latter need to be actively involved if sustainable solutions to their concerns are to be found (Stewart and Gray 2006: 375). This section will discuss in greater detail how participation efforts are implemented by some UNCSD water partnerships, and what potential they have with respect to input legitimacy.

The literature often identifies commercialization and private sector involvement as impeding community participation. However, the three partnerships Agua Para Todos, PROASNE and WSUP try to present themselves as distinct from 'traditional' public–private partnerships in the water sector, and particularly as more pro-poor and participatory than these. For example, WSUP highlights that in difference to the 'traditional' approach, it requires involvement and empowerment of poor stakeholders (WSUP 2005: 12–13). Furthermore, it suggests that its 'bottom-up' design 'builds local capacity and actively involves local communities from the start' (WSUP 2004: 1), in addition to emphasizing cooperation with local service providers. Nonetheless, the duration of the stakeholder consultation and phase has deliberately been reduced, as consultations may take more than a year and thus slow down the pace of implementation (Campe and Beisheim 2008: 23). This demonstrates the potential trade-offs between input and output legitimacy, where in this case a conscious choice was made to limit the room for participation and deliberation in favour of a quicker delivery of results.

In the formal governance structure of WSUP, representation and voting rights are restricted to the (currently seven) formal partners, which include businesses (e.g. Unilever), NGOs/non-profit (e.g. WaterAid) and academic institutions (Cranfield University) (WSUP 2010). These partners also have clearly established rules and obligations, specified in a contract and making them accountable to each other (Campe and Beisheim 2008). However, while the membership is mostly composed of large multinational companies and international NGOs, with the exception of one partner all of them are based in Europe. Patterns of limited participation by local actors and actors from southern countries in public–private partnerships have been identified as a broader trend that may undermine their democratic quality (Bexell, Tallberg and Uhlin 2010), and in the case of WSUP indicate that representatives from the areas of implementation are not involved as formal partners. Nonetheless, some stakeholders in the areas of implementation do have a more formalized agreement with the partnership: local private sector partners sign contracts with WSUP, documenting implementation commitments (WSUP 2005). However, although other stakeholders, such as local NGOs and community representatives, are recognized and consulted by the partnership, their involvement is not formalized, and they have no clear influence on decisions. Thus, WSUP is an example of the distinction between partners (in this case, large Western organizations) and stakeholders (which are further broken down into local private sector providers with a contract, and local civil society actors with no guaranteed involvement).

PROASNE also has a governance structure that is more participatory than what is associated with the 'traditional' public–private water partnership, although here again there is a distinction between formal partners and stakeholders. The main governing body of this partnership was a steering committee composed of lead partners in Canada and Brazil, as well as a technical and social coordinator from each of the Brazilian states that were involved (PROASNE 2005a). Thus, local actors from the country of implementation were strongly represented in the steering committee, providing 10 of its 12 members, and all states were equally represented (PROASNE 2005a). Despite this inclusiveness, one concern may be that with exception of the two lead partners in the project, the Geological Survey of Canada and the Geological Survey of Brazil, agreements with all other partners were informal, 'verbal and sealed with a handshake' (PROASNE 2005a: 59), a situation that potentially marginalizes the position of these informal partners within the partnership. As the partnership's self-evaluation indicates, this also led to problems in continuity whenever one of the informal partners experienced a change in management or senior staff (PROASNE 2005a: 59). At the same time, more formal agreements could have reduced the partnerships' flexibility, suggesting trade-offs between formal partner status and effectiveness. Furthermore, while the partnership also involved local communities by complementing its capacity building/technology transfer and implementation activities with a broad set of participatory socio-economic and educational activities at the request of its main donor, CIDA (PROASNE 2005a: 13), there is no indication of local community involvement via consultations and decision-making regarding the actual drinking water infrastructure being implemented. Rather, the participatory activities included education activities on issues such as water conservation and environmental protection, and consulting communities on what income-generating activities they were interested in (PROASNE 2005a, b).

Agua Para Todos also mentioned community participation as a key aim. In this case, each individual neighbourhood where a project is implemented establishes a local water committee representing its inhabitants, which then signed an agreement with the partnership specifying the terms and goals of implementation (Agua Para Todos 2007). These water committees were involved in some aspects of decision-making and implementation, such as regarding the type and cost of water access (household or shared) (Heid 2006: 3; Agua Para Todos 2007). Still, their influence on the partnership in other decisions is limited: although they have an umbrella organization that has informal negotiations with the partnership, not all committees are part of this organization (Heid 2006: 8), which is also not involved in the decision process.

As this discussion indicates, the partnerships examined here fall short on supporting participation, which is one aspect of input legitimacy. In particular, the involvement of local partners and stakeholders is inconsistent. What is evident in all three cases is that decision-making power rests almost exclusively with the formal partners of the partnership, while local service providers may have some influence, and local community participation is limited to informal consultations, contributions in labour or choosing between service options that are pre-defined by the partnership.

CONCLUSIONS

What are the implications of private sector involvement in UNCSD water partnerships for input and output legitimacy? The ability of the private sector to provide adequate participation mechanisms for sufficient responsiveness to stakeholder concerns in water services is often viewed sceptically. Furthermore, while the potential benefits of business involvement for improved output legitimacy (e.g. through increased efficiency) are often mentioned, the literature also highlights drawbacks, such as possible exclusion of marginalized or poor consumers.

As the quantitative overview of UNCSD water partnerships indicated, partnerships with private sector participation have particularly good pre-requisites for high performance and thus output legitimacy: they tend to have more resources available than other water partnerships, they produce more output, and also implement more effectively, as it is indicated by their higher function–output fit. However, this does not necessarily translate into a focus on project activities that actually benefit the groups and regions with the fewest improvements in water access. Indeed, the data from the GSPD indicated that especially among technology transfer partnerships in the water sector, it is likely that partnerships with private sector involvement will focus more strongly on OECD countries rather than regions where more improvements in water access are necessary, such as Sub-Saharan Africa.

Overall, the examination of output legitimacy indicated that water partnerships do face some key concerns surrounding private sector involvement, such as reconciling commercially viable water services with services that are affordable to all, and providing improved water access not only to the commercially most interesting (urban or high-income) areas. However, the three cases of Agua Para Todos, PROASNE and WSUP also indicate that to some extent there is room to address these issues. Thus, there is potential in innovative tariff structures, income-generating activities and cost-reducing measures to contribute to water services that are affordable to poorer communities while maintaining profitability.

However, these strategies also raise some concerns: relying on voluntary labour and providing services of lesser quality, to make water services affordable to poorer customers as well suggests that these partnerships may be implementing lower-quality services to still be able to access the thus far largely untapped market of urban poor water users. Countering such developments may necessitate the existence of adequate regulatory frameworks to ensure environmental responsibility, or the provision of subsidies for poorer consumers that cannot afford the service (Houghton 2002; Robbins 2003; Reed and Reed 2009). To what extent local authorities in the areas of implementation can provide such regulation or subsidies however remains an open question.

At the same time, these lower-quality services are not necessarily implemented for the partners' own commercial benefit, as only in the case of Agua Para Todos do the actual partners collect revenues for the service, while in the case of PROASNE and WSUP, the partners retreat from the area of implementation after the technology has been installed: as one partnership pointed out, partners work on the basis of cost recovery, yet partners do not 'own project infrastructure nor take responsibility for billing and collection', as these responsibilities are transferred to the local private sector (WSUP 2004: 4). However, marketing or market access is a motivation for the partnerships: WSUP highlighted 'full access to and use of the WSUP brand in marketing materials' as one of the benefits of membership (WSUP 2010: 3). And, in the case of PROASNE, the partnership documents highlight that the projects were seen as an opportunity for the business partners to advertise their technologies to the local authorities, as well as testing and improving them so that they 'may ultimately be brought back to Canada to benefit Canadians' (PROASNE 2005a: 64). As this indicates, these partnerships are not necessarily privatization mechanisms. However, as has also been suggested by other partnership studies, profitability, 'either directly or through reputational benefits' is an important driver for business involvement in partnerships (Kolk, van Tulder and Kostwinder 2008: 268).

However, irrespective of the profit gained from the activities discussed in this chapter, several issues remain open or ambiguous, warranting further analysis. On the one hand, the findings indicated that these public–private partnerships did not choose project sites based merely on their commercial viability. However, a more detailed examination of patterns of implementation and project site selection would be necessary to clearly identify what factors play a decisive role under which circumstances. And, on the other hand, while the partnerships examined here engage in attempts to make water services more affordable, barriers to access may not only be financial. For example, for some users, water quality, reliability, location and distance to shared water stands may also be important. Such issues would also need to be examined for a more complete picture of partnership output legitimacy.

Regarding input legitimacy, these partnerships reflect the emphasis placed on stakeholder involvement in the context of the Johannesburg Summit. In this sense, they appear to encourage more user participation than the literature generally expects of conventional public–private partnership types in the water sector. However, while this may encourage support from governments and donor agencies for the partnership activities (as was clearly the case with PROASNE, which included more community participation upon request from CIDA), it remains unclear how substantial representation and involvement in decision-making of local stakeholders are. Indeed, the analysis on these issues indicates that there is in all three cases a distinction between formal partners with decision-making power, local (business) partners with some influence and/ or contracts, and the local communities, which can express comments in consultations, and/or contribute voluntary labour. At the same time, the data examined in this chapter can only provide insights on certain facets of stakeholder participation, such as the existence of contracts or consultation sessions with partners and stakeholders. However, scholars have emphasized that rather than focusing only on issues such as who participates and in what ways, we must also examine the deliberative quality or if any stakeholders can dominate deliberations (Dingwerth 2007; Dryzek and Stevenson 2011). Thus, more empirical evidence (for example regarding the actual processes and outcomes of consultation sessions) would be needed to strengthen the observations on stakeholder participation in these partnerships.

The analysis also leads to some observations regarding tensions and trade-offs between input and output legitimacy. First, there may be trade-offs within partnerships, such as between the need for stakeholder consultations and speedy implementation, or flexible relations between partners with no contracts. Second, trade-offs between partnerships are also possible, with some focusing more on output, and others more on input dimensions: recent studies have observed that public–private partnerships with significant private sector involvement may be more output-focused, while partnerships with more NGO participation are more focused on providing input legitimacy (Kaan and Liese 2010). With respect to the water partnerships discussed in this chapter, the observation of partnerships with significant private sector involvement as output-oriented is supported by the fact that the three partnerships all implement sophisticated, medium to large-scale technologies that are suitable for reaching many users. However, fast and swift implementation of these technologies sometimes meant cutting back on aspects of input legitimacy (e.g. WSUP reducing consultation periods to focus more on implementation). This clearly contrasts with some of the UNCSD water partnerships with strong NGO participation but no business involvement (such as The Desert Rainwater Harvesting Initiative and The Global Rain Water Harvesting Collective), which implement infrastructure that is cheaper and small-scale (such as rainwater harvesting), and rely heavily on local communities to 'be responsible for designing, planning, implementing, assessing and maintaining their own projects and programmes' (DRHI 2010: 1).

NOTES

1. The nine major groups are women, children and youth, indigenous groups, NGOs, local authorities, workers and trade unions, business and industry, scientific and technological community, and farmers.
2. The UNCSD database registers UNCSD partnerships, as well some self-reported basic information on their membership, goals and targets.

3. These same trends are also clear in the general GSPD sample. Thus, while partnerships from all sectors are notably less likely than water partnerships alone to have any resources, among all partnerships those with business participation are still more likely to have resources than the partnership average (e.g. 40 per cent of partnerships with business participation have their own staff, while only 25.7 per cent of partnerships without business participation do). This is an interesting observation, also because 230 out of the 330 partnerships included in the GSPD do not have any business participation.
4. The numbers add up to more than 100 per cent because some partnerships implement projects in more than one continent/region.

REFERENCES

Agua Para Todos (2007), *Reporte 2007*, Cochabamba, Bolivia: Agua Tuya, available at: http://aguatuya.com (retrieval: 20.05.2011).

Andonova, L.B. and M.A. Levy (2003), 'Franchising global governance: making sense of the Johannesburg Type II Partnerships', in O.S. Stokke and O.B. Thommessen (eds), *Yearbook of International Co-operation on Environment and Development*, Oxford, UK: Earthscan, pp. 19–31.

Bäckstrand, K. (2006a), 'Democratizing global environmental governance? Stakeholder democracy after the World Summit on Sustainable Development', *European Journal of International Relations*, **12**(4), 467–98.

Bäckstrand, K. (2006b), 'Multi-stakeholder partnerships for sustainable development: rethinking legitimacy, accountability and effectiveness', *European Environment*, **16**(4), 290–306.

Bakker, K. (2003), 'Archipelagos and networks: urbanization and water privatization in the South', *The Geographical Journal*, **169**(4), 328–41.

Bakker, K. (2007), 'The "commons" versus the "commodity": alter-globalization, anti-privatization and the human right to water in the global South', *Antipode*, **39**(3), 430–55.

Bakker, K. (2008), 'The ambiguity of community: debating alternatives to private sector provision of urban water supply', in *Water Alternatives*, **1**(2), 236–52.

Beisheim, M. and K. Dingwerth (2008), 'Procedural legitimacy and private transnational governance. Are the good ones doing better?', *SFB-Governance Working Paper Series*, **14**, Berlin: DFG Research Center.

Benner, T., H.W. Reinicke and J.M. Witte (2004), 'Multisectoral networks in global governance: towards a pluralistic system of accountability', *Government and Opposition*, **39**(2), 191–210.

Bernstein, S. (2005), 'Legitimacy in global environmental governance', *Journal of International Law and International Relations*, **1**(1–2), 139–66.

Bexell, M., J. Tallberg and A. Uhlin (2010), 'Democracy in global governance: the promises and pitfalls of transnational actors', *Global Governance: A Review of Multilateralism and International Organizations*, **16**(1), 81–101.

Biermann, F., P. Pattberg, M.S. Chan and A. Mert (2007a), 'Multi-stakeholder partnerships for sustainable development: does the promise hold?' in P. Glasbergen, F. Biermann and A. P. J. Mol (eds), *Partnerships, Governance and Sustainable Development. Reflections on Theory and Practice*, Cheltenham, UK: Edward Elgar, pp 238–60.

Biermann, F., P. Pattberg, M.S. Chan and A. Mert (2007b), 'Partnerships for sustainable development. An appraisal framework', *Global Governance*

Working Paper, **31**, available at: http://www.glogov.org/images/doc/wp31.1.pdf (retrieval: 10.10.2008).

Campe, S. and M. Beisheim (2008), 'Transnational water public–private partnerships: explaining their success or failure', paper presented at the Annual Meeting of the American Political Science Association, Boston, USA, 28–31 August 2008.

Cashore, B. (2002), 'Legitimacy and the privatization of environmental governance: how non-state market-driven (NSMD) governance systems gain rulemaking authority', *Governance*, **15**(4), 503–29.

Casey, J.F., J.R. Kahn and A. Rivas (2006), 'Willingness to pay for improved water service in Manaus, Amazonas, Brazil', *Ecological Economics*, **58**(2), 365–72.

Cleaver, F., T. Franks, J. Boesten and A. Kiire (2005), *Water Governance and Poverty: What Works for the Poor?*, Bradford, UK: Bradford Centre for International Development.

Desert Rainwater Harvesting Initiative (DRHI) (2010), 'Desert Rainwater Harvesting', available at: http://www.yogaindailylife.org.au/Humanitarian-Care/Care-Projects/Desert-Rainwater-Havesting.html (retrieval: 12.02.2010).

Dingwerth, K. (2007), *The New Transnationalism: Transnational Governance and Democratic Legitimacy*, Houndsmills, UK: Palgrave.

Dryzek, J. and H. Stevenson (2011), 'Democracy and global earth system governance', *Ecological Economics*, **70**, 1865–74.

Finger, M. (2005), 'The New Water paradigm: the privatization of governance and the instrumentalization of the state', in D.L. Levy and P.J. Newell (eds), *The Business of Global Environmental Governance*, Boston, MA: MIT Press, pp. 275–304.

Finger, M. and J. Allouche (2002), *Water Privatisation: Transnational Corporations and the Re-regulation of the Water Industry*, London: Taylor & Francis.

Galiani, S., P. Gertler and E. Schargrodsky (2002), 'Water for life: the impact of the privatization of water services on child mortality', *Journal of Political Economy*, **113**(1), 83–120.

Hale, T.N. and D.L. Mauzerall (2004), 'Thinking globally and acting locally: can the Johannesburg partnerships coordinate action on sustainable development?', *The Journal of Environment and Development*, **13**(3), 220–39.

Hall, D. and E. Lobina (2006), *Pipe Dreams: The Failure of the Private Sector to Invest in Water Services in Developing Countries*, London: Public Services International Research Unit.

Hall, D., E. Lobina and R. de la Motte, (2005), 'Public resistance to privatisation in water and energy', *Development in Practice*, **15**(3–4), 286–301.

Heid, E. (2006), *Agua Para Todos: Water for All. Case Studies of the 2005 Seed Award Recipients*, Berlin: GPPi.

Houghton, G. (2002), 'Market making: internationalisation and global water markets', *Environment and Planning A*, **34**, 791–802.

Kaan, C. and A. Liese (2010), 'Public–private partnerships in global food governance: business engagement and legitimacy in the global fight against hunger and malnutrition', *Agriculture and Human Values*, **27**, 1–15.

Kolk, A., R. van Tulder and E. Kostwinder (2008), 'Business and partnerships for development', *European Management Journal*, **26**(4), 262–73.

Lederer, M. (2011), 'From CDM to REDD+: what do we know for setting up effective and legitimate carbon governance?', *Ecological Economics*, **70**, 1900–1907.

Maurice, Y. and R. Dumont (2003), *Groundwater Exploration and Management in Brazil*, Ontario: Geological Survey of Canada.

Otero, I., G. Kallis, R. Aguilar and V. Ruiz (2011), 'Water scarcity, social power and the production of an elite suburb: the political ecology of water in Matadepera, Catalonia', *Ecological Economics*, **70**(7), 1297–308.

Parker, D. and C. Kirkpatrick (2005), 'Privatization in developing countries: a review of the evidence and the policy lessons', *Journal of Development Studies*, **41**(4), 513–41.

Prasad, N. (2006), 'Privatisation results: private sector participation in water services after 15 years', *Development Policy Review*, **24**(6), 669–92.

PROASNE (2005a), 'Closing report', Geological survey of Canada/Serviço Geológico do Brasil.

PROASNE, (2005b), GSC [Geological Survey of Canada] saves lives through science and social work in Brazil', available at: http://proasne.net/The_Source_Aug_05.htm (retrieval: 09.02.2010).

Reed, A.M. and D. Reed (2009), 'Partnerships for development: four models of business involvement', *Journal of Business Ethics*, **90**, 3–37.

Risse, T. (2004), 'Transnational governance and legitimacy', paper presented at the Fifth Pan-European Conference on International Relations, available at: userpage.fu-berlin.de/~atasp/texte/tn_governance_benz.pdf (retrieval: 10.02.2010).

Robbins, P.T., (2003), 'Transnational corporations and the discourse of water privatization', *Journal of International Development*, **15**(8), 1073–82.

Rogers, P., R. de Silva and R. Bhatia (2002), 'Water is an economic good: how to use prices to promote equity, efficiency, and sustainability', *Water Policy*, **4**, 1–17.

Scharpf, F. (1999), *Governing in Europe. Effective and Democratic?*, Oxford, UK: Oxford University Press.

Schouten, G. and P. Glasbergen (2011), 'Creating legitimacy in global private governance. The case of the roundtable on sustainable palm oil', *Ecological Economics*, **70**, 1891–9.

Seppälä, O.T., J.J. Hukka and T.S. Katko (2001), 'Public–private partnerships in water and sewerage services: privatization for profit or improvement of service and performance?', *Public Works Management Policy*, **6**(1), 42–58.

Steffek, J. (2010), 'Public accountability and the public sphere of international governance', *Ethics and International Affairs*, **24**(1), 45–68.

Stewart, A. and T. Gray (2006), 'The authenticity of "type two" multistakeholder partnerships for water and sanitation in Africa: when is a stakeholder a partner?', *Environmental Politics*, **15**(3), 362–78.

Swyngedouw, E.A. (2005a), 'Dispossessing H$_2$O: the contested terrain of water privatization', *Capitalism Nature Socialism*, **16**(1), 81–98.

Swyngedouw, E.A. (2005b), 'Governance innovation and the citizen: the Janus face of governance-beyond-the-state', *Urban Studies*, **42**(11), 1991–2006.

United Nations (2002), *Report of the World Summit on Sustainable Development A/CONF.199/20*, New York, USA: United Nations Department of Economic and Social Affairs.

UNDP (2006), *Human Development Report 2006. Beyond Scarcity: Power, Poverty and the Global Water Crisis*, New York, USA: UNDP.

WHO/UNICEF (2010), *Progress on Sanitation and Drinking-Water: 2010 Update*, New York, USA: WHO and UNICEF.

WSUP (2004), *Working in Partnership to Progress Delivery of the UN Millennium Development Goals for Water and Sanitation*, London: WSUP.
WSUP (2005), *WSUP Alliance Business Plan*, London: WSUP.
WSUP (2009), *How Can Water and Sanitation Services to the Urban Poor be Scaled Up?* London: WSUP.
WSUP (2010), WSUP membership invitation, available at: www.wsup.com/intro/documents/WSUPMembershipInvitation26May10.doc (retrieval: 03.12.2010).

10. Assessing the legitimacy of technology transfer through partnerships for sustainable development in the water sector

Ayşem Mert and Eleni Dellas

Since the early 1980s, multi-stakeholder partnerships have been promoted as a solution to problems of urban environmental management, such as waste management and water provision. Business partners would sign a binding contract with the governmental or municipal partners, thus ensuring their accountability. More recently, partnerships have become mechanisms of transnational governance, often with limited public authority overseeing their activities (see Chapter 8). Since their promotion as 'type-2 outcomes' of the WSSD, public–private cooperation for sustainable development has been institutionalized based on this loosely defined concept. Their legitimacy and effectiveness have been debated extensively in the discipline of IR, focusing on questions such as whether partnerships are sufficiently participatory, inclusive, transparent, accountable and deliberate to be considered legitimate, and contribute sufficiently to problem-solving to be effective. In this chapter, we argue that it is necessary to complement these considerations with a focus on the content and rationale of partnership projects. We are particularly interested in whether the changes initiated in the recipient communities can be identified as legitimate and desirable as opposed to interventionist and impoverishing. This judgement will depend on whether the technology transfer process does or does not create new dependencies in recipient communities, increase inequalities or limits future consideration of alternatives to the proposed technology. From this point of view, technology transfer lies at the heart of several questions regarding the legitimacy of novel global governance arrangements.

In the run-up to the Johannesburg Summit, water was declared one of the five major issue areas (along with energy, health, agriculture and biodiversity) 'in which progress is possible with the resources and technologies at our disposal today' as UN Secretary-General Kofi Annan put it then (Rai 2002). To halve, by 2015, 'the proportion of the population without sustainable access to safe drinking water and sanitation' (UN 2010: 58) is also one of the environmental targets of the Millennium Development Goals. Considering this focus on water-related issues, it is not surprising that water partnerships (including the provision of drinking water, sanitation, urban infrastructure, irrigation capacity farming and purification of polluted water) make up the greatest fraction of partnerships registered with UNCSD. They introduce various technologies to the countries of implementation via technology transfer. Some of these technologies build on the existing 'indigenous' techniques and aim at increasing their efficiency, whereas others are cutting-edge techno-practices that claim to be more efficient in the exploration, extraction, distribution, irrigation, or cleaning of water.

The extent to which these technologies could be swiftly and widely implemented has been an important part of the (self-)assessment of partnerships. The focus often appears to be on the efficiency and urgency of drinking water problems, rather than the self-organizing skills and choices of communities. However, this preference may at times undermine the long-term sustainability of the projects.

The aim of this chapter is consequently to examine this dilemma, and to study in more detail how the overall package transferred by water partnerships (i.e. both the technological artefacts *and* the accompanying social measures) influence both the legitimacy of these technologies as well as the transfer process. The argument is structured as follows: first, two subsections provide an introduction to water governance under the United Nations (UN), and how partnerships and technology transfer processes may affect its legitimacy. Second, we introduce our framework of assessment of legitimacy of technologies. Lastly, a concluding section provides reflections on this framework and technology transfer by water partnerships. The empirical assessment is based on the GSPD (see Chapter 1).

WATER GOVERNANCE UNDER THE UN AND THE UNCSD WATER PARTNERSHIPS

Water scarcity has been linked to poverty in the UN sustainable development frameworks since the Rio Conference. Agenda 21 devotes its chapter 18 to the protection of the quality and supply of freshwater resources, suggesting that integrated management approaches to water would not only protect this critical 'resource', but also alleviate poverty, hunger, and famine. This understanding was reified in several UN reports in the following years, as well as by the UNCSD (WHO/UNICEF 2004; UNCSD 2006). To this end, Agenda 21 (UN 1992: 193) suggests, 'innovative technologies, including the improvement of indigenous technologies, are needed', but does not specify what kind of technologies are in line with its conceptualization of sustainability. This ambiguity raises several questions, such as whether innovation as such is identical to sustainability, whether indigenous techniques actually need to be improved by modern innovations, and whether these 'improvements' can alleviate poverty.

Six years after the Millennium Development Goals were set, *The 2nd UN World Water Development Report* argued that the problems regarding water have reached a point of crisis, and that this was 'largely a crisis of governance' (UN 2006: 1). The same report made two important points: firstly, there was little improvement in water-related services in Sub-Saharan Africa and least developed countries of Asia since 2002 (ibid: 53). Secondly, neither governments nor water multinationals [could] 'provide the type of technology that developing countries need' to reach the Millennium Development Goal target (ibid: 72). In short, place-specific technologies were not supplied. In terms of ODA, allocations for water and sanitation have been relatively static at about 15 per cent and 8 per cent of total aid, respectively; and assessments of water and sanitation plans suggest that aid flows are insufficient to reach the Millennium Development Goals (UN 2008: 10). The share of aid for the water sector as a percentage of all sector-allocable ODA has furthermore fallen sharply from the 2000-level (ibid: 11). Finally, the success of water projects was not evenly distributed within and among countries (Martens and Deibel 2008: 4–5).

This general failure of global water governance does not imply that partnerships as a mechanism of global water governance are an inevitable failure. Partnerships are neither directly, nor solely the responsible institutions for water governance. Nor can we assume that water governance has frustrated all stakeholders. The complex web of governance would not allow for such a simple causal relationship.

Water partnerships are perceived as more successful than partnerships in other areas. According to the GSPD, more water partnerships (68.8 per cent) generate output than partnerships on other issue areas (62.1 per cent). They are also on average more transparent than the overall sample: 83.3 per cent have a website on their activities and 37.5 per cent have monitoring mechanisms, while for the rest of the sample these ratios are 75.9 per cent and 22 per cent, respectively. In a series of expert interviews, respondents consistently evaluated water partnerships as more successful than others with regards to filling the implementation and regulation

Table 10.1   Comparison of expert evaluations on partnerships on water versus other issues

Expert Evaluation (Scale=1–5)	Water Ps		Other Ps	
	Mean	Std. Dev.	Mean	Std. Dev.
filling implementation deficit	3.70	0.83	3.36	0.98
filling regulation deficit	3.96	0.65	3.57	0.85
creating new financial resources	3.70	0.81	3.18	0.96
creating innovative solutions	3.66	0.69	3.51	0.88
focusing on an urgent issue	4.22	0.70	3.80	0.89
filling participation deficit	3.53	1.10	3.27	0.95

deficits, in their ability to create new financial resources, and as being innovative and addressing urgent issues (Table 10.1).

In sum, water partnerships are, by some measures, more successful than others while water governance in general is failing – according to UN sources. One reason for this discrepancy may be that the Millennium Development Goals focus on drinking water and sanitation access, while the UNCSD water partnerships focus on a far more diverse set of water-related issues. Furthermore, the discrepancy between achieving the Millennium Development Goal target and the success of water partnerships may be related to the global economic and political context in which water partnerships operate: since the 1990s, this background is characterized by commodification of drinking water and privatization of water and sanitation services in both the North (e.g. Germany and UK) and the South (e.g. Bolivia). In this context, water partnerships have been invoked mostly as privatization mechanisms (Finger and Allouche 2002; Hall and Lobina 2002; McDonald and Ruiters 2005). Thus, to some extent, the perceived success of partnerships may be related to being perceived as consistent with the current neo-liberal order. These developments received varying degrees of social acceptance, due to concerns regarding their affordability, accountability and equity (Hall and Lobina 2006). In short, while equity-related problems are an important dimension of legitimacy in water governance, there is no direct causal relationship between public and/or private involvement and social acceptability. Another reason for their positive image could be that water partnerships are more often geared towards transfer and implementation of technology than others (Table 10.2). However, the choice of technology and its implementation have implications on a number of issues, including equity in access, self-reliance in collection, storage and maintenance, and environmental impact. In order to write an account of these aspects, we focus on the

Table 10.2   *Technology transfer and technical implementation ratios of water and other partnerships*

	Technical/Technological function		Other functions		Total
	Frequency	%	Frequency	%	
Water Partnerships	17	35.4%	31	64.6%	48
Other Partnerships	77	27.3%	205	72.7%	282
Total	94	28.5%	236	71.5%	330

potential implications of the technology transferred, the features and the logical end results of its implementation for the societies they are transferred to. Partnerships also maintain some flexibility during technology transfer, to the extent that two very similar technologies have on occasion been implemented with very different outcomes. Analysing such interlinkages must focus not only on the implications of any given technology choice in terms of infrastructure costs, maintenance needs, operational models but also 'what the technology choice brings to the communities' in terms of autonomy, reversibility, flexibility, inclusiveness and freedom to self-organize.

TECHNOLOGY

Apart from the effectiveness narrative that justifies the partnerships regime in general, since Agenda 21, partnerships have been justified by an assumption of democratic legitimacy, presumably achieved through stakeholder participation (Bäckstrand 2006; Mert 2009; Chapter 8). In other words, the participatory ideal of the UN's development discourses also underlies partnerships. However, participation is not so clear-cut on the ground, and in partnerships the participatory principle is operative only to a very limited extent. In extreme forms, a false singularity of opinion is assumed among all stakeholders in a community, among all communities in a country of implementation or across countries of implementation: for example, if there is a local partner from the country of implementation, the partnership and its activities appear sufficiently democratic. Yet, this is not sufficient to ensure the general social acceptability of the technologies transferred. For example, any partner from the country of implementation can be regarded as a 'developing country stakeholder', even if this partner has no connection to the recipient communities. Moreover, in some partnerships there are fewer local partners than there are countries of implementation; hence a local partner in Angola presumably represents all developing countries or communities involved. Problems of representation and participation are beyond our scope; however, it is clear that the participation of any 'developing country stakeholder' in the partnership cannot be equated with a participatory technology transfer process. Transnational development aid in the form of technology transfer requires us to apply a different approach.

The UN governance platforms assert that innovation is causally linked to better water management and poverty alleviation, while simultaneously emphasizing participation. However, what is meant by participatory approaches in innovation and the causality between poverty and these other factors remain unspecified. The assumptions underlying such ambiguities reveal a certain technological determinism. Scholars of science and technology studies (STS) and critical theory reject this position: against the technologically deterministic idea that technology is the main cause of social change, they suggest that technological innovation is influenced by socio-political and cultural contexts.

On the other hand, studies that critically engage with legitimacy of technological innovation often rely on a democratic legitimacy model (e.g. democratic rationalization work of Feenberg 2004: 210–12; democratic politics of technology as suggested by Sclove 1995).

There are several problems regarding the application of these models on technology transfer. For one, these models assume that the more participatory the *innovation or selection processes* are, the more legitimate the resulting technology or product is. However, technology *transfer* operates differently: once the innovation process is completed and the resulting technology and/or products are installed, it is only possible to appropriate the technology to a very limited extent, not to redesign it from scratch. While studying the legitimacy of technologies introduced by water partnerships, this assumption must be juxtaposed with the democratic deficit in transnational governance (i.e. in the formation of partnerships): partnerships are vehicles through which a certain technological innovation is brought into societies that have neither produced them, nor deliberately choose them. As we noted, local partners might act as the vehicle of official justification and legitimation for a new technology and they often have a top-down approach: only a certain proportion or sector of the local communities, e.g. local companies, universities, chemical or agricultural producers are involved so as to receive trainings, therefore have some control over the technology. Such top-down installation of a technology does not easily fit the participatory and democratic picture painted by partnership projects.

These models are also difficult to universalize in the context of technology transfer, particularly when the democratic context and background of the countries of implementation differ, or the accountability and partici-pation of the transfer process cannot be guaranteed.

In general, technologies are products of political and cultural negotia-tions of a certain context. When introduced into an alien one they are more difficult to re-negotiate. This is in line with two concepts (1984) defined by Bijker and Pinch in their seminal article 'The social construction of facts and artefacts': *flexibility* and *closure*. While *interpretative flexibility* refers to the different interpretations of a technological artefact among different stakeholders, *design flexibility* refers to the multiple ways of constructing technologies. In time, flexibility diminishes as closure takes place. This can for instance be a rhetorical closure: when the problem is perceived as solved, the demands for alternative designs disappear; or the artefact in the focus of conflicts can be stabilized through the redefinition of the problem, or by prioritizing another problem it actually manages to solve. Closure is not a permanent state: new social demands can always reintroduce flexibility. When a technology is transferred, the receiving society, too, has choices: it can accept, reject, or appropriate it. It is however almost impossible to return to the design stage, for structural and psychological reasons: the new technology is often either presented as superior or as the only immediate and present solution for the problem. This does not mean that the interpretative flexibility completely disappears. However, in the development of a new technology interpretive flexibility would generate different problems related to the new technological artefact to be solved, different aspects or functions to be prioritized in the further development of the technology, before the artefact is stabilized. This does not happen in cases of technology transfer, as rhetorical closure had already taken place and the design is already stabilized. Often the infrastructure for redesign does not exist. However, the design of the technology and the extent of appropriation is not the only issue – similar technologies are often trans-ferred with differing accompanying 'packages', addressing issues such as education programmes, pricing, job creation, etc. These issues may also have implications for the way infrastructure is implemented, even if design closure has already taken place.

Thus, the difficulty of redesign and renegotiation turns the problem-solving and appropriation process (which may involve many adaptations, re-negotiations, consultations, etc.) into a success or failure factor for the technology, the partnership or even at times for the society in question. Therefore, the question of legitimacy requires a new framework that can assess the technologies in question in terms of their desirability, equita-bility and plasticity. In search of principles covering the problems listed above, we turned to the work of Ivan Illich, who suggested that the litmus test for the legitimacy of a technology would be its transfer to a so-called 'developing' country. Illich's writings on the perceptions of water (1985), technology and institutions (1973, 1974), as well as development and ecology (1973, 1978) have been influential on critical thinkers of technology, ecology and development. But most importantly, his critique of institutionalization allows us to scrutinize the aforementioned specificities of technology transfer undertaken by water partnerships.

FRAMEWORK OF ASSESSMENT FOR LEGITIMACY OF TECHNOLOGIES

In his institutional spectrum, Ivan Illich (1970: 52–64) studies different types of institutions extensively. Institutions on the left side of the spectrum are enabling: they support users without intervening in established habits and lifestyles. Conversely, on the right extreme of the spectrum are institutions considered constraining and manipulative, for example by creating new needs that previously did not exist. In this context, technologies too are institutions.

Central to Illich's thinking is the idea that many institutions and technologies reach a threshold, where they progress from supporting self-help and reuse, to negating their original usefulness. One example is transportation infrastructure (Illich 1973: 141–2), which Illich presents as having undergone two watersheds. At the first watershed, automobiles and improved roads facilitated mobility. At the second watershed, the magnifying scale and scope of the technology led to counterproductive results: the increasing focus on speed required smoother, expansive highways demanding ever-increasing sums of tax money. Modern highway infrastructure began to dominate lifestyles, which frustrated ways of living without cars and highways.

New technologies often enter lives through advertisement of a certain product or artefact: this necessarily includes the suggestion that there is a lack, a need to be fulfilled (Žižek 2001). Simultaneously, the institutionalization of each technology discourages competitors. The same is true for communities receiving a new technology: technology transfer includes advertisement campaigns, conducts of corporate social responsibility and public relations, trainings for users and supervisors, and infrastructural investment that creates path-dependency. The possibility for an autonomous citizenry to employ a certain technology and appropriate it (even partially) depends on the need, the nature of the technology, and the transfer process at once: autonomous appropriation is possible on condition that there is in fact a need for the technology; that the technology does not (1) manipulate the wishes of its users through creating a new set of needs (what Illich terms the creation of *'false public utilities'*), and (2) disable autonomous action against the cause of the perceived problem or obstruct subsistent or autonomous production of alternative solutions (the formation of *radical monopolies*). Otherwise, the appropriation of the technology by the community in question is impossible, because the technology 'subvert[s] the very purposes for which [it] had been engineered and financed originally, [resulting in] paradoxical counterproductivity – the systematic disabling of citizenry. A city built around wheels becomes inappropriate for feet' (Illich 1970: 28).

Counterproductivity is caused by the institutionalization of technologies and economic models based on *heteronomous* production that ignore use-values. These can be called *manipulative technologies*, as their ignorance of use-values lead to commodification and manipulation of the citizenry through the creation of newly designed needs (ibid: 29–32). This understanding of use-value relates to Marx's conceptualization of the term:

1. when the utility of a thing is not due to labour, that thing can possess use-value without having value (e.g. air, soil, etc.);
2. when labour is involved to directly satisfy desires and needs of the labourer, the product can be useful without being a commodity;
3. a commodity is only produced when the labourer not only produces use-values, but also *social* use-values (i.e. use-values for others);
4. lastly, only objects that are useful have value, irrespective of the time and labour dedicated to its production.

For Marx, someone who uses her own labour to satisfy her own needs is not producing a commodity, but only use-value. Illich focuses on the ability to satisfy one's own needs as the critical factor separating heteronomous production based on commodification, and autonomous production based on use-values: the latter has a quality of self-affirmation that professional production cannot satisfy. These two distinct production models can co-exist only to a limited extent, because:

> There are boundaries beyond which commodities cannot be multiplied without disabling their consumer for this self-affirmation in action. [. . .] Only up to a point can heteronomous production of commodities enhance and complement the autonomous production of the corresponding personal purpose. Beyond this point, the synergy between the two modes of production, i.e. self-guided and other-directed, paradoxically turns against the purpose for which both use-value and commodity were intended (Illich 1977 [2002]: 31–3).

This boundary is a result of the observation that commodities cannot completely replace use-values. From the viewpoint of the thing, which is the concern for Marx, a thing (or the labour involved in that thing) has no value unless it is an object of utility. From the viewpoint of the individual, which is Illich's concern, there is a certain value in the process of putting her labour into a product: 'Needs that are satisfied rather than merely fed must be determined to a significant degree by the pleasure that is derived from personal autonomous action' (ibid: 31). Beyond a certain point, commodities only serve the interests of the professional producer, while the consumer's satisfaction is limited by her non-involvement.

Similarly for communities, Illich recognizes the disabling potential of technologies that are suggested, transferred, implemented, produced and often maintained externally, by professional producers. When the community itself does not solve its unique problems, through its unique culture, its satisfaction is curbed. Another factor that limits heteronomous production is the environmental impact of mass production, including the mass production of services. But even if the environmental effect of the technology is minimal, its mass production would disable autonomous production:

> Medicine makes cultures unhealthy; education tends to obscure the environment; vehicles wedge highways between the points they ought to bridge. Each of these institutions, beyond a critical point of its growth, thus exercizes a radical monopoly [and] deprives the environment of those features that people need in a specific area to subsist outside the market-economy. [It] paralyzes autonomous action in favour of professional deliveries. [. . .] This radical monopoly would accompany high-speed traffic even if motors were powered by sunshine and vehicles spun of air. [. . .] At some point in every domain, the amount of goods delivered so degrade the environment for action that the synergy between use-values and commodities turns negative. Paradoxical counterproductivity sets in (ibid.).

Illich regards certain technologies (e.g. transportation by cars on highways, large-scale energy production or modern medical technologies) and institutions as the most extreme examples of manipulative institutions. Others, such as pavements, telephone lines, bicycles, small-scale and/or subsistence-level markets and industries he regards as *convivial.* Most technologies and institutions lie between these extremes. Moreover, as institutionalization of a concept, product, artefact or technology continues, it can move from left to right, from facilitating activity to organizing production. To highlight that technologies and institutions lie on a continuum and are mobile through time, Illich calls this an 'institutional spectrum.' The characteristics of the institutions that are at the right and left extremes of the institutional spectrum can be listed as follows: According to Illich (1970), manipulative institutions are characterized by:

1. Manipulation of clients:
    - The service is imposed; the client is subject to advertising, aggression, indoctrination, medication, imprisonment, electro-shock etc.;
    - The product results from complex and costly production processes, which include expenses from convincing consumers of their need of the product.
2. Counterproductivity:
    - They tend to develop effects contrary to their initial aims, as the scope of operations increases;
    - Many assume a therapeutic and compassionate image to mask this paradoxical effect.
3. Coercion:
    - The rules that govern them call for unwilling consumption or participation;
    - Membership is achieved by forced commitment or selective service.
4. Being 'addictive':
    - Socially: the prescription of increased treatment if smaller quantities do not yield the desired results;
    - Psychologically: clients' continuous need for more of the product.
5. Inviting compulsively repetitive use.
6. Creating radical monopolies:
    - Systematically frustrating alternative ways of achieving similar results.
7. Creating a demand for false public utilities:
    - Manipulating public taste such that a particular need is articulated into a demand that requires public services (which in turn boost their use).

Convivial institutions are characterized by:

1. Spontaneous use:
    - They do not require advertisements to induce their clients to use them;
    - They exist to be used rather than to produce something.
2. Being self-limiting:
    - The rules that govern them set limits to their use, with the purpose of avoiding abuses which would frustrate their general accessibility.
3. Amplifying opportunity:

- The service they provide is amplified opportunity within formally defined limits.
4. The client remains a free agent:
  - They tend to be networks, which facilitate client-initiated communication or cooperation;
  - They are often self-activated institutions.
5. Serving a purpose beyond their own repeated use:
  - They do not identify satisfaction with the mere act of consumption.

Our assessment framework based on Illich's critique of technology and his institutional spectrum is depicted in Table 10.3. Our assessment scale is based on a convivial–manipulative coordinate. On the left hand side of the table, the features of the convivial/autonomous institutions and technologies are listed, while on the right hand side we list the manipulative/ heteronomous characteristics. Each numbered line is a defining feature of such institutions (in bold script), followed by a list of indicators that might (individually or in combination) help us determine the extent to which manipulation, commodification, dependency, monopoly and coercion (and their convivial opposites) take place. Some of these features are interrelated, and appear repetitive, but as our assessment is not quantitative, we do not regard such overlaps as problematic.

ASSESSING LEGITIMACY OF WATER TECHNOLOGIES

UNCSD partnerships employ the UN discourse on water, highlighting the interlinkages between water problems and all other social, environmental and developmental issues. For example, the Global Rainwater Harvesting Collective relates its water access improvement aims not only to providing drinking water for the poor and isolated, but to enabling children to attend school instead of collecting water, to make communities less dependent, contribute to gender equity, reduce water-borne diseases and with all this contribute to poverty alleviation (Global Rainwater Harvesting Collective 2005). The Rainwater Partnership (2008) states that 'rainwater harvesting [is] an excellent, low cost and simple technique in combating *water related poverty*'. Similarly, the Desert Rainwater Harvesting Initiative (2009) states that it aims at 'alleviating poverty by providing a reliable water supply'. This apparent consensus that water access in general would have positive implications for poverty levels, equity between and within communities, and environmental sustainability, inherently affects the

Table 10.3   Framework for assessing manipulative and convivial technologies

Left (Convivial/Autonomous technologies)	Right (Manipulative/Heteronomous technologies)
1. Allows spontaneous use:	**1. Is manipulative:**
(a) Technology exists not as a service or a commercial product, but an opportunity to facilitate water access.	(a) Water provision involves complex and/ or costly processes, the financial costs of which are passed on to the users.
(b) Water provision and maintenance is without financial constraints.	(b) The technology and its maintenance are expensive.
(c) Initial infrastructure costs are low.	(c) Advertisements stimulate demand, suggesting the service is necessary or irreplaceable.
(d) Advertising is not involved as users need not be convinced of the value.	
2. Is self-limiting:	**2. Is counter-productive:**
(a) The inherent characteristics of the technology limit its *commercial* viability.	(a) The technology has side effects that may contradict the original intentions.
(b) The technology limits overconsumption of water.	(b) It is inserted, in the form of aid, assuming a compassionate image to mask its counterproductivity.
3. Leaves the client a free agent:	**3. Is coercive / exclusive or creates dependence:**
(a) Users have a right to the service, extent of usage is not defined by level of payment.	(a) Users must pay for the service, or face exclusion.
(b) Users and communities are involved in decisions regarding implementation and maintenance of the technology.	(b) Users have limited or no input in the design, implementation and maintenance of the technology.
(c) Users are essentially self-reliant, and responsible for use and repair of the technology.	(c) Maintenance of the new technology cannot be provided by the community itself and requires professionals.
4. Serves a purpose beyond its repeated use:	**4. Has monopolistic tendencies:**
(a) The aim of the service provider is not to expand the technology to other areas for the sake of market access.	(a) The aim of the service providers is to expand the technology to other areas in search of new markets.
(b) Communities retain other ways of accessing water.	(b) Customers have no option but to obtain the water-related service or product from one provider.
	5. Creates false public utilities:
	(a) The technology is propagated as a solution for the entire public, but is in reality only accessible to a certain (e.g. non-poor, non-rural) group. Public taste is manipulated in favour of this solution.

self-reporting process. As we depend on these self-descriptions and reporting in our analysis, we try to distance ourselves from this assumption. The assessment framework outlined above allows for a less partial study of the technologies in question, as it does not assume a relationship between access to water and reduced levels of poverty, inequality and environmental degradation. When evaluating projects and technologies, the self-reported positive statements are thus neutralized to a large extent.

Airborne Geophysical Exploration

The PROASNE partnership aims to develop a more dependable water supply in drought-prone northeast Brazil. For one of its numerous projects, it maps the subterranean conditions in pilot regions to identify suitable locations to drill through the rock, and build wells. The lead partners (Serviço Geológico do Brasil and the Geological Survey of Canada) assessed the technology to conduct this water exploration to be highly successful after the pilot studies (PROASNE 2004a). The outcomes were described by one partner as 'nothing less than spectacular' although their replicability was limited due to high exploration costs (Maurice and Dumont 2003: 2–3).

Airborne geophysical exploration is a highly complex and expensive procedure, and in the case of PROASNE, the companies involved in its promotion essentially had a monopoly on it. The advertisement opportunity seems to have been a key aim of the pilot projects: some of the actual and potential outcomes of the project that are highlighted are that 'Canadian companies win new contracts to carry out similar surveys elsewhere' and 'Canadian companies offer services worldwide based on a genuine test case' (PROASNE 2005). Even excluding the way the pilot projects were used, advertisement was a central part of the project in the form of education programmes. According to the partnership website, 'every project activity includes a technology transfer/capacity building component which involves training [. . .] provided through seminars, short courses, hand-on training in Brazil and in Canada, technical visits to Canada, joint project activities, long-term support of implanted technologies, etc.' (PROASNE 2004b). The PROASNE executive evaluation acknowledges that there were several shortcomings concerning these seminars and training programmes: the high cost of paying Canadian specialists to go to Brazil, severe language barriers, and the unfamiliarity of Canadian specialists with the local Brazilian context, made it difficult for them 'to address the problems directly without subjecting themselves to a lengthy learning process' (PROASNE 2005: 55–6). While the method appears successful in exploring water, it does not guarantee access to water. After a new source has been discovered using airborne exploration, wells must be drilled and water must be transported to settlements. Water thus becomes a complex product that is only accessible after a long chain of costly and complicated processes, for many of which the local communities become dependent on external support. As these observations indicate, airborne geophysical exploration has manipulative tendencies such as advertising, creating dependency, and monopolizing the ways in which water can be provided.

Solar Pumping and Desalinization Stations

The technology of solar pumping and desalinization is designed to pump highly saline groundwater for unelectrified communities using solar power, and then make it potable through reverse osmosis.[1] Special motors attached to solar panels provided the electricity for water pumps and desalinization by reverse osmosis. As the technologies are powered with solar energy, they seem especially suitable for small, unelectrified communities. The partnerships associated with these technologies are PROASNE and the Global Rainwater Harvesting Collective.

The PROASNE partnership also used these solar pumping and desalinization stations as advertising opportunities to gain access to new markets, taking the form of pilot studies which, among other things, aimed to create 'commercial opportunities for Canadian companies and consultants' (PROASNE 2005: 64). The high costs associated with the process can be prohibitive, and warrant a demonstration of the technologies' benefits via advertisement and education. Indeed, one report suggested that the cost of exploring water using the airborne exploration method and then installing the solar pumping and desalinization plants in suitable areas so that it can achieve a 'major impact' would amount to about USD 100 million (Maurice and Dumont 2003: 3).

These high costs of implementing the technologies are furthermore counterproductive because they not only severely limit its replication beyond pilot projects, but also the ability to make a substantial contribution to creating a more reliable water supply to northeastern Brazil. Additionally, the combined solar pumping and desalinization stations are so complex and difficult to reconstruct that monopolistic tendencies and dependence may arise because the technology cannot be built locally. Thus, in cases of problems, most spare parts need to be imported (PROASNE 2005).

Despite the manipulative characteristics suggested above, these technologies have been appropriated by the local communities to a large extent, once implementation has started. Although initially the technologies were costly and complex, particularly because the solar-powered motors had to be imported, in the case of PROASNE these engines were altered in such a way that they were compatible with a type of pump that is manufactured and available locally (PROASNE 2004c). In the case of the Global Rainwater Harvesting Collective, a solar-powered reverse osmosis desalination plant was installed in India, and all except for one part of the desalination plant could be obtained locally. This indicates not only that these technologies were adaptable to local needs and constraints, but also a conscious effort to lower the costs for the end-users. Maintenance and repair by the local community is also possible. Maintenance of the solar devices is very simple, and for the reverse osmosis device a local partner was to be trained in the case of PROASNE (Jensen 2001: 2). In the case of the Global Rainwater Harvesting Collective, a long development process for the solar-powered reverse osmosis technology led to the development of a desalination plant 'that could be managed, repaired and operated by the community themselves' (Global Rainwater Harvesting Collective 2009). Thus, it seems that concerning the usage of these technologies after the implementation stage, communities have become more self-reliant.

Rainwater or Rock Water Harvesting

Rainwater or rock water harvesting is a simple, low-cost technology, involving the construction of water collection and storage facilities made from easily available local materials. Variants of rainwater harvesting differ according to factors such as collection and storage sites (rooftops, pans/ponds, subsurface dams, soil water storage systems) (UNEP 2007: ix). Thus, different options may be suitable to different local characteristics and rainfall conditions. For example, some variants help improve the quality of water supplied (rooftop harvesting may prevent contamination of water where this has been a problem) or improve storage capacities in areas that experience extended dry periods alternating with excessive rainfall. In addition to being very low-cost and low-maintenance, another convivial characteristic of rainwater harvesting is that it is self-limiting and reduces dependence on groundwater. In the partnerships we have studied, such as Community Water Initiative (in Kenya and Sri Lanka), the Desert Rainwater Harvesting Initiative (India), Rainwater Partnership (Sub-Saharan Africa and Asia), and the Global Rainwater Harvesting Collective (India, Afghanistan and several African countries), the technology transfer often involved small initiation costs. These partnerships highlight not only rainwater harvesting benefits in areas where groundwater is scarce, contaminated or saline, and droughts are frequent, but also its environmental and financial sustainability (Community Water Initiative 2006; Desert Rainwater Harvesting Initiative 2009). However, rainwater harvesting may pose access constraints for some community members, depending on potential access disputes and the distance to communal storage tanks. Such issues are particularly relevant in the case of rainwater harvesting and hand pump technologies, which tend to be implemented with shared water access. According to recent data, most regions have seen a substantial increase in the number of individual household connections since 1990, however in two regions most improvements remain shared (WHO/UNICEF 2010: 25). In particular, 'in many African countries, one third of the improved drinking water sources that are not piped on premises need a collection time of more than 30 minutes' (ibid: 28), a situation which does little to reduce the water-collection burdens of women and children and allow them to earn an income or receive an education.

According to the criteria defined by our framework, rainwater harvesting has a number of convivial qualities. In addition to their self-limiting quality, communities are involved in decisions, implementation and maintenance of the technology. The development and implementation of the projects are heavily dependent on communities that will benefit from these technologies. Harvesting is usually free of significant financial constraints or advertisement, thus greatly contributing to spontaneous use. It is simple, replicable and reversible. It is an inherently self-limiting technology and enables communities to be as involved and self-reliant as possible: while it is not impossible to associate it with commercial use and service-based delivery, it is less profitable and less suitable for this than other technologies. Communities can collect water themselves and are able to maintain and repair without having to pay or rely on external support. This makes harvesting favourable in isolated areas where both the availability of finances and adequate technical support cannot be taken for granted. It does not unnecessarily complicate water access with machines that need to be repaired, maintained, and controlled. All in all, rainwater harvesting does not seem to have manipulative properties as defined in our framework.

Hand Pumps

Another low-cost technology, transferred especially to Africa and South-East Asia is the hand pump. Although there are numerous types of pump-based mechanisms (e.g. bush, rope, treadle and fuel-powered pumps), the analysis below is based on the India–Mali Mark II hand pump, used by the West African Water Initiative (WAWI), which has dug (or rehabilitated) more than 1500 wells and fitted with hand pumps in Ghana, Mali and Niger (WAWI Secretariat 2008: 13). Other types of pumps could be studied in a similar fashion, and would be likely to result in different levels of conviviality. In addition to WAWI, the Global Rainwater Harvesting Collective, Community Water Initiative and Total Water Programme also use pumps, often in combination with other technologies.

The particular choice of pump technology needs to fit the local setting (the groundwater levels, irregularities or limits of water supply etc.), which often means that any technology must be adapted to local conditions. But more importantly, the suitability of hand pumps is critically dependent on how it is implemented: for example, the cost for local communities associated with implementation and use might undermine its sustainability. Conversely, where water pumps are suitable to the context and financial capabilities, they may be a viable solution to improve long-term water access. Thus, depending on the approach taken by a partnership, the outcomes of a hand pump installation may be more or less convivial.

One manipulative characteristic is the continuous costs. In a survey, it was found that the high costs curbed the hand pump usage: while 62 per cent of villagers had at one point paid for access to the hand pumps, only 17 per cent continued to do so and 80 per cent of water was taken from other wells. Other reasons were unreliability and the time it consumed to pump water (Gleitsmann, Kroma and Steenhuis 2007). The partnership that installed these hand pumps expected villages to contribute the equivalent of 175 USD per installation, furthermore, in this case, households desiring access to the pump had to pay regular fees and contribute to maintenance costs, which the villagers considered burdensome (ibid: 147). In this sense, the commodification of water was coupled with the treatment of the community-members as customers, resulting in high and continuous fees, and their exclusion otherwise.

Despite these discouraging examples from one study, depending on the suitability of the hand pump technology and the way it is implemented, convivial tendencies are also possible. Hand pumps are particularly beneficial for the provision of access to safer water to isolated communities on a wide scale, without dependency on external products or sources. Hand pump variants are widespread technologies, they are easily available and inexpensive, and so is their maintenance. Most importantly, they can be applied in areas far away from urban electricity and water infrastructure networks, without forcing urban technologies on rural areas, or lifestyles of the rural or indigenous peoples. If implemented, taking these characteristics into account, hand pumps can be convivial technologies.

Piped Household Connections

In urban life, running water at your tap and shower is regarded as the most desirable form of water provision. The introduction or widespread use of this water technology was by no means obvious until the twentieth century. While its introduction to urban areas appears commonsensical to our modern day perceptions, it is also an indication of how dependent the modern citizen is on infrastructure. Hence, it is important to recognize that it may have manipulative outcomes for the affected communities, depending on the context of its application. For example, its desirability has been discussed in a study of the various attempts to connect the entire population of Jakarta to water pipes since colonial times: while universal service may seem like the most desirable option, the urban poor may nonetheless not wish to be 'connected' to hydraulic infrastructures which demand specific, constrained patterns of income, land tenure and water use which may be far less reconcilable with their volatile income and legal status than buying water from informal vendors (Kooy and Bakker 2006). While in the expansive megacities of the South the piped water supplied to richer areas is far cheaper than the water sold through vendors and other informal channels in slums, one problem that has been observed is that the installation of regular pipes drives rent and land values up, and the original inhabitants out of an area (also because these technologies require legalization and land registry) (Kooy and Bakker 2006). All these points reinforce that this technology option is not automatically the most desirable, and it is important that all such possible implications are considered and addressed. Partnerships that implement this type of infrastructure are Agua Para Todos in Bolivia and WSUP in Kenya, Bangladesh, Ghana and Mali.

Water pipe installation can be costly. What is often promoted as a universal solution may become accessible to only a fraction where the costs of installation are high, or where the constraints faced by users after installation are insupportable. However, partnerships implementing this technology have attempted to find ways to limit the costs for the eventual users. Among the most common approaches are identifying innovative tariff structures, income-generating programmes to help users afford the service, and offsetting the cost of installation by contributing manual labour. For example, Agua Para Todos (2008) gives customers the choice of financial contributions or mixed financial and labour contributions: users can offset part of the cost by digging trenches and laying pipes themselves. Concerning pricing structures for the water consumed that might enable access for the very poor, one recommended solution are bloc tariff pricing structures where the first bloc is provided for free (Cleaver et al. 2005: 18), and the progressively higher prices paid for higher blocs cross-subsidize the first level. WSUP is one partnership that relied on such tariff structures to make minimum water levels accessible to the poorest community members as well (WSUP 2008). Compared to flat-rate water prices, bloc tariffs have the added benefit of encouraging water conservation. Nonetheless, piped household connections are also a rather complex technology that creates dependence of users on external actors for maintenance and provision.

There seems to be a readiness among partnerships providing piped water supplies to adapt to the often informal or even illegal situation of the inhabitants where they implement. Communities are involved in decisions regarding the final design in ways that enable them to reduce costs and allow for a communal water supply that is more easily reconcilable with the needs of the communities. For example, in the case of Agua Para Todos, communities could choose to have the piped water delivered to a community storage tank rather than having individual household connections, thus also lowering the price of the water and giving the community members a choice concerning the balance between type of access and costs implied (Heid 2005). Indeed, local involvement also seems to be a way for these partnerships to reduce reliance on external actors. This is best illustrated by the WSUP partnership, which indicates that the international companies and organizations involved in the project implementation will retreat once the projects are fully established and sustainable, handing all maintenance and billing responsibilities over to the local private sector (WSUP 2004, 2009).

A manipulative characteristic of many technology transfer projects is the inclusion of 'education' programmes. In the case of WSUP, education programmes are also part of the partnership's implementation plan, which may be a disguised tool for advertisement and business expansion. It seems that these educational activities were mostly intended to increase awareness about behavioural changes that will reduce infection with diseases like diarrhoea (WSUP 2008). However, full details on these activities are not available. Nonetheless, the possible manipulative characteristics are highlighted by other partnerships where WSUP partners such as Unilever also engage in 'health education' (WSUP 2007). Thus, a report by Unilever on another rural hygiene education partnership (Swasthya Chetna, translated 'Health Awakening') provides insights:

> to grow in India in the twenty-first century will require extending the usage of soap to the 600 million Indians living in rural areas. For this to have any chance of success means that we will have to educate these people at the 'bottom of the pyramid' on why soap is important for personal hygiene (Neath 2006: 3).

Clearly, a secondary intention of these education programmes is for the company to extend its market access beyond the limited urban population. While the promotion of hygiene products can be easily coupled with running water, this makes the specific programme and not the technology itself manipulative. Piped connections often have convivial characteristics, suiting the lifestyles of the local population and reducing exclusion due to excessive pricing.

Sodium Hypochlorite Disinfection

While they are not directly related to water provision, water disinfection technologies also have implications for accessibility of drinking water. Partnerships promoting such measures are the Community Water Initiative (in Sri Lanka) and Safe Water System (in Africa, Asia, Central and South America). Sodium hypochlorite is the most widely used water disinfection agent, providing point-of-use disinfection of potentially contaminated water. In these partnerships, it is coupled with a suitable carrying and storage device, and 'behaviour change techniques' aimed at demonstrating the value of disinfecting water (Safe Water System 2008). Disinfection is needed when there is no water infrastructure and communities rely on potentially contaminated water from ponds and wells, or where not everyone can afford access to the existing infrastructure.

While Safe Water System was only initiated in 2002, several of its members, including the CDC and Procter and Gamble, have been involved in the development of disinfection products and in a number of partnerships intended to promote them. Procter and Gamble has been developing portable products to make existing water sources safe for use since the cholera outbreaks in the early 1990s, but the products had difficulties in becoming accepted by the communities they were intended for: attempts at using a filter were unpopular because it clogged fast, and sales of its first soluble disinfectant, 'PUR', remained low (despite proven record of reducing potential waterborne diseases and low prices) due to the taste and colour of the treated water (Hanson 2007). Later, 'PUR' was reintroduced through several partnerships 'to test three marketing strategies: social marketing, commercial marketing and disaster and humanitarian relief networks', and eventually succeeded at selling the product to non-profit organizations for humanitarian relief purposes: it seems that the partnership helped make this product commercially viable (ibid.).

Water disinfection products are also associated with much advertisement (often in the form of behaviour change or hygiene education) and advertisement-related costs. Indeed, if the partnerships to promote 'PUR' are any indication, it seems that SWS's 'behaviour change strategies' might be considered a successful marketing strategy. The advertisement efforts of Procter and Gamble in regard to making 'PUR' commercially viable included employee campaigns (to buy 'PUR' as donation) and introduction of the product to the NGOs working on disaster relief. Hence, it is difficult to argue that the advertisement campaign was to create a certain need that would manipulate the users, but rather the buyers. On the other hand, Procter and Gamble's strategy was not to limit the use of 'PUR' to such emergencies, but to make it abundant and accepted such that it would become a product of convenience in areas with water scarcity. It is in this sense that sodium hypochlorite disinfection approximates a manipulative technology. Despite the relatively low costs of the product, at least one study found that in Malawi the cost associated was considered prohibitive (Stockman et al. 2007: 1077).

A convivial characteristic that may be associated with water disinfection is that such products are not associated with their own overuse or increased use of water; they simply make existing sources of water safer for use and consumption under extreme circumstances, particularly in disaster hit areas. Despite its simple application for the end-user, the users have no influence on the chemical design of the product, and it is universally applied instead of being customized for each particular disaster zone.

CONCLUSIONS

Assessing the legitimacy of technology transfer by UNCSD water partnerships by the new framework implies three sets of conclusions: about the framework itself, about the technology transfer process, and about partnerships in relation to these technologies.

Convivial technologies run the risk of appearing less appealing than technologies that tend towards manipulation, such as piped water. This is mainly because they are small-scale projects which cannot be replicated universally, and more importantly, since they frustrate the image of bridging inequality that development aid often suggests. Nonetheless, when the results of our assessment with the new framework are checked against the existing literature we see that at least two studies supported the framework's assumption that convivial technologies have higher social acceptability (Gleitsmann, Kroma and Steenhuis 2007; Heid 2005). Recipient communities prefer accessible, flexible, and free- or low-cost sources of water, even if access is less convenient over resources that are costly or that require frequent repairs by professionals.

The choices of the communities appear to be influenced by a complicated web of factors rather than the price. In this sense, the assessment framework proved useful in enriching the dimensions on which poor communities and users make decisions. Agua Para Todos, for instance, demonstrates that the price factor is one among many: the local communities supplied with the pipes preferred to have the water in a communal tank from where they would purchase it individually, according to their needs and abilities. The price difference might be one factor here, embedded in a host of other social factors, such as fluctuating incomes or reliance on communal availability of water. It proves to be a research bias to assume that the social acceptance of the technology by poor communities is solely determined by the price of the water provided (possibly due to easy access to price information).

On the other hand, the fact that the less appealing technologies tend to be more convivial also masks another issue that needs to be highlighted: while partnerships such as Agua Para Todos succeeded in extending water access to more users by lowering costs, this involved compromising house-hold connections. What this glosses over is that in the same urban area of implementation, official water utilities provide subsidized household water access to richer neighbourhoods, while leaving the poorer, less profitable neighbourhoods to be helped by partnerships and NGOs. Thus, 'the crea-tion of parallel networks entrenches the fragmentation of the water supply system, creating two tiers of service with vastly unequal levels of state support [. . .] in celebrating community resourcefulness, we risk condon-ing both government inaction and corporate misconduct' (Bakker 2008: 239). Perhaps the lack in legitimacy of technology transfer by some of the partnerships examined here is still rather insignificant compared to the failure of the responsible official public water utility or private concession to provide long-term sustainable water access in these poor areas.

Other than these specific observations, the framework appears useful in suggesting the legitimacy (in terms of social acceptability and enabling of autonomous citizenry) of the technologies transferred. While including the economic dimension (without reducing it to prices), it scrutinizes the effects of technologies to the economic organization of communities systemati-cally. The indicators point to the potential systematic effects of a technol-ogy, rather than focusing on the effectiveness logic that is omnipresent in the development aid narratives of the UN. In this sense, the framework discredits the win–win argument that is at the core of technology trans-fer through partnerships. On the other hand, the framework gives mixed results when a technology has various applications and implementation varies, such as hand or solar pumps and desalinization stations. In short, the framework suggests that some technologies (regardless of their appli-cation) are manipulative due to complex and expensive production and professional use and maintenance procedures, while others with mixed characteristics remain contingent on the application by the partnership.

The analysis reveals more variance among technologies that tend towards the manipulative side of the spectrum than the convivial end.[2] What does this tell us about the different technologies? It is not that those on the convivial end are without faults, as we identified flaws not related to the framework with technologies such as rainwater harvesting. However, considering their impact on the societies involved and provision of access for the poorest sections, convivial technologies seem to fare better than manipulative ones. Technologies such as rainwater harvesting are essentially tools for spontaneous use, the users of which define how they are used, and communities remain self-reliant in their water governance. These technologies are not associated with a strong potential for commercialization or service provision. Technologies where convivial characteristics prevail most clearly are rock and rainwater harvesting. The other technologies assessed here (piped water, hand pumps and solar desalination) have both convivial and manipulative attributes, mostly because the outcome depends upon the way the project is implemented. The partnerships examined in this chapter demonstrated that there is at least some potential for adaptation of the technology so that spontaneous use and self-reliance are likely (e.g. communities can take care of maintenance).

Furthermore, we do not suggest that piped water, for instance, is in every instance less desirable than rainwater harvesting. In areas where absolute poverty is rare, access to and payment for tap water is possible for nearly everyone. Neither is it intended to discredit the work of partnerships that transfer technologies on the manipulative end of the spectrum, piped water or solar pumps or even desalinization projects appear to have been appropriated by some of the communities and even constructed locally.

The assessment framework assumes that heteronomous technologies provide services that are often not absolutely necessary, and as a result have to resort to manipulative actions such as advertisement to entice communities to invest in them, thus creating false public utilities. This is most obviously exemplified in airborne geophysical exploration and in the non-emergency use of 'PUR'. The costs associated with the promotion of these technologies limit access, not only making the technology an exclusion mechanism, but also indicating its counterproductivity as the aim appears to be (the universal) provision of water in the first place. For such technologies, partnerships offer an opportune platform: even when their effects are contrary to their initial aims, these technologies can, through partnerships, assume a therapeutic and compassionate image to mask this paradoxical effect, which according to Illich is another feature of counterproductivity. The separation of end-users and buyers (donors) in the case of 'PUR' was an effective strategy for Procter and Gamble in this regard, while other examples include the use of pilot projects as advertisement by PROASNE and education strategies in general.

Moreover, the technology transfer is assumed to be identical to

Table 10.4   Overview of technology characteristics

	Convivial characteristics	Manipulative characteristics
Airborne geophysical exploration		• pilot projects serve as an advertisement opportunity • the technology is costly and complex, additionally further investments (into drilling etc.) are needed before water is obtained • monopolistic tendencies
Solar pumping & desalinization	• adaptation to communities needs in price and construction is possible, users thus could remain free agents • self-reliance may be possible where all parts necessary to construct/repair the technology are locally available	• pilot projects serve as an advertisement opportunity • the technology is costly and complex • dependence continues where not all parts necessary to maintain the technology are easily available
Rainwater harvesting	• spontaneous use: no advertisement or notable financial constraints are involved in the projects • self-limiting: its inherent characteristics (no service or commodity) make commercial exploitation less straightforward and overuse unlikely • self-reliance: low-maintenance, easily replicable, community-based	
Hand pumps	• may be a tool for spontaneous use due to low costs, easy maintenance and adaptation to local conditions and that it can facilitate water access in remote areas	• where it is cost-associated, the financial burden falls on users • dependence: where the design is not adapted to local requirements, hand pump breakdowns are frequent. Repair is difficult and maintenance requires outside help

Table 10.4   (continued)

	Convivial characteristics	Manipulative characteristics
Piped water	• there is room for adaptation of the technology to local needs and requirements	• costly process: water access involves payment for water services, and potentially payment for infrastructure installation
Water disinfection		• advertisement and education to convince of necessity, masked as 'behaviour change techniques'
		• monopolistic characteristics, as only one company produces the product
		• dependence: users must buy new disinfection product regularly

'having water to drink' which has implications for the implementation deficit in water governance. For example, in one case it was suggested that the key aim in the NGO head offices seemed to be meeting the WHO water quality standards with their technology choices, but they failed to adapt and implement it in such a way that the amount supplied could sustain an entire village (Gleitsmann et al. 2007). The consequence in this case was that villagers continued to make use of more abundant water sources of lower quality. Other than the quality versus quantity dimension, even when the number of people that gain access to water may increase as a result of these projects, their ability to initiate solutions to problems that they define themselves may simultaneously be curbed. The dependence of the communities on some partnerships concerning all design and implementation-related issues is an indication of this.

Another role that partnerships assume in the process of technology transfer is more subtle, but equally important: they become a process through which flexibility reappears. In this sense partnerships may end the closure and the consensus over the technology in question (that took place in the society of origin), and re-introduce interpretive and even design flexibility. Even some of the technologies with some manipulative characteristics (such as piped water or solar pumps or even desalinization projects) have been appropriated by the receiving communities and made locally constructible during the implementation process. The extent to which this is due to partnership organization or the technology in question would be an appropriate next step in the development of our assessment framework.

The promotion of a manipulative technology by a certain sector of the receiving community (or sometimes by external NGOs or governments) implies two things: first, it means that diverging interests have not been reconciled in the partnership process, although it looks participatory. This can be termed *the paradox of selective participation* in partnerships, resulting from the assumption of democratic legitimacy based on stakeholder representation. Second, it indicates that preferences for a specific technology are often 'hard-wired' into development politics even where more suitable options would be possible and available (Lovell 2000, in Moriarty et al. 2004: 34). In this sense, partnering as a governance arrangement is transferred into the logic of the communities that are receiving development aid. As a business representative at UNCSD suggested: 'Everybody is leveraging the others. [. . .] What is your alternative? Your alternative is non-partnering, which, you know. . .doesn't sell well. . .'[3]

Although this does not directly denote disempowerment of the communities in question, it certainly implies that partnerships become a part of the package that is transferred, which not only includes the transferred technologies but also the political and social arrangements that they are embedded in. Hence, inefficiencies and failures in partnerships can as well be interpreted as the resistance of the poor communities to the imported logic of governance through partnerships, technology transfer and the win–win logic.

NOTES

1. In the case of PROASNE, pumping and desalinization technologies are employed simultaneously and powered by the same energy source. This is why the two technologies are discussed together here.
2. For a table summarizing manipulative and convivial implications of technologies, see Table 10.4.
3. Personal communication with business representative to the CSD, New York 2008.

REFERENCES

Agua Para Todos (2008), 'Agua Para Todos', available at: http://www.aguatuya. com/html/water_for_all.html (retrieval: 14.09.2010).

Bäckstrand, K. (2006), 'Democratizing global environmental governance? Stakeholder democracy after the World Summit on Sustainable Development', *European Journal of International Relations*, **12**(4), 467–98.

Bakker, K. (2008), 'The ambiguity of community: debating alternatives to private sector provision of urban water supply', *Water Alternatives*, **1**(2), 236–52.

Bijker, W.E. and T.J. Pinch (1984), 'The social construction of facts and artefacts: or how the sociology of science and the sociology of technology might benefit each other', *Social Studies of Science*, **14**, 399–441.

Cleaver, F., T. Franks, J. Boesten and A. Kiire (2005), *Water Governance and Poverty: What Works for the Poor?*, Bradford, UK: Bradford Centre for International Development.

Community Water Initiative (2006), 'Community Water Initiative Project portfolio overview', available at: http://www.energyandenvironment.undp.org/undp/indexAction.cfm?module=Library&action=GetFile&DocumentAttachmen tID=1796 (retrieval: 05.12.2009).

Desert Rainwater Harvesting Initiative (2009), 'Desert Rainwater Harvesting', available at: http://www.yogaindailylife.org.au/Humanitarian-Care/Care-Projects/Desert-Rainwater-Havesting.html (retrieval: 12.02.2010).

Feenberg, A. (2004), 'Democratic rationalization' in D.M. Kaplan (ed), *Readings in the Philosophy of Technology*, Oxford, UK: Rowman and Littlefield, pp. 209–25.

Finger, M. and J. Allouche (2002), *Water Privatisation: Trans-national Corporations and the Re-regulation of the Water Industry*, London: Taylor and Francis.

Gleitsmann, B.A., M.M. Kroma and T. Steenhuis (2007), 'Analysis of a rural water supply project in three communities in Mali: participation and sustainability', *Natural Resources Forum*, **31**, 142–50.

Global Rainwater Harvesting Collective (2005), 'Summary of the partnership's goals and objectives', available at: http://webapps01.un.org/dsd/partnerships/public/partnerships/1101.html (retrieval: 23.05.2011).

Global Rainwater Harvesting Collective (2009), 'Sweet drinking water: the first solar powered de-salination plant in Rajasthan', available at: http://www.glo balrainwaterharvesting.org/desalination.asp (retrieval: 02.01.2009).

Hall, D. and E. Lobina (2002), 'Water privatisation in Latin America', Paper presented at the *PSI Americas' Water Conference*, available at: http://www.dev-zone.org/kcdocs/6154latam.pdf (retrieval: 05.12.2009).

Hall, D. and E. Lobina (2006), *Water as a Public Service*, Ferney-Voltaire, France: Public Services International.

Hanson, M. (2007), 'Pure water', available at: http://www.managementtoday.co.uk/news/647187/ (retrieval: 12.12.2009).

Heid, E. (2005), *Case Study Project: Agua Para Todos: Water for All*, Berlin: GPPi.

Illich, I. (1970), *Deschooling Society*, New York: Harper and Row.

Illich, I. (1973). *Tools for Conviviality*, New York: Harper and Row.

Illich, I. (1974), *Energy and Equity*, New York: Harper and Row.

Illich, I. (1977[2002]), *Disabling Professions*, London: Marion Boyars Publishers Ltd.

Illich, I. (1978), *Toward a History of Needs*, New York: Pantheon.

Illich, I. (1985), *H₂O and the Waters of Forgetfulness*, Dallas, TX: Dallas Institute of the Humanities and Culture.

Jensen, N.E. (2001), *Northeastern Brazil Groundwater Project Field Report*, Alberta: Sunmotor International Ltd.

Kooy, M. and K. Bakker (2006), 'Zersplitterte Netzwerke? Wasser, Macht und Wissen in Jakarta: 1870–1945' in S. Frank and M. Gandy (eds), *Hydropolis: Wasser und die Stadt der Moderne*, Frankfurt: Campus, pp. 265–93.

Lovell, C. (2000). *Productive Water Points in Dryland Areas: Guidelines on Integrated Planning for Rural Water Supply*, London: ITDG.

Martens, J. and T. Debiel (2008), *The MDG Project in Crisis: Midpoint Review and*

Prospects for the Future, Duisburg, Germany: Institute for Development and Peace (INEF Policy Brief 4/2008, September).

Maurice, Y. and R. Dumont (2003), *Groundwater Exploration and Management in Brazil*, Ontario: Geological Survey of Canada.

McDonald, D.A. and G. Ruiters (2005), *The Age of Commodity: Water Privatization in Southern Africa*, Oxford, UK: Earthscan.

Mert, A. (2009), 'Partnerships for sustainable development as discursive practice: Shifts in discourses of environment and democracy', *Forest Policy and Economics*, **11**(5–6), 326–39.

Moriarty, P., J. Buttersworth, B. van Koppen and J. Soussan (2004), 'Water, poverty and productive uses of water at the household level', in P. Moriarty, J. Buttersworth and B. van Koppen (eds), *Beyond Domestic: Case Studies on Poverty and Productive Uses of Water at the Household Level*, Delft, The Netherlands: International Water and Sanitation Centre, pp. 19–48.

Neath, G. (2006), 'Business as a partner in reaching the Millennium Development Goals', paper presented at the *Business, NGO and Development Conference*, Washington DC: World Bank.

PROASNE (2004a), 'Airborne geophysical surveys', available at: http://proasne. net/airbornesurvey.html (retrieval: 08.01.2009).

PROASNE (2004b), 'Northeastern Brazil Groundwater Project (PROASNE)', available at: http://webapps01.un.org/dsd/partnerships/public/partnerships/847. html (retrieval: 08.01.2009).

PROASNE (2004c), 'Solar Power Development Project', available at: http:// proasne.net/solarpower.html (retrieval: 08.01.2009).

PROASNE (2005), 'Closing report', Geological Survey of Canada/Serviço Geológico do Brasil.

Rai, V. (2002), 'If WEHAB today, we have tomorrow', available at: http://find-articles.com/p/articles/mi_m1309/is_3_39/ai_93211722/ (retrieval: 07.03.2011).

Rainwater Partnership (2008), 'Rainwater statement', available at: http://www. unep.org/depi/rainwater/ (retrieval: 24.02. 2009).

Safe Water System (2008), available at: http://www.cdc.gov/safewater/ (retrieval: 20.02.2009).

Sclove, R.E. (1995), *Democracy and technology*, New York: The Guildford Press.

Stockman, L., T. Fischer, M. Deming, B. Ngwira, C. Bowie, N. Cunliffe, J. Bresee and R.E. Quick (2007), 'Point-of-use water treatment and use among mothers in Malawi', *Emerging Infectious Diseases*, **13**(7), 1077–80.

UN (1992), *Agenda 21*, New York: UN.

UN (2006), 'The 2nd UN World Water Development Report: Water, a shared responsibility', available at: http://www.unesco.org/water/wwap/wwdr/wwdr2/table_contents.shtml (retrieval: 02.01.2009).

UN (2008), *Delivering on the Global Partnership for Achieving the Millennium Development Goals*, New York: UN.

UN (2010), *The Millennium Development Goals Report*, New York: UN.

UNCSD (2006), 'A gender perspective on water resources and sanitation', *Background Paper No. 2*, New York: Commission on Sustainable Development.

UNEP (2007), 'Mapping the potential of rainwater harvesting technologies in Africa: a GIS overview on development domains for the continent and ten selected countries', *Technical Manual No. 6*, Nairobi: UNEP.

WAWI Secretariat (2008), 'WAWI Final Evaluation Report', available at: http:// www.wawipartnership.net/wawi_implementation.php (retrieval: 15.11.2008).

WHO/UNICEF (2010), *Progress on Sanitation and Drinking-water: 2010 Update*, New York: WHO and UNICEF.

WSUP (2004), *Water and Sanitation for the Urban Poor (WSUP): Working in Partnership to Progress Delivery of the UN Millennium Development Goals for Water and Sanitation*, London, UK: WSUP.

WSUP (2007), 'Frequently asked questions', available at: http://www.wsup.com/intro/faq.htm#05 (retrieval: 05.06.2009).

WSUP (2008), 'Report from the Programme Implementation Workshop', London: WSUP.

WSUP (2009), *How can Water and Sanitation Services to the Urban Poor be Scaled Up?*, London: WSUP.

Žižek, S. (2001), *The Fragile Absolute: Or, Why is the Christian Legacy Worth Fighting For?* London: Verso.

11. Conclusions: partnerships for sustainable development

Philipp Pattberg, Frank Biermann, Sander Chan and Ayşem Mert

This chapter summarizes our key findings and provides a number of policy recommendations on partnerships for sustainable development. Our research was motivated in particular by the existing knowledge gaps in relation to three distinct areas. First, we sought to better understand the emergence of partnerships for sustainable development, including questions such as: what was the political context surrounding the emergence of partnerships for sustainable development? Who benefitted from the emerging system of partnerships? How can the observed variation in sectoral, functional and geographic spread of partnerships be explained?

Second, we were interested in measuring and explaining the effects and broader impacts of partnerships for sustainable development both as an aggregate phenomenon of more than 340 partnerships and as individual partnerships. Here we analysed their concrete problem-solving effectiveness (i.e. partnerships' contribution to the Millennium Development Goals, the Agenda 21 or the Johannesburg Plan of Action) along with their broader influence in global environmental governance (including unintended effects).

Third, we scrutinized the legitimacy of partnerships for sustainable development, including questions such as: how do partnerships perform in terms of their input and output legitimacy? Are partnerships for sustainable development effectively closing the participation gap in global environmental politics? Are partnerships democratizing environmental governance? How legitimate are specific technologies and practices promoted through partnerships for sustainable development?

In addition to addressing these knowledge gaps, our research on partnerships for sustainable development was motivated by three more practical concerns. First, the lack of empirical data on the role and relevance of partnerships in world politics in and beyond the environmental and sustainability realm might lead to distorted political assessments of this new mechanism of governance. Lack of knowledge could result in dismissing of non-state governance as peripheral and unimportant. However, lack of a sound assessment could also lead to exaggerating the real influence of public–private, multistakeholder partnerships and other forms of governance beyond the state. In both cases, limited public resources and attention could be directed in wrong directions, and policies could be mistargeted.

Second, a better understanding of partnerships for sustainable development might also offer new insights on how to increase their effectiveness, and it could provide valuable recommendations for policy reform.

Third, a better understanding of partnerships might also assist in addressing the democratic deficit of the current system of global governance. Knowledge about their democratic legitimacy, accountability and transparency might hence become immediately practically relevant.

KEY FINDINGS

Emergence: What did we Learn?

The emergence of transnational public–private partnerships has been analysed in the broader context of an alleged shift in governance from public sources of authority to those that are hybrid or private in nature (Kersbergen and van Waarden 2004). However, our analysis of the more than 300 partnerships for sustainable development agreed around the 2002 Johannesburg summit showed that partnerships are firmly embedded in an intergovernmental context. Consequently, our research has focused on the political negotiation process in and around the Johannesburg Summit and the resulting type-2 agreements on partnerships for sustainable development. This research has shown that while partnerships have been portrayed by the UN as mere implementation instruments for global sustainability goals, they have also a strong political dimension. The negotiations that resulted in partnerships as the type-2 outcome of the WSSD was marked by contestations over partnerships between different governments, business representatives and civil society delegations. This process resulted in a definition and operationalization of the partnership idea that was heavily influenced by powerful actors such as the United States or business interests. While the resulting institutional framework for partnerships was sufficiently vague to allow for the inclusion of many divergent interests, the insufficient monitoring and reporting requirements placed limits on the effectiveness of partnership governance from the very beginning. Analysing the Johannesburg partnerships as the outcome of a political bargaining process rather than the functional answer to a number of governance demands opens up the possibility of addressing the question of performance and broader impacts beyond a narrow focus on problem-solving effectiveness.

In addition to highlighting the political nature of the WSSD partnership regime, our research also addressed the question of functional and geographic distribution of partnerships for sustainable development. Here we found that – in contrast to many functionalist accounts – partnerships are not necessarily filling functional gaps. They also do not necessarily emerge in the geographic spaces where the demand for partnerships is greatest. Policy network theories go a long way in explaining the geographic dimension of emergence, with partnerships emerging in countries that are member to many international organizations. However, network theories do not seem to be applicable to the participatory dimension of partnerships. While non-state actor representation is considerable, most partnerships are still led by traditional actors in international relations. Some evidence for an institutional explanation for partnership distribution can be found in the fact that partnerships are often active in issue areas that are already densely populated by international law and agreements. However, no prevailing organizational model or best practice could be identified for the overall WSSD process.

Effectiveness: What did we Learn?

In terms of the effectiveness of partnerships for sustainable development, the balance of evidence in our large-*n* analysis of all WSSD partnerships suggests that these new mechanisms of global governance fall short of the high expectations that were placed in them. While we acknowledge that some partnerships are highly effective and make important contributions to global sustainability governance (see Chapters 6 and 7 for examples of such effective partnerships), overall, our comprehensive analysis of more than 300 partnerships that have been agreed around and after the 2002 Johannesburg summit leads to a rather critical assessment. To start with, many partnerships are simply not active. In addition, partnerships do not seem to address core functions where their particular role and comparative advantage was believed to lie: to initiate new global governance norms in areas where governments fail to take action; to help implement existing intergovernmental regulations; and to increase the inclusiveness and participation in global governance by bringing in actors that have so far been marginalized.

Even though there are undoubtedly a number of individual partnerships that make highly useful contributions in their areas, the overall system of partnerships for sustainable development does deliver much less than expected in 2002. Our research shows, among others, that partnerships are most frequent in those areas that are already heavily institutionalized and regulated; that they are predominantly not concerned with implementation but rather with further institution-building; that for many of them it is doubtful whether they have sufficient resources to make any meaningful contribution towards implementation in the first place; and finally, that the vast majority of partnerships strengthens the participation of those actors that already participate: governments, major international organizations, and those civil society actors that have had a say in global governance already before the partnership phenomenon emerged. In many cases, those that had been marginalized before have also been marginalized in the partnership process.

If the entire system of partnerships does not help much in supporting global sustainability governance, what is then their main rationale? Other reasons for partnerships to emerge can be conceived. While it has been suggested that 'self-regulatory institutions remain subject to takeover by opportunistic individuals and to potentially perverse dynamics' (Dedeurwaerdere 2005: 4), the whole partnership idea might be closer to realizing joint gains among partners than producing broader societal benefits. On this account, considering the amount of time and funding invested in each partnership, it seems not surprising that partners themselves tend to be the primary beneficiaries of their partnerships.

In addition to addressing the entire system of public–private partnerships agreed upon at the 2002 WSSD, our research has further investigated the effectiveness of individual partnerships. Here, we have focused on identifying the success conditions for partnerships for sustainable development. Based on a sample of partnerships that focus on energy, we conclude that the involvement of powerful actors is necessary but not sufficient for the success of a partnership. As our quantitative analysis has shown, the participation of industrialized countries, along with that of private for-profit partners, is strongly correlated with effectiveness. The in-depth qualitative analysis further suggests that the influential partnerships link many powerful states and businesses. By contrast, most of the least effective partnerships include weaker and poorer countries. However, a more detailed analysis also suggests that powerful actors alone are not a sufficient condition for partnership success. A key point emerging from the qualitative analysis is that the level of institutionalization and the internal organizational structure of an initiative matter. Effective partnerships have to be institutionalized into real organizations. If they are, partnerships become operational and can work towards achieving their goals. Depending on the scale of these goals, the activities of a partnership may require more or less resources. In addition, the decision-making styles and the governance culture might also play a role, but only in the context of a functional partnership. If a partnership is operational and well institutionalized in the form of an organization with functional forums of decision-making, then (and only then) can the factor of deliberation make a difference.

A third conclusion on the effectiveness of partnerships for sustainable development derived from our research is that the political and institutional context matters. Comparative analysis confirms that the potential for partnership governance varies from country to country with regard to political, societal and economic contexts. In China, where formal political participation exists but there is a lack of political pluralism and real influence for citizens, the potential for partnerships is rather limited. In India, on the contrary, the relative freedom and autonomy of civil society allows for more partnership initiatives that include NGOs and social organizations. Within the same partnership, differences in organization can be observed depending on whether activities are implemented in China or India. Despite the global reach and universal goal formulations of these partnerships, we observe considerable variation at the domestic level. However, the analyses of partnerships for sustainable development in China and India are not static assessments. While our research shows a limited potential for partnership governance in China and greater compatibility of domestic governance with partnerships in India, in the long-run, it is difficult to assess whether China or India will emerge as a more suitable context for partnership governance. In the end, this will depend on domestic reform at large, rather than reform in the relatively limited area of sustainable development.

Our regional analysis of partnerships in Africa has also highlighted the limitations of partnership governance. For example, partnerships for sustainable development were tasked to 'compensate for weak institutions or institutional deficits across levels of governance' (Andonova and Levy 2003: 20). However, our research indicates that they are not designed to overcome the policy implementation deficits resulting from weak governmental capacity in many developing countries, especially in Africa.

Taken together, partnerships for sustainable development do not bring about a radical transformation of development aid patterns, and the shift towards participatory governance that is part of the partnership discourse is by and large rhetorical. The fact that some partnerships have limited outputs, or no outputs at all, raises the question of whether the partnership phenomenon can be considered an instrument of global sustainability governance after all.

A fourth and final conclusion on the effectiveness of partnerships for sustainable development is that partnerships have broader impacts beyond problem-solving that need to be critically analysed. For example, we have analysed cases in which partnerships, due to the lack of a strict screening and follow-up process, create a platform for highly controversial technologies to gain recognition at the UN level. These technologies and practices introduced by partnerships for sustainable development include nuclear energy, biotechnologies, biofuels, PVC and vinyl, to name a few. On this account, partnerships are not just neutral instruments for implementing internationally accepted sustainability norms, such as the Millennium Development Goals and Agenda 21, but rather sites of contestation over distinct technologies and practices. We contend that this broader critical view on partnerships beyond problem-solving is a helpful corrective to the more common measurement of the effectiveness of the partnership regime.

Legitimacy: What did we Learn?

With regards to the question of legitimacy, we have three main conclusions. First, we have attempted to answer the question whether global public–private partnerships can be regarded as democratic. A central argument emerging from our research is that partnerships can be considered democratically legitimate if they fulfil core democratic values, such as participation, accountability, transparency and deliberation. A conclusion from almost a decade of research on the Johannesburg partnerships is that their democratic credentials are weak in terms of incorporation of core democratic values. The Johannesburg partnerships consolidate rather than transform asymmetrical patterns of participation between North and South, between established and 'marginalized groups', and between state and non-state actors. Furthermore, the accountability mechanisms are weak and the deliberative potential of the partnerships remains limited.

A second conclusion on the legitimacy of partnerships that emerges from our research on partnerships in the water sector, is that these partnerships reflect the emphasis placed on stakeholder involvement in the context of the Johannesburg Summit. In this sense, WSSD partnerships appear to encourage more user participation than the literature generally expects of conventional public–private partnerships in the water sector. However, while this may encourage support from governments and donor agencies, it remains unclear how substantial the involvement of local stakeholders in decision-making is. Thus, more empirical evidence (for example regarding the actual processes and outcomes of consultation sessions) would be needed to strengthen the observations on stakeholder participation in water partnerships.

Our third conclusion takes issue with the widely held assumption that the legitimacy of partnerships can be assessed independently from the technologies and governance practices that are embedded within individual partnerships. Analysing the water sector, technology transfer through partnerships is often presented as a tool not only to combat water scarcity, but also to alleviate poverty, ensure gender equality, and to improve health and environment indicators. However, the implications of technological improvements are not straightforward, as different technologies have varying implications for the autonomy, flexibility and self-reliance of communities. Reflecting these limitations of technology transfer through partnerships provides a novel perspective on the legitimacy of governance for sustainable development.

POLICY RECOMMENDATIONS

Reform of Partnerships for Sustainable Development at the UN Level

One of the key weaknesses of the WSSD partnership process after Johannesburg has been the weak monitoring and reporting practices. As discussed in more detail in Chapter 2, while partnerships were expected to be voluntary, self-organizing, transparent and accountable, the agreed upon Bali Guidelines did not stipulate any screening or monitoring mechanisms to ensure these qualities. Instead, partnerships should prove to be transparent and accountable by self-reporting. Moreover, the Bali Guidelines refer to the need for identifying funding resources, formulating tangible goals and specifying clear timeframes without clear reference to how these goals should be achieved. In sum, neither UNDESA nor the UNCSD were given authority to effectively review and monitor partnerships. The UNCSD's authority and resources were limited to screening and selection at a very minimal level.

Here we see a particular need for policy reform. The UNCSD needs to be institutionally strengthened, while the rules and regulations specifying reporting and monitoring requirements for partnerships need a substantive overhaul. As a minimum requirement, partnerships should provide regular proof of activity. The UNCSD should be responsible for removing inactive partnerships from the database. As a more far-reaching requirement, we see the possibility to introduce a peer-review process among partnerships according to a joint protocol. Based on a generic reporting form, partnerships would engage in reviewing other partnerships, creating peer pressure, circulating best practices and subsequently increasing the overall coherence of the partnership process. Needless to say, a more detailed reporting mechanism would require additional financial and administrative resources within the UNCSD and UNDESA. In addition to this procedural reform,

UNCSD should also be given authority to assess whether the overall sample of partnerships for sustainable development are in line with broader UN policy goals such as the MDGs and Agenda 21.

Finally, we know that the universe of transnational public–private partnerships working on sustainability issues is much broader than the limited set of WSSD partnerships. To increase coherence and effectiveness, as many partnerships as possible should be incorporated in a reformed partnerships for sustainable development process. To this end, the UNCSD, together with other relevant UN bodies, should engage in a broad stock-taking exercise to identify existing partnerships outside the WSSD framework.

Improving Partnerships on the Ground: Prerequisites for Success

While our research has painted a rather gloomy picture of the overall sample of WSSD partnerships in terms of contributing to the much needed sustainability transition, we acknowledge that individual partnerships can make a distinct contribution to sustainable development. In answering the question why some partnerships perform better than others, we have highlighted the importance of organizational structure, resources and powerful actors (see Chapter 5). We conclude that in terms of problem-solving effectiveness, there is something like an ideal model or best practice of partnerships for sustainable development. Hence, the main policy-conclusion emerging from our research is that partnerships, in order to be effective, need to be institutionalized, preferably in the form of an organization with an executive board that should include the representatives of major stakeholders, and a permanent administrative secretariat with adequate material resources, dedicated to the goal and mission of the initiative. The involvement of powerful actors can help by bringing in necessary resources, and is crucial in the case of large-scale partnerships established to perform difficult and costly activities.

Addressing Shortcomings: Participation, Legitimacy and Unintended Consequences

This book concludes, among others, that the overall positive expectations in the system of partnerships for sustainable development have by and large not been fulfilled. In particular, the promise of making global governance more inclusive and democratic by means of partnership governance was not met (see Chapters 4, 8 and 9). Addressing these shortcomings will have to become a prime target for governments and stakeholders involved in partnerships, if the idea of solving key global problems by means of public–private partnerships is to survive. In particular, we see here a prime responsibility for those governments that have taken a leading role in the WSSD partnership regime. What is needed is a more orchestrated approach towards partnerships, weighting the benefits of an unconstrained bottom-up process against the necessity to involve all relevant stakeholders.

In addition to the lack of democratic legitimacy and balanced representation, we also see a problem emerging from the largely unnoticed unintended side-effects of partnership governance as discussed in Chapter 2. Here, we are particularly worried about the broader impacts of introducing contested technologies into the sustainable development domain via the UN. To safeguard against an overly broad portfolio of partnership themes, governments – within the context of the UNCSD (see also above) – should define unambiguous criteria on how to link partnerships with the goals of the Millennium Development Goals and the Agenda 21, among others.

CONCLUSION

As the introduction to this book has suggested, the study of transnational public–private partnerships is complicated because there is no consensus on the definition of the object to be studied, a consensus that, by comparison, had been quite early reached in the literature on intergovernmental regimes, which allowed for a substantive comparative research programme. The existing variety in terminology reflects, on the one hand, the unconsolidated nature of the current partnership research. On the other hand, it puts strict limits on cumulative empirical research and theory building. This leads to a second shortcoming of the current academic literature on public–private partnerships: most research so far has been case-study based. Detailed case studies are important for inductively generating hypotheses and deductively testing different propositions. Carefully devised theory-driven study programmes can employ the case study method to a meaningful result as well (cf. Beisheim, Campe and Schäferhoff 2010). Nevertheless, with the wide diversity of partnerships at hand, most case studies build on different definitions and focus on different sectors. These problems have complicated the comparison of findings and the accumulation of knowledge.

We believe that the GSPD – which provided the data basis for large parts of the research reported in this book – provides a meaningful corrective to these shortcomings. First, by the systematic large-*n* evaluation of influence of partnerships in global sustainability politics we have assessed whether partnerships matter. This assessment of the influence of partnerships is central to a critical analysis of new mechanisms of global governance as additions or even substitutes for intergovernmental policy-making. Second, understanding reasons for variation in the influence of partnerships of different types or in different sectors has also resulted in crucial policy advice. In the end, the GSPD not only advances scholarly understanding of whether and how private–public cooperation matters. It also offers tools and avenues to improve the performance of this new and emerging type of global governance in daily practice.

Public–private partnerships for sustainable development are widely seen as the most prominent outcome of the 2002 WSSD in Johannesburg, South Africa. In 2011, 10 years after the Johannesburg summit, it was time to take stock and to provide a comprehensive assessment of what the hundreds of Johannesburg partnerships could achieve, of the reasons why they emerged, and of the problems and potentials associated with this new governance mode. This 10-year assessment was the main goal of this book. While our assessment has been rather critical with regards to the overall effectiveness of partnership governance in its current form, we have also highlighted positive examples, factors for success and concrete ways to improve partnerships for sustainable development. The exact future of partnerships as a governance instrument for sustainable development is unknown. However, we believe that – given the substantial amount of material and intellectual resources invested – partnerships will stay with us for the foreseeable future, making their assessment not only an academic but also a practical question.

REFERENCES

Beisheim, M., S. Campe and M. Schäferhoff (2010), 'Global governance through public-private partnerships', in H. Enderlein, S. Wälti and M. Zürn (eds), *Handbook on Multi-Level Governance*. Cheltenham, UK: Edward Elgar, pp. 370–82.
Dedeurwaerdere, T. (2005), The Contribution of Network Governance to Sustainable Development. Paris: Institute du Development et des Relations Internationales and Chaire Development Durable Ecole Polytechnique.
Kersbergen, K. van and F. van Waarden (2004), 'Governance as a bridge between disciplines: cross-disciplinary inspiration regarding shifts in governance and problems of governability, accountability and legitimacy', *European Journal of Political Research* **43**, 143–71.

Appendix

THE GLOBAL SUSTAINABILITY PARTNERSHIP DATABASE: AN OVERVIEW

This appendix provides an overview of the sample of partnerships that have been agreed upon and implemented as a result of the 2002 WSSD, and/or subsequently been registered with the UNCSD. General characteristics of partnerships covered in the GSPD include: (1) the geographical scope of partnerships; (2) the issue areas covered; (3) the overall number and type of partners, membership and other organizational characteristics; and (4) the countries of implementation, i.e. the geographic areas in which on-the-ground partnership projects are implemented. This overview shall provide the background to the analyses provided throughout this book.

Geographical Scope

Within the sample of the GSPD, half of the partnerships are global in scope, while the other half has a regional or sub-regional scope. National or local partnerships are very rare (Figure A.1).

Issue Areas

The UNCSD statistics on currently registered partnerships use the self-reported 'primary and secondary themes' questions on the registration form, which often results in ambivalent and inaccurate categorization, and more importantly, overlapping categories. To avoid this, the GSPD data has been coded in a different way, as a result of which a more clear-cut list of issue areas emerged. Instead of accepting the self-description of partnerships in the UNCSD database, in the GSPD partnerships were coded according to a list of pre-defined issue areas. Partnerships working on interlinkages of issues or more than one issue had two values for issue area, as long as these issues were equally important in the activities of the partnership. The results of this re-coding suggest that knowledge production/dissemination, water, and energy are the most frequent issue

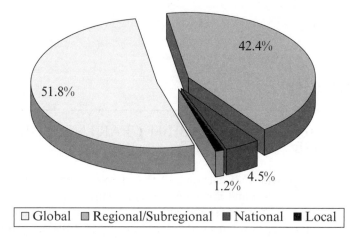

42.4%

51.8%

4.5%
1.2%

□ Global ▪ Regional/Subregional ■ National ■ Local

*Figure A.1   Geographical scope of partnerships for sustainable
development*

areas partnerships are engaged in (Figure A.2). Settlements, oceans/
coasts/rivers and river basins as well as biodiversity were also popular
themes. The smaller number of partnerships working on climate change,
health and poverty can be explained by the presence of other platforms
or UN organizations focusing on these issues. However, the presence of
some partnerships working on these issues, particularly the numerous
energy *and* climate partnerships prompts the question: why they chose
the UNCSD for registration instead of alternative platforms? In other
words, the possibility of the UNCSD partnerships being a green/blue-
washing mechanism (a possibility voiced by several NGOs and Southern
delegations during the WSSD process), must be scrutinized (see Chapters
2 and 10).

Number of Partners

Among the 330 partnerships in our dataset, 235 provided information
about the exact number of partners involved, with a mean of 24.8 and a
standard deviation of 45.3. This reflects the diversity in the organization
of partnerships (Table A.1).

Lead Partners

Partnerships for sustainable development are predominantly led by state
actors (23.8 per cent) and UN and other intergovernmental agencies

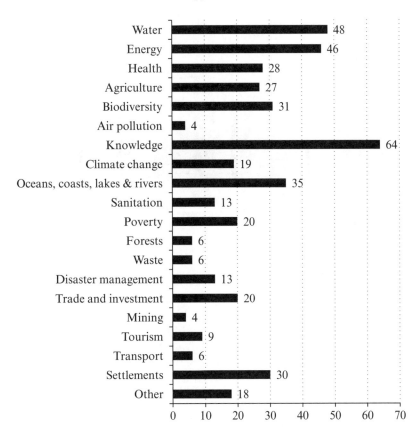

Figure A.2   Issue areas partnerships for sustainable development focus on

Table A.1   Number of partners in partnerships for sustainable development

	N	Mean	Std. Deviation
no of partners	235	24.82	45.331
Valid N	235		

(29.2 per cent); they are, however, rarely led by private actors. While business-lead partnerships are very few (3.2 per cent), NGOs and research and science networks represent only 7.9 per cent and 11.5 per cent of lead partners, respectively (Figure A.3). This prompts the question why partnerships are conceptualized as private governance mechanisms in much of the literature. A part of the answer lies in the process in which

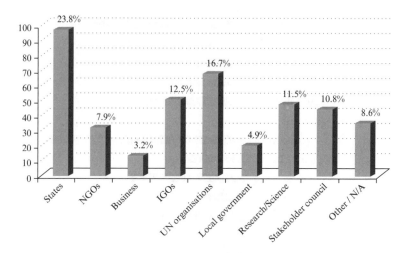

Figure A.3   Type of lead partners in partnerships for sustainable development

partnerships were negotiated: the main supporters of partnerships have been the business actors, although later, once a voluntary partnerships regime was endorsed by governments and the UN, they had no obligation to initiate partnerships (see Chapter 2). The NGOs were not supportive of the concept in the beginning, which might explain their hesitation in initiating new partnerships. Science networks and research institutions are the lead partners especially when the partnership's primary target is knowledge production (43 per cent of all partnerships with a scientific lead partner focus on knowledge production).

Partners

The number of individual partners from each sector varies from one partnership to the other. States and international organizations are present in just over half of the partnerships, while subnational and municipal governments are absent in most. This is a healthy way of assessing the presence of state partners, since different state agencies can act as NGOs, science institutions, or even for-profit organizations at different times. The presence of partners from specific sectors is depicted in Figure A.4.

Nevertheless, it is also important to survey the total number of partners from different social groups or societal actors across the board. The exact number of state actors cannot be exactly determined due to definitional

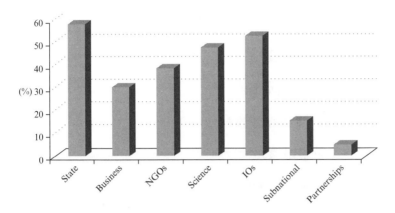

Figure A.4   Percentage of partnerships for sustainable development with at least one partner from. . .

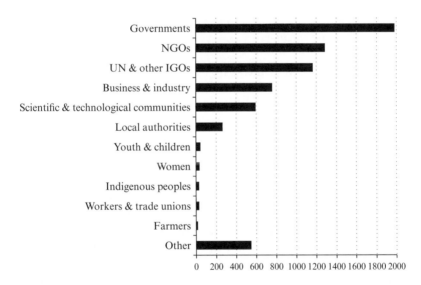

Figure A.5   Number of partners from specific sectors

problems as well as the lack of accessible data. Hence, we employ the UNCSD's statistics and categorization from 2008 to establish a general profile (Figure A.5). When the UNCSD partnerships are taken as a whole, the partner distribution shows the dominant presence of state actors, IGOs and NGOs, whereas major groups (such as women, youth groups,

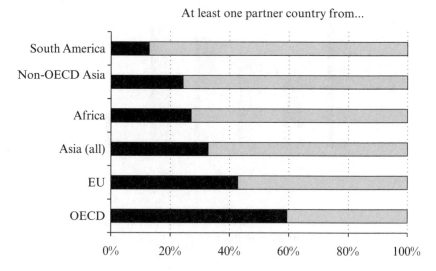

At least one partner country from...

*Figure A.6   Presence of state partners in partnerships for sustainable
        development*

indigenous peoples and workers) are largely underrepresented. This raises
the question to what extent partnerships fulfil their role as participatory
mechanisms often ascribed to them in the literature (see also Chapters 4,
8 and 10 for an assessment of partnerships as mechanisms of participatory
governance).

The distribution of state partners also illustrates existing power imbalances. More than half of the partnerships have at least one state actor
from an OECD country, as opposed to recipient governments that are
less often present as partners (Figure A.6). To some degree, the presence of donor countries in more partnerships is expected, while recipient
governments can participate in the local implementation of partnerships in their own countries. In fact, our data supports this assumption.
However, this is also the case with global partnerships, supporting the
worries in much of the literature that partnerships re-enact the already
existing power imbalances in global politics (Figure A.7). Furthermore,
this brings to mind the concerns that have been raised by Southern
country delegations during the WSSD negotiations: that partnerships in
fact could be a way to circumvent recipient governments. These concerns
can be affirmed, albeit to a limited degree according to our data (Figure
A.8).

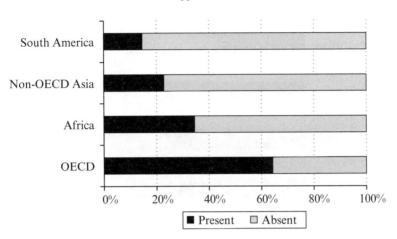

Figure A.7   Presence of state partners in partnerships for sustainable development with global scope

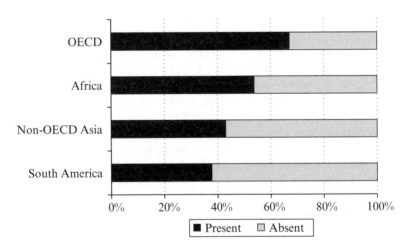

Figure A.8   Presence of state partners in partnerships of their region

Countries of Implementation

The countries in which partnership projects are implemented include most states. The number of countries of implementation per partnership ranges from 1 to 200; but most partnerships implement projects in only a few countries: 30 per cent of the partnerships have only up to 2 countries of

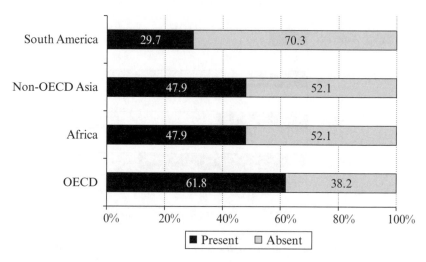

Figure A.9   Regional distribution of countries of implementation in all UNCSD partnerships

implementation, and 71 per cent have less than 10 countries of implementation. On average, UNCSD partnerships have 9.9 countries of implementation with a standard deviation of 17.5. The geographical distribution of partnerships is interesting for our research: most UNCSD partnerships have at least one country of implementation from among the OECD countries, whereas regions with predominantly developing countries have fewer partnership projects (Figure A.9). This prompts the question whether partnerships are indeed implementation projects for the Millennium Development Goals, as 24 per cent of all partnerships have no country of implementation from Africa, South America, or non-OECD Asia.

Membership and Organization

Partnerships are often assumed to represent a network-type governance mechanism, participatory in nature, flexible and adaptable to new conditions. One of the reasons for this conception is the Bali Guidelines, which state that flexibility would be an important feature of UNCSD partnerships. Nevertheless, the partnerships in our sample appear rather restricted in terms of their organizational structure. Only a small minority of partnerships are open to new members, while most of them restrict membership either by function or by sector (Table A.2). In total, 37 per cent of UNCSD partnerships are closed to new members.

Table A.2   Restrictions on membership

Membership style	Frequency	%	% within semi-open partnerships
closed	122	37.0%	
open	10	3.0%	
semi-open	184	55.8%	
restricted by function	*89*	*27.0%*	*48.4%*
restricted by geographical area	*51*	*15.5%*	*27.7%*
restricted by number	*10*	*3.0%*	*5.4%*
restricted by sector	*164*	*49.7%*	*89.1%*
restricted by time	*131*	*39.7%*	*71.2%*
No info	14	4.2%	
Total	330	100.0%	

Table A.3   Protocol, contract, or MoU between partners in partnerships for sustainable development

	Frequency	%
Not indicated	313	98
Indicated	17	5.2
Total	330	100.0

According to the GSPD, most partnerships do not have a protocol, contract, or a non-binding memorandum of understanding (MoU) between partners that would define the overall goal and functioning of the partnership (Table A.3). The lack of contracts in UNCSD partnerships raises additional questions: where and how are the so-called joint rights and responsibilities specified among parties of significantly divergent interests? Who carries the risk in case of failure? Which partner is responsible for the effective implementation of the partnership?

Other indicators show low levels of institutionalization in UNCSD partnerships (Figure A.10). For example, 38.5 per cent of all UNCSD partnerships indicate no budget plan, office space, staff, organizational structure, logo, or activity reports on their respective UNCSD webpage or their own websites. Particularly the lack of budget plans and activity reports raise serious questions about the transparency and accountability of partnerships in relation to the democratic deficit in global environmental governance.

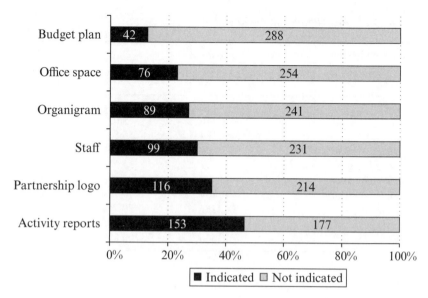

Figure A.10   Indicators of institutionalization

Index